The Writer's Handbook
Guide to Writing
for Stage and Screen

Barry Turner has worked on both sides of publishing, as an editor and marketing director and as an author. He started his career as a journalist with the *Observer* before moving on to television and radio. He has written over twenty books including a best-selling biography of the actor Richard Burton.

His recent work includes a radio play, travel articles, serializing books for *The Times*, editing the magazine *Country* and writing a one-man show based on the life of the legendary theatre critic James Agate. He has edited *The Writer's Handbook*, an annual best-seller, for sixteen years and is in his sixth year of editing *The Statesman's Yearbook*.

The Writer's Handbook
Guide to Writing
for Stage and Screen

EDITED BY BARRY TURNER

MACMILLAN

First published 2003 by Macmillan
an imprint of Pan Macmillan Ltd
Pan Macmillan, 20 New Wharf Road, London N1 9RR
Basingstoke and Oxford
Associated companies throughout the world
www.panmacmillan.com

ISBN 1 4050 0098 8

1 3 5 7 9 8 6 4 2

A CIP catalogue record for this book is available from
the British Library.

Printed and bound in Great Britain by
Mackays of Chatham plc, Chatham, Kent

Contents

LISTINGS

Introduction

It is said of Tom Stoppard that when asked what his first play, *Rosencrantz and Guildenstern are Dead* was about, he replied, 'It's about to make me very rich.' The story is apocryphal but it contains an often ignored truth that, if you get it right, playwriting can be a highly profitable craft. Getting it right, of course, is none too easy which is why in *The Writer's Handbook Guide to Writing for Stage and Screen* advice and guidance is from those who themselves have made successful careers but are also practised in the art of encouraging newcomers to make the best of their talent.

Tackling stage and screen writing in a single volume might seem to be over ambitious. But the overlap between the two media, already extensive, is growing. The writer who makes his mark in the theatre, thus proving the skill of creating exciting and convincing dialogue, is soon diverted into television. Even if the days of the stand alone screenplay are long since gone, the long-running series like *East-Enders*, *The Bill*, *Brookside* and *London's Burning* have an insatiable appetite for top-class dramatists.

From the writer's point of view, the rewards of television are more immediate. A full-length stage play can take up to a year to write and even longer to bring together a producer, director and actors to mount a performance. TV is now; the commission to write a script for an established production team with a cheque to follow soon after delivery. Longer term, live theatre has the advantage; whereas there is a limit to the number of repeats and overseas sales for a television drama, a popular stage play can run and run. Royalties vary between 4 and 10 per cent of box-office receipts with the highest returns earned from the big subsidized companies. Then there are the proceeds from touring and overseas productions, movie rights and even hard-print sales. In part fulfilment of Stoppard's prophecy, *Rosencrantz and Guildenstern are Dead* sells 20,000 copies a year, many of them to students. The overlap between stage and screen can also pay off handsomely. One of the best things to happen on television in recent years was Peter Flannery's social drama, *Our Friends in the North*. However, it started as a modestly produced stage play at the Pit, the small theatre in London's Barbican complex.

But enough talk about money. For anyone new to playwriting, there is much to accomplish before recognition brings its rewards. The aim of *The Writer's Handbook Guide to Writing for Stage and Screen* is to take the rough edges off the learning process, pointing out what must be done to achieve a breakthrough and, every bit as important, spotlighting the common mistakes that could, if left uncorrected, hold up a promising career.

When the time comes for the creative imagination to take off, there will be a period of lonely effort. 'Writing plays,' John Mortimer reminds us, 'like any other literary pursuit, begins with sitting alone in a room.' It is an awesome thought, not least because there will be disappointments along the way. But take comfort from the experience of one of our greatest playwrights. Harold Pinter's first important play, *The Birthday Party*, closed after one week with receipts totalling £207. Soon after, a production of *The Caretaker* in Düsseldorf was booed off on its opening night, the cast doggedly taking curtain calls until there were only two people left in the theatre, both still booing.

GUIDE TO WRITING FOR STAGE AND SCREEN

Writing for the Theatre

James Roose-Evans

Writing for the theatre is a hazardous business. Even if you have a play commissioned the work can take up to a year, or even longer, and you won't be able to live on the advance. Most of the time you will be living off savings, or a partner or, like Trollope, rising early to put in three hours writing before going off to a paying job. Having written your play, what do you do? You can consult a periodical like *Contacts* and start sending off copies to theatres and managements. But be warned! Almost every one of these will take months, rather than weeks, to consider a script and many will not even be acknowledged, even though you have included a stamped addressed envelope. This is because most theatres receive several hundred scripts a year and unless there is a special script reading department attached to the theatre, the director will only be able to spare time to read half a dozen a week, simply because of the sheer pressure of work involved in running a theatre and directing plays. Also, let's face it, some directors of theatres, including many commercial managements, are lazy! The odds, therefore, against an unsolicited script being accepted are a hundred to one. So, when it comes to sending out your play, circulate as many copies as you can, together with a short synopsis. Make sure the script is neatly typed, using double spacing. It is important to be clear eyed about all this from the start. Too many ill-prepared scripts pile up in theatres which are already strapped for cash for staging plays.

But even if you get the essentials right, don't be disheartened by rejection slips, or total silence! Even well-established authors have scripts regularly turned down. The fact is that there are too many plays chasing too few opportunities. In addition, plays go in fashions and you may well have written a very workmanlike play, but its style or content is not what producers or directors happen to be looking for at that moment.

Let us assume, however, that you are not going to be put off. You want to write for the theatre. Why? What is it about theatre that makes it different to other media? One answer is that theatre is a communal activity. There is a buzz about the performance of a stage play that you just don't get with a movie. You can tell from the sudden silences that happen in the theatre, the ripples of amusement, waves of laughter, as well as the buzz of voices in the interval, when a play is working. Unlike the cinema, in the theatre there is a special relationship between the actors and the audience which changes each night. That great actress, Dame Edith Evans, used to compare acting to riding a horse. Each night she would stand in the wings and listen to the audience before she came on. Some nights, she would say, the audience was so unruly that as you came on you had to pull on the reins and dig in your stirrups before you could start to canter; on other nights, you could gallop away from the start. And so your play is a living breathing thing, constantly shifting and changing, however subtly, from performance to performance. You can go and swan about the south of France (if your play is successful) or drown your sorrows in the local pub (if it is a flop) but it is the actors who have to make it live from night to night. That is why the text per se is not theatre, but becomes theatre through the actor's use of it.

So what is a play? A play consists of a plot, character, dialogue. Character, wrote Galsworthy, is situation. By this he meant that if the author gets his characters right they will precipitate the action, as his *Forsyte Saga* perfectly illustrates.

But where, you may ask, am I to find my characters? The American poet Emily Dickinson who, although a recluse, was a great observer of people, wrote:

The show is not the show
But they that go.
Menagerie to me
My neighbour be.

From the start you must make a practice of observing people, empathizing with them, metaphorically wearing their shoes and clothes. Your neighbour, the passer-by, the man in the pub, this is your potential material. Watching, but also listening. A good dramatist must develop not only a photographic eye but a recording ear, noting people's different speech patterns, accents and styles. Joyce Grenfell based most of her one-woman sketches on people she observed, often blending two or three into one character. Sometimes, seated on a bus, she would become so absorbed in an overheard conversation that she would stay on long past her own stop. Ruth Draper, another famous solo performer, based her very first sketch on the little old Jewish tailor her mother employed to do the sewing and make dresses. She observed his accent, his gestures, the stoop of his shoulders, the way he walked.

You never know when a character you meet is going to be the one that sparks off the play you are meant to write. The writer Jack Rosenthal tells the story of how he once employed some men to redecorate his house. In conversation with them he found out that they were firemen, doing decorating on the side. He had the nous to probe and question them each day during their breaks, learning all he could about firemen, and out of this was born his successful television series, *London's Burning*.

An ear for dialogue is crucial in the theatre. I recall working with Hugh Whitemore on his play, *The Best of Friends*, which I directed. This was about the friendship between three people: George Bernard Shaw, Sir Sydney Cockerell (who was Director of the Fitzwilliam Museum in Cambridge) and Dame Laurentia McLachlan OSB who was abbess of Stanbrook Abbey in Worcester. I pointed out to Hugh that while I happened to know a great deal about enclosed contemplative nuns, few in his audience would be so well informed. What was needed, I suggested, was a speech explaining what an enclosed nun at that period would do with her day. And so, when we were staying at Stanbrook researching the archives, Hugh asked one of the senior nuns, Dame Felicitas Corrigan, what a day in the life of a nun would have been like at that time. The long reply which Dame Felicitas gave went straight into the play. Yet Hugh made no notes, nor did he tape-record anything. As a writer he had so developed his powers of memorizing, that the exact phrasing and detail of her reply were not lost.

That incident illustrates another important point about writing for the theatre: a play is not just people talking. Actions often speak louder than words (as film and television especially demonstrate), as also can a sudden pause or a silence. And so the playwright has to consider what his characters are doing, or not doing, from moment to moment. Two of them might be arguing while a third is silent, perhaps knitting or reading, but that third character is not 'dead'. If such a character suddenly stops knitting and looks up, that becomes a dramatic moment, whether anything is said or not. And so with this long speech of the abbess in Hugh Whitemore's play. If it had been spoken straight it would have been very static. Since, however, a few lines earlier there had been a reference to the apple-picking harvest at the abbey, I suggested that Rosemary Harris, who created the role of the abbess, wear an apron and be seen packing crates of apples throughout the speech, and that she should do it without looking down once, as though it were something she did year in and year out, thereby helping to emphasize the practicality of nuns.

As a writer you will often find in rehearsal an actor saying to you: What am I *doing* in this scene? And that is why a playwright needs to know much more about his characters than will actually be used in the text. You will need to research thoroughly into each character's background, job, place of work, home life, habits, family and childhood. Hugh Whitemore recalls how, when working on his play *Breaking the Code* about the brilliant mathematician Alan Turing, he spent a year learning mathematics so that he could write with some inside knowledge. Of course this is the kind of detail that any conscientious actor will seek out when working on a part, as Zoe Caldwell recounts in her recent autobiography *I Will Be Cleopatra*: 'to know as much as possible about the time my character lived in, what she wears and why; what she sits in and how; what she eats and how she eats. What the state of the society she lives in and so on.'

The questions, therefore, that the dramatist has to ask are the same as the actor has to ask of the character she or he is playing. Similarly, as a director, after having read the script several times, I construct a biography of each character: writing down everything the author has to tell me, either directly, or through the comments or reactions of the other characters in the play.

These basic questions are: Who am I? Where have I come from, as I enter the stage, and where am I going, once I leave the stage? When is it: what time of day, year, season? What is the weather like? What am I wearing? What can I see outside the window? What is in the next room? What have I come to do or say? In other words, the dramatist has to visualize the life of the character off stage, before the play begins, as well as when the play has ended. Of course only a little of this information can be fed into the script, otherwise an audience would have indigestion! A play is not a lecture. Observe how skilfully Shakespeare, in the opening of *Romeo and Juliet*, slips in so many facts. We learn Juliet's age and the exact date of her birth; that Lammas Eve is 20 August, that Lady Capulet is 26, that the Nurse's daughter, who has died, was called Susan, and also that the Nurse's husband is dead. We learn that there was an earthquake eleven years ago, that the Capulets were away in Mantua at the time of the earthquake – and all this in the first scene with Juliet.

Hugh Whitemore's play *Breaking the Code* also provides a splendid model of how to weave in information without the audience being aware of what the dramatist is doing. At the start of the play we are told nothing about the central character, Alan Turing, other than that he is reporting a burglary to the police. It is only at the end of

Scene 4 that we learn he worked for the Foreign Office and 'got to be their big chap during the war. Quite a big fish, our Mr Turing. Winston thought the world of him'. And then, only towards the end of the next long scene are we shown the extent of Turing's brilliance when he launches into a long speech about his theory of compatible numbers.

Before rehearsals began there was some concern about this speech, whether it should be cut: would an audience understand it? But so remarkable was Derek Jacobi's rendering of it that although most people still did not understand it, what came through – and this is what makes theatre – was Turing's passion for higher mathematics and his quality of genius. The actor made the speech work!

This play also demonstrates the first essential in setting out to write a play for the theatre: the importance of having one central character who has a story to tell, and a strong motive, or desire, which has to be realized. Then creating a character, characters or situation which thwarts this desire and thereby produces conflict. In Turing's case this was the law which, at that period, made homosexual behaviour illegal. As Arthur Miller has expressed it: the business of a play is to explore and resolve a conflict.

If you have never written a play before you may want to consider taking a writing course. Formal teaching of creative writing in any form took much longer to catch on here than in the US. The best known of the university courses is the one-year M.Phil. in Playwriting Studies at Birmingham University, set up by David Edgar, who ran it for ten years. It is now run by the playwright April de Angelis and many of its graduates are gaining a reputation.

There are well over a hundred and fifty other courses at different levels aimed at writers for theatre or screen. Some are attached to education institutions but there are also writers' groups run by theatres or companies to encourage writers in particular areas. The best source is the Internet site Writernet (www.writernet.org.uk), which has full listings of most courses.

Although bringing playwrights into creative contact with theatres is exciting and rewarding, the way a playwright really develops is by going through rehearsal and seeing her or his work in front of an audience.

There are many books on writing for the theatre (some of the best are listed on pages 17–18) but all emphasize the importance of learning the craft. And the best way to do this is through exercises. Just as Dylan Thomas learned his craft as a poet by writing poems in the style of Keats, Wordsworth and others, so Hugh Whitemore records how he wrote plays in the style of those dramatists who most influenced him when he was young. The best way to start is by aiming at one-act plays of five to ten minutes in length, with two to three characters (but no more than that). A useful model here are the one-act plays by Jean McConnell (published by Samuel French) which have proved very popular with amateur groups. *Deck-chairs*, for example, is a set of five plays, each of which is about fifteen minutes in length, each calling for just two actresses and each set on a seaside promenade. Some are funny, some poignant. In the first, *Shoppers*, two well-to-do shopaholics have a rather surprising secret. *Early Blight* is a moving exploration of a doomed mother–daughter relationship. *Dancers* dissects the tea-dancing world of two skittish women. *Late Frost* is a drama in which one woman finds out her best friend had an affair with her late husband, and *Doggies* is a hilarious tale about two very different types of dog owner.

In writing such exercise pieces try and keep to a contemporary style, and to one setting. Writing is a craft that must be learned, as with any other art. Unlike a novel, which can tell and deal with past action, a play must reveal through action on the stage what a character is thinking, feeling. A play is more than people talking. There has to be a subtext beneath the printed text. A character may be saying something as banal as 'I'll go and put the kettle on' but what she is really thinking/feeling could be 'I don't know what to say. I need time. I must get out of the room.' Again, observe how often in real life, in the middle of a conversation, someone gets up to go to the toilet, and when they return they start off with a fresh burst of excitement or come up with a new idea, and this gives impetus for the next scene, or phase.

Richard Eyre, the former director of the Royal National Theatre, in a speech he gave on presenting the Lloyds Banking Award for Best New Play, observed how the playwright 'by sleight of hand engineers confrontations, love affairs, battles, deaths and births, as if each action effortlessly and inevitably followed another, leaving an audience with the impression that the play happened rather than was written'.

Playwrights are essentially practical thinkers and their storylines are well constructed. And so, at this apprentice stage, it is invaluable to write out a synopsis of your play, noting its theme, its characters, its structure – that is, its beginning, middle and end – and to keep this pinned up before you as you write. It will save you a lot of time and keep you from getting bogged down or going off at tangents. Of course the detail will change as you write and most plays go through several revisions, but this will ensure you have the basic ingredients. When you have several plays under your belt and have gained a mastery of your craft, you need not stick to such a rigid scheme. Indeed, experienced playwrights find they go through many drafts and the final play emerges in the process. But that is for later!

You may say: Having found my characters and researched their background, where do I start in the story? That is a sound question. Alan Ayckbourn, who has written and produced more plays than any other dramatist of the twentieth century, has this advice: 'To begin at the beginning and carry on until the end sounds like good advice, but it can become ponderous! My rule is to start as late as you can without leaving the audience terminally perplexed.'

Hugh Whitemore's *Breaking the Code* was inspired by and based on the book *Alan Turing, The Enigma* by Andrew Hodges. It has 526 pages but, exemplifying Alan Ayckbourn's dictum, Whitemore commences his play towards the end of the book, starting the action with Turing reporting a supposed burglary, a complaint that leads to the police discovering he is homosexual.

So it is invaluable to a novice writer to read and study as many plays as possible, making notes at the time, analysing how each author achieves his or her effects. And, parallel with this, to go to the theatre as frequently as you can. I am amazed how often young writers expect their plays to be staged professionally and yet have seen or read very little in the theatre. If you find a play that fires you, go and see it more than once, if you can afford it. Not only analyse why and how it works but also observe how subtly it changes in performance. Why does one scene work and not another? Is it due to some weakness in the writing or to the way it is being acted or directed? Equally, it is very instructive to attend a bad play. The point is to observe, analyse, and observe again!

Perhaps the single most useful preparation for writing plays is to be an actor: one has only to think of Shakespeare, Molière, Coward, Osborne, Pinter, Whitemore, Ayckbourn and many more, including Julian Fellowes who won an Oscar for his film script of *Gosford Park*. A writer will learn much by watching actors, and especially experienced actors. I remember directing a play in the West End when I had to take the author to one side (it was his first stage play) and point out that certain scenes needed rewriting. He exploded with anger: 'I have slaved over every word and punctuation mark at my desk over the past two years. I do not intend to rewrite!' My answer? 'Then you are being very foolish. This is your first play in the West End and you have a very experienced cast, and the actors are telling you that certain scenes are not working. You should listen to them.'

Don't just sit in your room but get to know actors and others in the theatre. Hang around your local theatre, whether it is professional or amateur. Make yourself useful, offer your voluntary services, be prepared to do anything. Get to know people, make friends. It is often said in theatre: Make friends on your way up because you will need them on the way down! Above all, if you can get a job as prompter on a production, that is the best way of learning about actors and what goes on in rehearsal. Observe perpetually, as Virginia Woolf says on the final page of her journal.

And, having made friends with your local theatre, you will find it much easier when the time comes to have someone look sympathetically at your play, even to be given a rehearsed reading of it – which is an excellent test for an author to see where certain scenes need editing or rewriting, or a character needs to be developed – or a full-scale production. But, if you do get your play staged, and even if it is a resounding success, don't give up your day job. All too often an author's second play proves to be an equally resounding flop. Be cautious, for theatre is as fickle a profession as politics.

Writing for Children's Theatre

C. S. Lewis once said that the best children's writers were those who wrote for the child within themselves. Theatre for children is a separate art form with qualities that make it quite distinct from adult theatre. It is not, repeat not, simplified adult theatre. If this is an area that interests you then the best introduction is *Theatre for Children* by David Wood with Janet Grant, published by Faber & Faber, with an introduction by Cameron Mackintosh. For over thirty years David Wood has had the ability to captivate children's minds, both as a writer and as a director. He has fought passionately against the disparaging tag of 'children's theatre'. The challenge is, he says, to give a unique experience of theatre to an audience many of whom will be first-time theatre-goers. He also knows that children are the most challenging and, at the same time, rewarding audiences. Irving Wardle, reviewing David Wood's *The Gingerbread Man*, wrote in *The Times* of 'the loudest audience participation I have ever heard and, much more remarkable, the most absolute breathtaking silences'. Children remain the most critical audience and the best test of whether a scene is boring or not! As Cameron Mackintosh remarks in his introduction to David Wood's book: 'What has certainly surprised me is the huge number of children, some of whom are only six years old, who go and see or study the stories of *Les Misérables* and *Miss Saigon*. Not only do they empathize with the characters, they also follow the story and often ask more probing questions about the motivation of the story than some adults.'

David Wood's book examines the dynamics of a children's audience; stories and themes that children love; the craft of writing an original play; adapting a children's book for the stage; and everything you want to know about directing and the production side, and concludes with a valuable section on marketing, acquiring the rights of a book you would like to adapt, and getting your play published.

In addition, both the Unicorn Theatre and the Polka Theatre have new literary managers (Carl Miller for the former) as well as new policies for plays. The Unicorn is opening a purpose-built theatre for children in London in 2004. Indeed, every city ought to have a children's theatre. In Antwerp they have one right next to the adult theatre but in the UK children's theatre still has a low priority. However, there are signs that children's writing could be on the verge of the same exciting breakthroughs that we have seen happening in children's fiction with authors such as Philip Pullman and J. K. Rowling.

The Amateur Theatre

No one knows the full extent of amateur drama, although there are at least 3,000 amateur companies affiliated to the Central Council for Amateur Theatre throughout the UK. Tom Williams, Chairman for the CCAT, believes that these 3,000 represent no more than 25 per cent of the total. Samuel French Ltd, which has the largest publishing list of plays, has a mailing list of more than 11,000.

The Arts Council of England has recently commissioned Jonathan Newth of Writernet to produce a guide to new writing for the amateur theatre. CCAT and the Writers' Guild both serve on the working party overseeing this work. According to Tom Williams, there seem to be three ways in which new work is produced by amateurs. A writer may create a play for his group to perform or create his own group to ensure that it is performed. A second possibility is for new work to emerge from a writing competition. One of the usual features of such a competition is the promise of a production. Regular competitions are held by the National Drama Festivals Association (annually for one-act plays), the Drama Association of Wales and the Little Theatre Guild of Great Britain. The third way forward is the production of what has now become known as a community play. This seems to have replaced the old-fashioned pageant as a means of involving the whole community in a drama-based event.

Most amateur groups are reluctant to seek to commission plays directly from an established playwright. Either they do not have the confidence that a playwright would agree to work just for them or they fear that the exercise would be too costly. It is to try and overcome these fears that the commission was given to Jonathan Newth.

One amateur theatre company with a long and distinguished track record for promoting new drama is The Questors at Ealing in London. The Questors was one of the founder members of the Little Theatre Guild of Great Britain, which comprises amateur theatres who own or control their own premises. The guild now includes nearly one hundred members from Galloway to Exeter and from Bangor in Northern Ireland to Whitstable in Kent, many of whom have their own writers' networks.

As regards a writer having his play published, the largest promoter is undoubtedly Samuel French Ltd. Paul Taylor, performing rights director at French's, comments that for a full-length play to be published, amateur theatre groups would expect the play to have been professionally produced either in the West End, or to have toured nationally, or have been done in a regional repertory theatre. This means that a completely unknown play which has never been staged is at a considerable disadvantage.

French's catalogue gives a detailed breakdown on cast, plot and ratio of male to female roles. The latter is important because most amateur groups tend to have a preponderance of females. There are also the women's guilds, for whom French's publish a special range of all-women plays.

A playwright cannot expect in general to live off royalties from the amateur theatre but in the case of musicals and pantomimes the case is somewhat different. Paul Taylor says, 'I can think of some cases, particularly musicals, where we are sending the author a four-figure sum every month and have been doing so for ten or twenty years. Now that is quite a significant income. If the same show was done professionally it might have, say, a repertory production at a good date such as the Theatre Royal, Windsor and turn up a royalty of £5,000, but it might not get another professional booking for eighteen months. Whereas the amateur income comes in month after month.'

When it comes to pantomimes, bear in mind that there are thousands of amateur groups around the country and every single one will do a pantomime at Christmas. So there is a lot of money to be made between October and March. An interesting new development reported by French's is the writing of more innovative and up-to-date pantomimes that have the traditional feel of a pantomime but with new subjects and new ideas. For example, French's publish pantomimes about the Three Musketeers, King Arthur and Hercules. And although the amateur theatre movement was at first reluctant, preferring to stay with the old familiars such as *Aladdin*, amateur groups are now much more willing to try new ideas. Paul Reakes, a successful writer for the amateur theatre, wrote one of the first new pantomimes, called *Santa in Space*.

In addition, the educational market provides another outlet for writers. Secondary schools often do annual plays, though mainly by popular mainstream authors. Colleges and universities tend to be more ambitious and sophisticated. Plays which twenty years ago might have been unacceptable are no longer so. Recently, French's published Patrick Marber's *Dealer's Choice* and also his *Closer*, both of which have done well even though full of expletives and difficult subject matter, with *Dealer's Choice* also being an all-male play.

In many ways, says Paul Taylor, the amateur theatre is a barometer of society. 'Often we are able to gauge opinion across the amateur perspective simply by what plays we are being asked about. If there is a play in the West End and we are asked about it several times as to when amateur rights will be available, that is a good way for us to realize that that is a property we should be interested in publishing.'

Samuel French, like other publishers of plays (Methuen, Faber, Oberon, Joseph Weinberger), do receive unsolicited scripts, but they require that the play has some professional history. Paul Taylor's advice to an author who has no professional experience would be to get the play tried out by a local amateur group, 'because, apart from anything else, it's a wonderful way to see whether it works. When you see it on stage you see its strengths and weaknesses, what works, what doesn't work. And then, having done that and rewritten the script in the light of the experience, to try and get a professional company interested. Or get an agent. But then you have the catch-22 situation: the agent is not interested if you haven't got a professional history, and professional theatres are not interested if you haven't got an agent!'

International Outlets

Some established writers (Edward Bond being the most famous) are more widely produced outside this country than here. Others do very well on the royalties which come in from productions of their work in, for example, the extensive German network of subsidized theatres. In addition, many of the younger writers who came to prominence in the 1990s have been widely performed outside Britain as examples of new 'shock' theatre. Sarah Kane is among the most famous, along with Mark Ravenhill and (less of a 'shocker') the young Scottish writer, David Harrower. Often work which is only seen in small theatres here is staged on much larger stages abroad.

There has been traffic in the other direction as well with much more contemporary writing from abroad being seen in London, thanks to the work of the Gate Theatre, LIFT (London International Festival of Theatre) and the Royal Court's International Department. The dialogue about theatre forms and content is now a global one. For further information, contact the Theatre Committee of the Writers' Guild of Great Britain.

James Roose-Evans

James Roose-Evans is the founder of the Hampstead Theatre and was its artistic director for ten years. Among his many West End productions are Hugh Whitemore's *The Best of Friends* and his own adaptation of Helene Hanff's *84 Charing Cross Road*, which he also directed on Broadway, winning awards on boths sides of the Atlantic for Best Play and Best Director. He also adapted Laurie Lee's *Cider With Rosie* for the stage and wrote, especially for Maureen Lipman, *Re: Joyce!* an entertainment about Joyce Grenfell. He is the author of *London Theatre: From the Globe to the National* (Phaidon); *Directing a Play* (Studio Vista), *Experimental Theatre* (Routledge) and *One Foot on the Stage: the biography of Richard Wilson* (Weidenfeld & Nicolson).

Websites

Samuel French: www.samuelfrench-london.co.uk
Amateur dramatics: www.amdram.co.uk

Further reading

The Crafty Art of Playmaking by Alan Ayckbourn (Faber & Faber, 2002)

Playwriting in Process – a book of exercises to develop techniques by
  Michael Wright (Heinemann, 1997)
The Playwright's Process, learning the craft from today's dramatists by
  Buzz McLaughlin (Backstage Books, New York, 1997)
The Dramatist's Tool Kit: the craft of the working playwright by Jeffrey
  Sweet (Heinemann, New Hampshire, 1993)
The Elements of Playwriting by Louis E. Catron (Macmillan, USA,
  1993)
New Playwriting Strategies by Paul C. Castagno (Theatre Arts,
  Routledge, 2001)
Writing a Play by Steve Gooch (A&C Black, 3rd edn, 2001)
Theatre for Children by David Wood with Janet Grant (Faber &
  Faber, 1997)
Connections – new plays for young people (Faber & Faber, 1997)
Contacts – (The *Spotlight*, October, annually)

> I don't pick up a pen and see how things will go. By the time I pick
> up a pen, I've gone through so much work. Once I have the vague
> idea of a structure, landmark moments occur which fit into the
> structure. I have an idea of how a scene will end, but I don't know
> how to get there.
>   I will begin by mapping something out on a single piece of paper
> without a line of dialogue, so I have a structure. In the actual writing
> I can't bash out a rough draft. It's a slow work-through, and each bit
> has got to be potentially 'it' before I can go on to the next bit.
>   – *Tom Stoppard*

Writing Plays Is Like Learning a Foreign Language

Hugh Whitemore discusses his philosophy of writing with James Roose-Evans

'Excuse me, Mr Roose-Evans,' said a student, stopping me in a corridor of the Royal Academy of Dramatic Art, 'but may I ask what was the music you used in your production of *Pericles*?'

The student was Hugh Whitemore and we were not to meet again for some 30 years when I was asked to direct his play *The Best of Friends*, but his passion for music is perhaps a key to his brilliance as a writer of dialogue. 'To my mind,' he told me recently, 'my dialogue is like music and if an actor changes it ... I remember Clifford Williams when he was directing *Pack of Lies* – which on the surface is a very mundane, suburban, ordinary play – saying to the cast at the read-through, "Don't change this, because if you do it falls to pieces."'

Hugh was an unlikely actor but had been accepted on the strength of his audition when, never having seen the play, he gave a rendition of Hamlet's 'Oh, what a piece of work is man' in the style of Frankie Howerd. The examiners all thought he was an original and accepted him on the spot.

He thinks now that what he most wanted to do was learn about theatre and get involved with the creation of plays. He had started writing full-length plays at the age of fourteen. He didn't go much to the theatre but he read a lot and started writing plays in the styles of Christopher Fry, John Whiting and Terence Rattigan.

On leaving RADA he acted a bit in repertory, failed, lived in a squat, then got a job in the piano department of Harrods. Learning that Associated Rediffusion Television was looking for someone to write what announcers say between programmes, he applied and got the job. 'One always thinks they make it up as they go along, but it is all meticulously scripted in order to fit in with the split-second timing necessary for TV schedules.'

This was splendid training for a young writer for, as he observes, 'I was writing the equivalent in airtime of a full-length television play every week. In this way I learned a great deal about the technique of writing for television. For four years I wrote a colossal amount. And got well paid. And it was at this time I started writing plays for television.'

Because Whitemore knew John Mortimer slightly, the latter said to him, 'If you want to be a writer you should get hold of my agent!' This was the famous Peggy Ramsay. Hugh wrote to her, saying he wanted to be a writer, could she help him? And she, typically, replied, 'I'm not interested in people who want to be writers, only people who are writers!'

So, after a year, when he had his play done on television, he wrote again to Peggy Ramsay, saying, 'You may remember I wrote to you and you were rather grumpy. Well, I've written a play and sold it, so who needs agents?'

She rang him within twelve hours and said, 'I can see you tomorrow afternoon at three o'clock.'

'I can't,' he replied, 'because I'm working in an office job.'

She didn't seem to hear him.

'No, no, tomorrow afternoon's fine. Three o'clock.'

'I arrived, and found her sitting on the floor, as she always seemed to be, surrounded by papers and scripts, and she said, "Do you know how much Bob Bolt made last week? Nine and a half thousand. [This was 1962–3.] Give up your job!"

' "But I'm married, I've a flat; I can't just give up my job like that!"

' "If you do, I guarantee you'll make at least £5,000 next year."

'That was a lot of money then, so I said, "Alright!" gave in my notice and, touch wood, I have never been out of work since. And I went on to do a tremendous amount of television.'

Then he adds ruminatively, 'I'm not sure I understand writing. I think that is the most alarming thing. Where does it come from? If you don't know where it comes from you are always desperately afraid that it might go away. I work obsessively and do lots of rewrites and fresh drafts. I keep a notebook and jot down ideas immediately they occur otherwise they'd be lost for ever.'

Hugh Whitemore's modesty belies him. He is hardly a one-play wonder. He has written successful plays that have been performed in the West End and on Broadway, and each has been led by outstanding actors such as Glenda Jackson in *Stevie*, Judi Dench and Michael Williams in *Pack of Lies*, Derek Jacobi in *Breaking the Code*, Sir John Gielgud and Rosemary Harris in *The Best of Friends* and Edward Fox in *Letter of Resignation*. His film and television credits include his adaptation of Anthony Powell's *The Dance of Time*, Laurie Lee's *Cider with Rosie*, as well as film adaptations of *84 Charing Cross Road*, Bruce Chatwin's *Utz* and much work for American television. His most recent television play is *The Gathering Storm*, with Albert Finney as Winston Churchill and Vanessa Redgrave as Lady Churchill.

With reference to this last he reflects that ultimately one is born with a talent or a certain knack which is perfected with practice.

'One has to have a certain instinct. For example, this recent film about Churchill. I knew exactly how the film should begin – with Churchill imagining the Battle of Blenheim. There was a lot of resistance at first. But I absolutely stuck to my guns because, instinctively, I knew it was right. And it turned out that it was right. It is purely instinct, because they asked me to explain why and I replied, I can't explain why. It is partly to do with a view of history that Churchill had, and a sort of rather naive patriotism. But above all it was this instinct. And also a belief. That, too, comes into it. You have to believe in what you are doing.'

In a collection of essays entitled *The Writer and Television*, Whitemore observes, 'I have learned to obey the voice of instinct; and on the rare occasions when I have over-ruled myself, I have always regretted it.'

But once he does believe in a project he hangs on to it. 'It took me about ten years to write *The Best of Friends* but I never gave up or thought, I'm not going to go on with this. Because I knew that somehow it would form itself.'

This leads us on to talk about plays based on real-life characters or situations such as Whitemore has explored in a number of his most successful plays. His original version of *Pack of Lies* was written first for television under the title *Act of Betrayal* and I asked him why he then chose to rewrite it for the stage and to explain the essential difference between writing for television and the stage.

'I did it for emotional reasons really. The television version was what is described often as docudrama and I wanted to open it out, to be more imaginative, to explore things that hadn't occurred to me to do on TV, and to characterize the family with more depth. I suddenly realized that the play is really about the powerlessness of ordinary people. This was during the Falklands crisis. I felt strongly that Margaret Thatcher was doing a very wrong thing, and realized suddenly how powerless one is. We elect these people and suddenly they take you into a totally indefensible war.

'I love real-life stories. I don't find it any different doing that and doing fiction or doing an adaptation of a book. I think you always find something if you are drawn to a subject. I adore the research. I love finding things out.'

It was through reading a review of Andrew Hodges' book *Enigma*, the story of the mathematical genius Alan Turing, of whom he had never heard, that Hugh came to write *Breaking the Code*, his most brilliant play. But, again, it took him years to write.

'I was very intrigued that a man like Turing should commit suicide by dipping an apple in cyanide when his favourite film was *Snow White*. I found that fascinating. And then there was this split between Turing's thinking and feeling, which is something I am very well aware of in myself, though less so now, but there was a time when it was very painful for me, as for many of my generation.

'I think Turing stopped growing emotionally at the age of fourteen. His tragedy was his inability to make adult sexual relationships, which was the result of not having grown out of adolescence at an emotional level. And so I saw Turing as a man flawed by this Jungian gap between thinking and feeling. Half of his tragedy – and it applies to heterosexuals as well as to homosexuals – was that he was driven by his sexual energies but could not relate them to his intellectual side.'

I comment on the marvellous economy in the writing of that play, where there is not a wasted word.

'I think this is where television helped me. You see I was forty before I wrote my first stage play. And so I had already done twelve years in television and film. And what you especially learn in working on a film is the collaborative process. It is also the same in television. You learn the importance of making the dialogue and the action really clear. And you work with the story editor, the producer and the director.

'I think structure is terribly important. And I don't think this is something you can learn from a book about writing for the theatre or for television. You learn by trial and error. I was lucky in that I came into the business at a very good time, when there was a lot of drama. I wrote about a hundred television plays, but I also learned by watching it in process as well as by working with directors and actors.'

What it comes back to always, Hugh stresses, is a question of personal commitment. There is a story which he often quotes, about Scott Fitzgerald when he was at the height of his fame as a writer. A woman who was a distant cousin wrote to him, enclosing a short story she had written. Fitzgerald took enormous pains with the letter he wrote back. 'I have read your story,' he said. 'Nice construction. Characters crisp and well delineated. The dialogue is witty. *But I see nothing of you in this story.*'

'After all,' adds Whitemore, 'nobody's interested in a soldier who is only slightly brave! And so you have to be as brave as you can be, and not worry about what your wife, your parents or your friends are going to say.

'I never know how things are going to end. This Churchill film,

The Gathering Storm, is a good example. I was sitting here with the director and he said, "Well, I don't think the ending works at all." And I said, "Neither do I." And as we sat there I suddenly improvised the ending.

'I actually find that one writes best when one doesn't think too much about it. So I am always doing this thing of giving myself impossible deadlines. And I await the call which says, "If we don't have it all on Monday then it's all off!" and that somehow frees one up to write. Harold Pinter said something similar to me about this, that writing is almost like free association, you don't know what's going to come up. You've just got to get it down. And in a way I think that's right. You have to ride the waves as it were.

'I remember when I was asked to write *The Gathering Storm*, this play about Churchill. I thought, I don't think I can do this because it's a very personal story, it's not to do with big affairs of state, but about the relationship between Winston and his wife. I didn't know quite what to do, and so I said, Let me think about it. And I went down to the country on my own. I sat down and just wrote a scene. I hadn't an idea for it, I just wrote it straight off the top of my head and I looked at it and I thought, Well, that's fine. And the odd thing is that it has stayed in the film. Writing plays is like learning a foreign language. You learn the grammar, you learn the words and the vocabulary and the syntax and all that. But actually when you launch out, you are flying by the seat of your pants.'

Hugh Whitemore playlist: *Stevie* (first produced 1977); *Pack of Lies* (1983); *Breaking the Code* (1986); *The Best of Friends* (1987); *It's Ralph* (1991); *The Towers of Trebizond* (1991); *A Letter of Resignation* (1997); *God Only Knows* (2001).

Catching Them Young

James Roose-Evans talks to Carl Miller, literary associate
at the Birmingham Rep where he introduces young
people to a life in the theatre

To meet Carl Miller is to encounter a man passionate about his
commitment to working with young people. He believes that more
theatres need to be open to hosting seminal work by young writers.

He was artistic director of the Royal Court Young People's Theatre
at a time when the Court was promoting new writing to reflect
today's society. It was a job that excited him because, he says, 'If we
don't do this, we are in danger of losing generations of potential
writers – not to mention audiences!'

When Carl Miller arrived at the Royal Court the programme
for young people had been going for a number of years and various new writers had already emerged from it, notably Andrea
Dunbar, a teenage girl from the kind of background where theatre
was not regarded as important. However, a teacher had encouraged her writing and she had submitted a piece to the Royal Court.
'It was formally a mess,' recalls Carl, 'in that it wasn't even laid out
in the right way, but it did have the most extraordinary combination of story, dialogue and character, the three basic ingredients of
a play.'

It was called *Arbor*, which was the name of the housing estate
where she lived. She then went on to write a play called *Rita, Sue
and Bob, too*, which was staged at the Royal Court, made into a film,
and successfully revived in 2001 on tour and in London. 'I suppose
Andrea Dunbar was the quintessential young writer from that
period in that here was someone who was writing about something

she knew from personal experience in the way that another writer could only have done at one remove, through research. But this does not mean, and should not mean, that if you are a black or an Asian, you should only write about black or Asian issues, any more than if you are gay you write solely about gay issues. What is important is to offer writers the chance to write the plays they have it in them to write.'

I ask him about his job at Birmingham where, each year, he works over several months with about twenty young writers before arriving at a three-week festival when all the plays are staged.

'What we aim to do at Birmingham is to make these youngsters feel part of the working environment of the theatre, because that's how one picks up a lot of the craft. If you see a lot of theatre and how it is made, that helps you as a playwright. It's the same process at the Royal Court, at the Hampstead Theatre and at the Traverse, where they have similar programmes.'

Because so many of the young people he works with have had comparatively little experience of theatre, he tries to find different routes to starting a play. But there is no simple process. 'At the Royal Court, there used to be a concept of something called the Royal Court process – but, like the rainbow, it falls apart the closer you get to it. If there really was a way you could train people in a particular way to produce masterpieces, then we'd all be doing it and become extremely rich!

'All that we can do is to work with writers and share with them the best we know. It's not like learning French! There is no guarantee, there can't be, that at the end of the process you will produce a good play. But one thing those taking part can be sure of, is that with commitment and hard work they will see their plays staged. That is crucial. It's important because the learning curve gets steeper and faster the closer you get to performance. There are things that can only be learned about writing for the theatre by being in rehearsal with actors saying "Why am I doing this?" or "How can I possibly get from here to there and do such and such at the same time?" Being challenged in this way about every detail teaches you a huge amount, just as sitting in the audience, listening and watching, teaches you something more.'

The Birmingham Repertory Theatre has the bonus of an M.Phil. course in playwriting at the university, founded by David Edgar and now run by April de Angelis. This brings in the question of funding. At Birmingham there is just enough money to assemble a group of actors to perform the plays over three weeks. But how do you stage the work of twenty writers in that time?

'You have to find ways of doing extracts, or rehearsed readings. It's a simpler way of staging but it pays off. The writing does get better.'

Some go on to full-time writing careers, but Miller has also worked with talented youngsters who, having written their play, decide that what they really want to do is to be a hairdresser or work with computers. 'For a lot of them that is enough and I don't find this a problem.' Jonathan Harvey is one of those who has become a professional writer. Before his play *Beautiful Thing* brought him to the attention of the critics, he had already had his first play staged at the Royal Court's Young Writers Festival.

I ask Carl Miller if he has ten commandments he could give to young writers. He laughs and replies, 'I'm no Moses so I can only offer five!' Here they are.

1 Write
Don't just keep talking about the play you are going to write. And then when you have completed that one, don't just sit waiting for the phone to ring. Write the next one.

2 Collaborate
Writing is a solitary business, but making theatre is about communicating with others. Find people who can help you make your work better: people who can read your work and offer their thoughts, people who can read your work out loud and try things so that you can think about what the play will be like in rehearsal

27

and performance. These could be other writers, actors, directors, who are starting out like you. Or they could be friends with an interest in theatre.

3 Go to the theatre
What contemporary plays do you like? What don't you like? What do other people seem to like? Watch and read plays and see how they work; what makes them effective on stage?

4 Rewrite
Your first draft may be great, but put it aside for a week, then try and make it better. It may just be a question of cutting; your draft will almost certainly benefit from that. Get feedback from people you trust and think about what advice from them to include before you send your play out into the world. Don't send out a play that you know has flaws. Solve them first. Don't give people an easy reason to set your work aside.

5 Don't be disheartened
Writing can be hard, lonely, frustrating work, particularly when you start out. It is important to be able to take criticism; some comments may be useful even though they are hard to take. But don't give up. It is your energy and commitment that are needed at this stage in your writing career. So make sure you find ways to keep yourself motivated – celebrate your achievements and try not to dwell on your disappointments.

Carl Miller was born in London. His first professional work in theatre was as assistant director at the Royal Court Theatre through the Regional Theatre Young Directors Scheme. He was artistic director of the Royal Court Young People's Theatre from 1997 to 1999 and continues to work with the Royal Court International Department. His writing includes the plays *Descent*, *The Last Enemy* and *Master Better*; the award-winning short film *Jean*; and the book *Stages of Desire: Gay Theatre's Hidden History*. He was editor of London magazine *City Limits* and has written for the *Observer*, the

Guardian, the *Independent*, *Time Out* and other publications. He is currently literary associate at Birmingham Rep Theatre where he co-directs an annual festival of new work by young writers, and literary manager of the Unicorn Theatre for Children.

Breaking the Screen Barrier

Bob Ritchie takes twelve simple steps to becoming a TV scriptwriter

Step 1: Be related to a producer

It may come as a surprise that I, a writer who can't in all honesty use the adjective 'successful' yet – or even 'full-time' – should presume to offer advice to other beginners. On the other hand, I have plenty of first-hand experience. Whether it is useful experience I leave you to judge. If you want to know how famous screenwriters got their breaks, you should stop reading now and get their autobiographies out of the library. Most of them are very entertaining, unfortunately not particularly helpful. Writers are a disparate bunch. They seem to have little in common except a burning desire to write. Some, judging by the extraordinary amount of complaining they do about what a thankless, lonely and exhausting job it is, don't even have that.

Previous career is not a reliable indicator. People come to screenwriting by a variety of different routes: redundancy, divorce, depression, journalism. This will be bad news for anyone who is thinking a couple of years as a shoplifter is only one short step away from a writing credit on *The Bill*. Similarly, being a doctor may be an advantage for an aspiring contributor to *Holby City*, but equally it may not; a doctor may find perfectly acceptable what a prime-time TV audience would find utterly revolting.

Coincidentally, some believe that a good bout of sickness helps, ideally something painless but requiring lengthy periods in bed.

Three hundred years ago William Congreve claimed to have written his first play 'to amuse myself, in a slow recovery from a fit of sickness'. Perhaps the solitude and tedium of the sickbed are supposed to stimulate creativity. In which case, if you genuinely desire for yourself the life of a writer, you should immediately cease eating well, wrapping up warm and in all other respects molly-coddling yourself, and instead start hanging around people with infectious diseases in the hope that you will soon come down with something suitable.

My own life has been devoid of such advantages. Yes, I had the usual crop of childhood illnesses, but none lasted long enough for me to get started on my first script. I did, however, have my first introduction to the world of drama when I was a child. Not the magical experience at the theatre which many playwrights claim to have had, nor the gaping fascination with the celluloid world of Saturday morning pictures. It was as a lowly Assistant Stage Manager in my older brother and sister's toy theatre productions, an experience shared by Michael Frayn (*Noises Off*, *Alphabetical Order*), who built his own theatre, made all the characters, wrote all the scripts and acted all the parts. I, unfortunately – though I used all the emotional blackmail the youngest member of a family is permitted to use on these occasions – was restricted to raising and lowering the curtain and playing the part of Messenger.

As James Roose-Evans says elsewhere in this guide, many playwrights were actors first. This is also true of screenwriters, Julian Fellowes (*Gosford Park*) and Lynda La Plante (*Prime Suspect*) to name two. Acting certainly provides plenty of first-hand experience of drama, but only a fool would deliberately adopt it as a strategy to break into writing, since it is even more over-subscribed. It is also absolutely terrifying. My only experience of acting (as a waiter in J. P. Donleavy's *A Fairy Tale of New York*) was a humiliating disaster. Not only did I have to say my lines in a Bronx accent (actually a bizarre mixture of cockney and Irish, the only two accents I can manage convincingly), but I also had to clear a restaurant table of place settings, then re-lay it. During my decidedly lacklustre performance I inadvertently provided a false climax by dropping a tray of cutlery, the loud crash waking the audience from its slumbers and a knife missing the foot of the leading actress by a whisker.

Nepotism is probably the most reliable way in. Dan Petrie Jr. (*Beverly Hills Cop*) comes from a film family. His father and brother are directors, his mother is a producer, one of his sisters an actress. Even so, he had to spend five years working in a talent agency, starting in the mail room, before he had enough money to leave and write his first script. Which, almost unheard of, was actually picked up by a studio and made into a movie.

He would probably claim that was down to luck. As Samuel Johnson wrote, 'There seems to be a strange affectation in authors of appearing to have done every thing by chance.' But luck probably plays less part than even the most becomingly modest writer would have you believe. Unless you're the kind of person who always picks the winning horse (in which case why write for a living?) you have to make your own. Success in writing, like most things in life that are worth doing, is down to hard work.

Step 2: Be passionate

My first attempt at writing drama was a stage play grandly entitled *The King is Dead; Long Live the King*. The method I used can only be described as bizarre. It was the end of the 1960s and like nearly everyone of my generation – or so it seemed at the time – I was heavily into radical politics. I was also shy, inarticulate and hopeless at arguing my point of view. In the evenings I would fill notebook after notebook with the brilliant ripostes I would have uttered if only I'd had the time to think of them. And in my notebooks they would have stayed, if I hadn't made the mistake of reading William Burroughs. Inspired by his 'cut up' technique, I proceeded to shred what I had written, scatter the pieces over the floor of my student bedsit, then stick them back together in a random yet, I was sure, more interesting and dramatically revealing order. I invented a cast of characters – hero: radical young student; villain: ruthless head of corporation – and distributed the resulting text among them. The result was, of course, gibberish. There was no plot, and the characters, predictably enough, all sounded the same. Yet – and here's the point of this story – there was passion, the key ingredient in all good drama.

Instinctively I also knew that I had to be upbeat. Although there was little to be cheerful about in my view of the world, I knew that very few people watch a play in order to be depressed. Even in my most naively radical phase, though my plays had little basis in reality, I always tried to make them end on a positive note: the workers taking over the factory, the general's daughter realizing she loves the handsome guerrilla leader just as he faces the firing squad. I had good precedent. At the end of the film of David Mercer's *Morgan, a Suitable Case for Treatment*, when Morgan (David Warner) has lost the love of his life (Vanessa Redgrave) to the wealthy dullard (Robert Stephens) and is seen tending a garden in the grounds of the mental hospital to which he has been confined, the camera pulls back to reveal that he has planted a floral hammer and sickle and that Vanessa Redgrave is pregnant with his child. He is unbowed.

Step 3: Be yourself

For years David Mercer was my hero. I wanted nothing more than to write like him. This is, as Kate Rowland says, one of the most common faults to which new writers succumb. When I interviewed her for this guide, her shelves were overflowing with pale rehashes of *The Royle Family*. Yes, it is brilliant. Yes, Caroline Aherne has changed the face of TV sitcom. But unless you have something new and heartfelt to say about deadbeat families living their lives in front of the TV set, don't go there. Professional script readers can see a bandwagon coming before you have even thought of jumping on it.

Step 4: Don't be a snob

Like many new writers I also went through a phase of dismissing everything that was popular. For no other reason than that it was popular. Perhaps it is the result of the strong Eng. lit. tradition in our education system or the snobbishness of most of our TV critics. Every week the highest TV viewing figures are for the soaps, yet many people feel slightly ashamed of watching them, as if they are confessing to taking crack cocaine. This is no way to think for a writer who wants to break into TV. The soaps (or 'continuing series', as people in the business prefer to call them) are probably the greatest enthusiasts for new writing talent. No, it isn't Shakespeare, as Andrew Collins (one-time writer for *EastEnders*) said recently, but to be able to grab the attention of millions of viewers day after day requires considerable skill. Samuel Johnson acknowledged this when he wrote of the then widely read poet John Pomfret, 'He pleases many, and he who pleases many must have some species of merit.'

Judging by the current TV schedules you should also be a fan of cops and docs. Perhaps it is just a phase TV is going through, or perhaps there is something perennially fascinating about crime and sickness, areas of life in which the cracks in people's façades are most easily widened for public view. On the other hand, police and medical dramas are often simply frameworks for stories in other genres. Story ideas I recently sent to the half-hour daytime soap *Doctors* had little medical content. One was a political story about asylum seekers, one was about a man who believed he was cursed, another was about a teenage girl who had an unhealthy obsession with a pop singer.

Mind you, they were all rejected, so I could be wrong.

Step 5: Try radio (but don't think it'll be easier)

Thankfully *The King is Dead* was never performed, but I was not discouraged. My second dramatic effort quickly followed. A group of work colleagues and I decided to enter a one-act drama competition, but when I visited the library to choose a play, nothing appealed. The staple amateur repertoire was far too conventional for my radical taste. I wanted something that would startle, shock, politicize. So in a wild mood of hubris, I decided to write my own.

At the time I was trapped in an office job I hated, so naturally enough I wrote about a person trapped in a hated office job. To make it less obviously autobiographical I cunningly changed my hero into a heroine. It had no real plot, but lots of modern dramatic devices – sudden blackouts, actors planted in the audience, chanting, even four-letter words and a masturbation scene – all of which I had shamelessly plagiarized from various productions I had seen in the preceding months. The judge was the artistic director of a west London theatre and at the end of our performance she asked me to send her any other scripts I'd written. Believing that life as a professional playwright was just around the corner I dashed off a script in a couple of months, put it in the post and waited confidently for the first royalty cheque to arrive.

A few weeks later the script came back. No.

I made a couple more attempts. One was an updated version of *King Lear*, the other actually won a competition judged by Michael Billington of the *Guardian*. But essentially that was the beginning and end of my career as a writer for the stage. If I was to get out of my awful job I needed a decent income, and even I knew there was no money in the theatre. The broadcast media were the obvious next step. I didn't own a TV at the time, so that left radio, on which successful playwrights like Anthony Minghella (*The English Patient*) and Joe Orton (*Entertaining Mr Sloane*) cut their teeth.

My first effort was a fiery half-hour drama exploring social conflict by way of the iniquitous class distinctions on British Rail passenger trains. I haven't read it for almost thirty years, so I can't say exactly how dreadful it was, but it wasn't rejected totally out of hand. Instead I received the first letter of a kind with which aspiring writers become all too familiar, the kind that says, 'No, thank you, but please send us anything else you write.' It was enough to keep me going. In the course of the next two or three years I wrote maybe half a dozen radio plays, all of which bar one – a crude, half-baked murder mystery written in an attempt to produce something popular – received the same response.

I realize now that I was attempting to write for perhaps the most difficult dramatic medium of all. It is a common misconception that because radio deals only in sound, it must therefore be easier to write for. In fact, this restriction confers a terrifying liberty. A writer can do almost anything on radio; you only have to listen to Douglas Adams's *Hitchhiker's Guide to the Galaxy*. And while on the screen a writer can capture the audience's attention immediately by a compelling image, on radio the writer has somehow to capture the listeners' imaginations. Otherwise one flex of a quarter of a million forefingers and they're all listening to Radio 2.

Step 6: Read the experts

For years I had little idea why my efforts were being rejected. One or two were worthy only of the BBC's standard rejection slip, but if they were promising – as most of them were – I received comments, usually a couple of paragraphs cut from a reader's report. Naturally, I took no notice of them. I was young. Who were these people to give me advice? It has taken me more years than I care to remember to realize how wrong I was. In writing, as in any walk of life, there are people who know what they are talking about, who are experts. And I should have listened to them a lot sooner than I did.

The trouble is, everyone thinks they can write. All it needs is paper and pen and a basic grasp of the language. We start telling stories almost from the moment we learn how to speak. How hard can it be?

Well, actually, very hard. Holding someone's attention for five minutes by the coffee machine is not the same as stopping a family like the Royles talking for an hour. I wasn't even very good at holding someone's attention for five minutes, so I had a long way to go. With the benefit of hindsight I now understand that while I had a very clear idea of *why* I was writing – to change the world, of course, to eliminate greed and exploitation, to bring equality and happiness – I had little idea of *what* I was writing. I had little idea what made one story more interesting than another, what made an audience desperately want to know the fate of a character, what hooked a listener from the first few lines of a play, what made them listen through to the end. In truth, I probably didn't even ask myself the questions. I knew what I wanted to say; the rest would just come naturally.

Thirty years later I like to think I know better. I've read all the experts (Field, Vogler, McKee, etc.) and I now know what makes a good screenplay. I still may not know exactly how to put this knowledge into practice, but at least I know the theory. I know about the hero's journey, the three-act structure, story arcs, inciting incidents, etc. If anything, I may have read too much.

Step 7: Watch a lot of TV

And how to tell good advice from bad? One successful TV writer explains the grip her scripts instantly exert on the viewer by the fact that 'they always start with a fuck or a fight'. But there are plenty of equally riveting dramas that don't. Watching TV with an analytical mind definitely helps. When I first decided to pitch ideas for *Doctors* I set the video for each daily episode, then watched all five back-to-back every Sunday for a month. For each episode I wrote down what I was watching: the number of scenes, the characters who appeared in each scene and what they did, how the scenes were divided between the running story lines and the daily storyline, and so on. My aim wasn't to discover the *Doctors* 'formula', but to understand how my story ideas could best be told within the constraints of a half-hour continuing series. I even wrote out some of the episodes in the form of story ideas, so that I could see how I might pitch my own.

All this may seem like unnecessary and tedious labour, but it has to be done. If you want to be a professional writer, you have to be dedicated to it; you have to think of it as a job. One of the current writers for the series watched fifty hours of taped episodes before he felt confident enough to contribute. Now, that's dedication.

Step 8: Have good ideas

Every book on writing for TV explains the importance of the 'sample script', the script that shows the writer's 'voice', arguably the most important script a writer produces. A sample script was therefore what I had to write. My problem was that I no longer knew what I wanted to write about. In my late forties I was no longer the left-wing firebrand I had been in my early twenties. Or rather, I still held the same views – somewhat softened round the edges – but was no longer naive enough to believe that everyone wanted to hear them.

New ideas, that's what I needed.

It's a common complaint even from established writers. Julian Mitchell, who wrote some of the *Morse* scripts, struggled to find ideas for stories but found the actual writing process relatively easy. Another *Morse* writer, Alma Cullen, on the other hand, reckoned that a glance through the newspapers would produce three or four usable stories; it was the writing she found difficult. In *Shakespeare in Love*, our greatest playwright gets his idea for *Romeo and Juliet*'s two warring families from a street preacher declaring, 'I say a plague on both their houses!' Americans seem to approach the problem more systematically. A *Frasier* writer scans a magazine until he comes across a word that seems promising, 'car', say. Within twenty minutes he has a dozen story ideas: Frasier has a crash, Daphne takes driving lessons, Niles takes auto repair classes, etc.

After his five years at the talent agency reading other people's scripts, Dan Petrie Jr. planned his sample script coolly. He wanted a strong male lead, a strong female lead – which meant it would probably be a love story – he also wanted some action without it being an action movie, plus humour as well as drama, and so on.

If it was to be a love story, he didn't want the two leads to be immediately compatible – that would be too predictable – so he came up with the most unlikely romantic couple he could think of: a crooked cop and the DA investigating him. It was the beginning of *The Big Easy*.

I had only one idea. In fact, it wasn't even an idea, it was no more than an image. The scene was outside the gates of a school, when all the children are coming out and parents are milling round. Two schoolkids are standing uncertainly; evidently their mother hasn't turned up. Typical. Suddenly a bright red Ferrari weaves between the cars and buses and screeches to a halt. Out stumbles a vision in blonde – sunglasses, high heels, lipstick, the works. Everyone stares open-mouthed. She calls to the two children, but they simply gape. Who is this madwoman? She pulls off the sunglasses and blonde wig and cries, 'It's me, your mother! Get in! Now!' They all squeeze into the car and it roars off down the street.

It didn't seem like much, but in my gut I felt it had possibilities. More than that, it felt exciting. Like the line from Scott Fitzgerald: 'Listen, little Elia, draw your chair up close to the edge of the precipice and I'll tell you a story.'

Step 9: Stop writing

Within a few days I'd teased my one small scene into an idea. The woman was Cinderella, the Ferrari was her coach, the driver her fairy godmother (well, godfather). The script adviser Raymond Frensham claims that Cinderella is one of only eight basic stories from which all others are derived, so I felt I was on the right track. The theme of transformation also chimed in neatly with the current fashion for 'makeover' programmes. And there's never any harm in being topical.

Like Petrie, I wanted to write a love story, but an unlikely one. I knew enough about writing by now to realize that I had to define my main characters first; the story would evolve from what these characters did. So I made my heroine into an anxious thirty-something mother of two with an unfaithful husband, and my hero (the godfather – there would be no handsome prince in my version) a recently bereaved would-be suicide. What I needed next was what Hollywood calls the 'inciting incident', the event that kicks off the story. Why not a bank robbery? And why not make my heroine inadvertently run off with the money? I now knew what my original scene was about. She was fleeing from the police (or the bank robbers); hence the fast car and the makeover.

At this point I should have spent at least a month or two making notes, scribbling down more ideas, working at the plot, rejecting things that just weren't good enough. In other words, planning. It is what all the experts say: Don't start writing too soon. Arthur Miller may have written *The Crucible* in six weeks, but only after he'd thought about it for ten years. I, of course, knew better. I was keen to begin what I always find the most exciting part of writing: putting words in people's mouths.

It was a mistake. One successful screenwriter says that when he goes to bed he imagines what his characters might be doing at the same time, whether they're out partying, or already asleep, with whom, and so on. I, in contrast, was so far from knowing my characters, I was even unsure what names to give them. But I went ahead and wrote the script anyway. The result was predictable: an hour and a half of frantic action, a bank robbery, a love story, a car chase, a makeover, even a dog. It couldn't possibly fail, could it?

Step 10: Rewrite, rewrite, rewrite

With a great effort of will I put the completed script aside for a week, then eagerly set about rewriting it. Again, it was far too soon. Experts recommend at least a month before writers can read their own work with an unprejudiced eye. In my case I think maybe I should have put it aside for ever.

Many successful writers say that rewriting is where the real skill lies. Victoria Wood amazed a writing seminar when she stated that she usually writes ten drafts of a script. Some authorities are specific about what each rewrite should concentrate on: structure, character, dialogue, and so on. But to my mind the best advice I've ever read about rewriting comes from Samuel Johnson (no apologies for quoting him again): 'Read over your compositions, and where ever you meet with a passage which you think is particularly fine, strike it out.'

Makeover – as my Cinderella story ended up being called – enjoyed numerous rewrites, most of them, unfortunately, after it had been rejected by the BBC and various commercial TV production companies, instead of before. Well, it's easier to spot mistakes after others have spotted them. What I also should have done first was show it to a few people I could rely on to provide constructive comments. The trouble is that I, in common with many would-be writers, react badly to criticism. I am likely to sulk for a week if my partner suggests so much as the replacement of a single word. I know my defensiveness is doing me no favours. I know that to welcome criticism is the only way to improve. I even have a glaring example from my own experience. After the dress rehearsal of the play I had written and produced in my twenties the husband of a cast member told me to 'lose the meaningful pauses'. At the time he was acting in a play at the Royal Court, so I did exactly what he suggested. Result: we won the competition.

Step 11: Think of it as a competition

Which brings me neatly to BBC Talent.

In the post office one day to send *Makeover* to the umpteenth script reader, I noticed the BBC Talent brochure. That year they were looking for sitcom writers. Sitcom? I had never written one before, but maybe I should have a go. I blew the dust off a comedy drama I had started a few years before, but for some reason never completed. An uptight man in his late thirties marries his wayward teenage daughter's best friend, the three of them forced by circumstance to share the same flat. Well, it seemed funny at the time. With considerable effort I changed it from a one-off 45-minute radio play into a 30-minute TV pilot, tried out some of the jokes down my local and sent it off.

One of the frustrating things about competitions is that the judges invariably take months to pick a winner. In the case of BBC Talent this was compounded by the fact that there were over 4,000 entries. So it was some time before I eventually learnt I had reached the final ninety scripts before getting the thumbs down. A considerable achievement, I was assured by the charming lady from the BBC when I phoned to find out why. As usual, the reasons were all sound, and I tried to take them on board for the next time. But the more significant aspect of her response, at least as far as I was concerned, was her urging me to send them anything else I had written.

It was enough to convince me – for a year, anyway – that sitcom was where my talent lay, despite a nagging voice in my head telling me I had been here before. Hadn't my competition win twenty-five years ago persuaded me that the theatre was my natural home? Nevertheless I quickly knocked off a black comedy about four incompetent nurses in an intensive care unit and sent it off.

Two months later: no.

Step 12: Don't take it personally

Maybe comedy wasn't really my forte, after all. Never mind. By then the next talent competition had come round. This time they wanted an episode of *Casualty*. All right, a medical drama. I was up for that. So, ignoring that same nagging little voice in the back of my mind telling me I was in danger of becoming a competition junkie, I wrote a *Casualty* script.

Writers are, as Samuel Johnson (yes, him again) said of John Gay, 'easily incited to hope, and deeply depressed when [their] hopes are disappointed'. It's true we are by and large a shy, self-effacing species, rarely seen in public or even daylight, preferring to spend our time alone in small rooms tapping away at keyboards, living second-hand lives through the actions of our invented characters.

We forget to eat, we have no social life, our marriages collapse. We are therefore often not best equipped to deal with rejection. Yet rejection is a fact of life for us all. One successful writer even goes so far as to say that you can't consider yourself a professional until you are receiving at least one rejection a day. So if the word 'no' makes you feel suicidal, perhaps you should consider another career.

The other solution is, as Paul Abbott (*Clocking Off*) says, to keep moving on. In a BBC Writers' Room interview he said that one of the most common faults of new writers is that they invest too much energy and expectation in their single masterpiece, when really they should be working on a number of different ideas. You could also try not to think of a rejection as definitive. After all, the difference between acceptance and rejection is only a matter of opinion, otherwise the people who make these decisions would produce nothing but hits. At low points I remind myself of what William Goldman (*Marathon Man*) famously said of Hollywood, 'No one knows anything.'

So yes, I was deeply attached to my *Casualty* script by the time I finally came to send it off. But I had learnt not to dwell on it. Three months later, when the result came through, I had almost forgotten it; I was already near the end of a script about three OAPs planning a robbery. So it came as a pleasant surprise to be told I was one of the fifteen finalists. I wasn't one of the three who had their scripts performed live on set by the actual cast and I wasn't the one who got her picture in the *Radio Times*, but as far as I was concerned I was a winner. More importantly, it was a view shared by the BBC. I was given an advance against any future commission and invited to pitch ideas.

Well, it's a start.

Further reading

Adventures in the Screen Trade by William Goldman (Time Warner, 1991)
The Hero with a Thousand Faces by Joseph Campbell (Abacus, 1975)
Screenplay: the Foundations of Screenwriting by Syd Field (Dell, 1984)
Screenwriting by Raymond G. Frensham (Hodder & Stoughton, 1996)
Story by Robert McKee (Methuen, 1997)
Twenty Master Plots and How to Build Them by Ronald B. Tobias (Piatkus, 1995)
The Writer's Journey: Mythic Structure for Writers by Christopher Vogler (Pan, 2nd revised edition, 1999)
Writing for Television by Gerald Kelsey (A&C Black, 1995)
Writing for Television by William Smethurst (How To Books, 3rd edition, 2000)

BBC writersroom (www.bbc.co.uk/writersroom

Updated weekly, writersroom should be a regular stopping-off point for any writer seriously interested in writing for television or radio. Aimed at all kinds of writers for BBC TV and radio, drama and comedy, it contains interviews with writers, writing guidelines, information about competitions and programmes that might be looking for material. In addition, major series such as *EastEnders* (www.bbc.co.uk/eastenders) and *Casualty* (www.bbc.co.uk/casualty) have their own web pages which may contain items of interest to writers, although they tend to be aimed mainly at fans of the series.

Regular writersroom pages include:

• *Message Board* For visitors to writersroom to exchange ideas, ask for information and have their say.

- *Stop Press* Information on the BBC's Northern Exposure scheme for funding commissions, master classes, pitching sessions, development rehearsals, etc. in collaboration with theatres and arts organizations across the north of England. Project manager: Melanie Harris (melanie.harris@bbc.co.uk)

- *Write Now* Details of the New Writing Initiative established to 'identify and champion talent and diversity for all BBC platforms across BBC Drama, Entertainment and Children's programmes'. In 2002 this covers a TV screenwriters' course, a radio drama writers' group, two TV popular series schemes, a children's comedy drama series scheme, a comedy writers' group, regional initiatives and writers' bursaries.

- *Q&A* Sessions of questions and answers with, for example, BBC writers Ashley Pharoah (*Paradise Heights*) and Paul Abbott (*Clocking Off*).

- *Insight* 'How to get your script on the BBC: interviews with people in the know.' Interviews on video (or sound only) with BBC personnel such as Patrick Rayner, BBC Scotland's head of radio drama, Richard Fell, head of BBC Fictionlab, Geoffrey Perkins, head of BBC Comedy and Tracey Scoffield, head of development/executive producer, BBC Films; plus a Q&A session held in Liverpool on the Northern Exposure initiative and an interview with Victoria Wood and Geoffrey Perkins.

- *Writers' Guidelines* Writing for television, writing for radio and useful addresses. Links to information on how the BBC commissions work (background and programming needs, how to pitch an idea, information on quotas) and help on script layout.

In Conversation with Kate Rowland

The BBC's Creative Director for New Writing
explains to Bob Ritchie the many and varied
ways of getting in to radio and television

BOB RITCHIE: Your title suggests a wide-ranging job. Does it cover the whole of the BBC?

KATE ROWLAND: Yes, but mainly for drama, entertainment and children's programmes. And that's across television, radio, online and also film. My main role is to find, to nurture and then to mentor writers through the BBC.

BR: Is this a recent initiative?

KR: The BBC has always been eager to attract new writing but when I started, it wasn't doing it across departments. I couldn't believe how divided it was as an organization. Each department was jealous of its writers. If, say, somebody was good at comedy, that's what they did, comedy. There was no question of them moving over to do drama or switching between radio and TV. Now, the BBC is a much more open place and is much more responsive to writers.

BR: So is it a lot easier now for a new writer to get started?

KR: Oh yes. Because the BBC is far more accessible. But there is still only one criteria for writing success and that's talent. We can do a lot of work in finding writers, but they have to have the basic craft and instinctive skills, then we are not wasting time and money. We have to be selective, supporting those who can actually do the job.

BR: How did you come to this job?

KR: I started as a drama teacher in a comprehensive. I've been

46

a youth worker. I worked in community theatre for quite a long time and then I was associate director at the Liverpool Everyman and Liverpool Playhouse. Most of my work has been with new writers. At one time I had my own new writing theatre company, Altered States, which won awards. I became a radio drama producer and then head of Radio Drama. I set up the New Writing Initiative because I just felt that there was so much more we could do to encourage writers and now I'm full time overseeing this policy.

BR: Clearly you felt that a lot of promising new writers were being missed.
KR: Yes, and for one major reason. We were not giving out enough information. How are things commissioned? What is the route through to TV series? What is the route to films? What are the chances of success? Being honest with the facts is so important. We sent out guidelines to thousands of writers. We have a really good website now – the writersroom website. Last year we spoke to 5,000 writers in our public face-to-face sessions. I go along with heads of departments and we talk in detail about the kind of writing we are looking for.

BR: So the BBC now goes out looking for writers rather than simply waiting for them to knock on the door?
KR: Not only that, we can offer constructive advice about where to place their script. There are writers who are ambitious to write for television but never think about writing for radio until we point out the opportunities. Radio takes more risks with writers and it has more original drama than probably anywhere else.

BR: And easier than television?
KR: It's not necessarily easier; it's a different medium. But what is true is that writers cross over now more than they did. It used to be that a writer concentrated on a single genre. Theatre writers wouldn't necessarily do much television or film, for example. Today, writers are very happy to try a radio play, then something for television,

and then something for theatre. We did a public session with Victoria Wood last year. It was packed, and we filmed it and put it on the website and she was talking about doing eight drafts. And some people were amazed. So many people think, I've written that then. I'll bang that off. And don't think about the work that's involved. But that's a later question.

BR: To get started, what is the very first thing a writer should do?

KR: The most important thing is to have an original piece of work, because we're all looking for a distinctive voice. And then we ask, do they understand the medium they want to write for? Can they write comedy or can they write strong characters, understand about storyline or what's needed to do a series.

BR: Should writers worry that their first script is very unlikely to be performed?

KR: No. If you think about it, life is like that. You go for lots of interviews before getting the job you want. But that's all right. You become more experienced as a person, you become more aware of what's right and what's wrong about your approach to work. A writer has to develop. I would urge any writer to watch good drama on television, listen to radio, go to the theatre, watch films, watch people who are good. It's such an obvious thing but many writers are simply too wrapped up in their own preconceived notions. And each script must say something that is special. That's the first thing we all look for, a calling-card script. You have to write what you passionately want to write. I think anyone at the BBC would say, 'Write about who you are, let's see who you are in that script.'

BR: A lot of writers do find it difficult to get over that first hurdle. They spend months, maybe years, working on one script and when they hand it in, even if it gets a favourable response, the chances of it being put on are very low. And so they think, Well I've worked hard, you like it, but you're still not going to do it, you want me to go away and do something else, or come in with some other idea. That can be a bit depressing.

KR: I know, but that is the nature of the business. It's the same in the theatre. You send a spec script and the theatre will either like it or not. But if we like a script, even if it's not used, we meet the writer and actively encourage a follow-up. Often a script isn't suitable because it duplicates something that's already been on or is under commission. It's often as simple as that. If, say, we've done a lot of plays about breast cancer, we will not take another one unless it has a very different perspective. It might be really good but it still might have to wait three years for us to return to the subject.

BR: How many scripts are we talking about? How many come into your department?

KR: If you take films, radio and for TV comedy drama and we're dealing with well over 10,000 a year. If we go out and do public seminars we often get an increase. Also, this helps to improve quality, which is great. People are thinking more about what they are sending off. We do a lot of workshops on craft skills. We've got four road shows coming up about writing for *Doctors*, the daytime drama series. The series editor will go out with a writer and talk through what works and what doesn't work. With the unsolicited scripts people always ask, 'Do you read them all?' No, we don't. We assess them all. All of them are looked at and we have a very good team. The readers we have are crucial to the whole structure of what we do, very committed and good at their job. Writers sometimes think we don't want to find anybody good. Not true. We're cock-a-hoop if we find somebody good. The first ten pages of every script is read and then we might look at more. But if we feel that nothing jumps out, that the dialogue's not working, then there's no point in going on. If there's nothing to recommend that script in ten pages, then we will send it back with a standard rejection. But the rest are taken away, and are given a close read. Each writer is then sent a considered response. We can't give everybody the same thing, we can't afford to give notes on 10,000 scripts. You can spend a lot of time finding the euphemistic words for not very good.

BR: There is one writer I know who says that you can't really count yourself a professional until you are receiving at least one rejection a week.

KR: You know it and I know it but a lot of writers don't. Rejection is part of the process but rejection doesn't make them bad writers.

BR: Do you ever feel that it would be a good idea to discourage some writers from writing?

KR: I don't think you can. Writing belongs to all of us. Writing is a great hobby, a great thing to do, a great release. The BBC is a public service organization and we have a responsibility to be fair but not to be cruel.

BR: Roughly what percentage of the scripts sent in are worth serious consideration?

KR: I would say 25 per cent get far more than a standard rejection, where we're really encouraging. I would say about five per cent are taken on in different ways, which is actually quite a high proportion. Writers for radio are most likely to have something commissioned. But for film I have known only one unsolicited script to be commissioned. But that doesn't mean that good writers haven't come to our attention through unsolicited scripts.

BR: Are there common failings? Failings that you keep coming across?

KR: An awful lot of writers describe everything that's happening. So there's no drama, it's almost like prose. They're telling us what the character's doing, what the character's thinking. It's long-winded descriptive writing. It's like someone colouring in; they've coloured in everything, so there's nothing left. The most important thing for a reader, or the audience, is wanting to know, wanting to find out what's going to happen. Every play should be like a thriller. Whether it's a monologue, or whatever. And most of them aren't. You know what's happening by page one. Some plays are just static. You can have four people in a room and a conversation is going on and it's dialogue but it isn't a drama. I have just read four scripts

50

for a competition and against each of them I wrote, 'Why? I don't know what I was meant to feel.' The other big danger is a lot of people now are very interested in concept and form. But they miss out the emotional core. Unless you engage with the characters and the story and want to know and care about what happens to them, you stop reading.

BR: Can good writing be taught?
KR: A lot of skills can be taught. Like how to get into a story. Often I read a script and find I could have started ten pages in. Now that's important because the opening is what should grab us. If all of it is a preamble, explaining why something is happening or whatever, it is just a switch-off.

BR: Should writers show their work to anybody else before they send it in?
KR: Having somebody that you trust to look at your work and give you an outside eye is important. Getting involved in a writers' group can help. It's good to have a friendly critic saying, 'I don't know why you've written that; that bit's really boring.'

BR: Your department reads 10,000 scripts a year but who is to say your judgement is right? Isn't it possible that you are just looking for novelty?
KR: No, we're not looking for novelty; we're looking for good writing. And that's in terms of dialogue, in terms of imagination, in terms of storytelling. But it is not just my department. When we think a script has potential we pass it on to a producer to look at. So there are many opinions that are brought to bear.

BR: So there's no such thing as fashionable themes?
KR: No, quite the reverse. Often we think well, that's quite good but it's been done. There is a tendency for writers to imitate what they see or hear at peak time. Like lots of Royle families. I would say to any writer, 'If something's on radio or television, don't copy it.'

BR: Would you say the same for topical subjects?

KR: Well the likelihood is if a script is accepted it will be at least a year before it gets produced. So if you're thinking topically, be alert to the time frame.

BR: What are the absolute no-nos?

KR: I've covered most of them but I would add, even though we don't judge scripts on the way they're laid out, pages that aren't numbered, or written with green biro, don't do anyone any favours. Also, we don't read synopses. A new writer will not be commissioned on a synopsis alone. We need to know that you can write. It's the same with big, heavy treatments. They won't get anywhere unless there are scripts attached. So if you've developed a series idea, then we must have at least one episode to make a judgement.

BR: It's often said that if you want to write for an existing series then your sample script shouldn't be an episode of that series. Why is that?

KR: Because we want to see who you are as a writer. The producer of *EastEnders*, for example, will judge you on the quality of your writing. If he's sold on that the next question is, can you write under the pressure? Some writers can't write at speed.

BR: One problem with the encouraging rejection is that a writer might think, They like it really, so I'll just tweak it and send it back in. Presumably, this is not a good idea.

KR: Right, unless you've been asked to re-submit a script. If you get a letter with notes and you're confused about something, then, of course, you can e-mail us with a query like, 'Is it worth me doing more with this?' But if you just get a standard rejection, then move on. You might come back to the idea in a couple of years. But it might be better to start again. It often is.

BR: It's been said that a lot of writers work away at their one masterpiece and don't spread themselves enough, don't try out enough new ideas. Is that a fault that you've come across?

KR: When you ask a writer, 'Well, what other ideas have you got?'

and they haven't got one, that's a problem. I do encourage writers to draw up what is a menu of ideas. A concept can be put across in a few lines. I can see, smell a good idea in eight lines. And you can say, 'That's great!' or, 'No, don't see the point of that one.'

BR: Maybe some writers feel that if they're going to write with passion, that writers can only write with passion about one or two subjects.
KR: Maybe, but then somebody's going to watch it, listen to it. It isn't just about you. If you've decided to do dramatic writing, then it is for an audience. Is this something people want to watch? That doesn't mean it can't be challenging or difficult but a lot of writers forget the audience.

BR: I came across a wonderful quote the other day, a producer or director saying to his writer, 'Yes, but what is the audience doing all this time?'
KR: A very obvious thing that's often forgotten.

BR: I went along to a meeting where Alan Plater was one of the speakers and Alan said that in his opinion television wasn't a visual medium, it was really just people in rooms talking. Do you have any truck with that or was he just trying to be controversial?
KR: Alan's very good at being controversial. I would say good television is a visual medium. For me one of the most inspiring pieces of drama ever was *Culloden*. I watch *Clocking Off* and I think some of those stories are just fantastic. They deal with universal themes, the characters are so strong, it's committed writing. It isn't just people in a room talking, it's drama. And that takes off from the room.

BR: Maybe there is something in what Alan says. Perhaps our approach to television drama is still too literary.
KR: It is literary. It is also quite literal. In radio drama, there's much more a tradition of breaking the rules, maybe mixing form and surrealism. We tend to work in a very real, naturalistic world. One of the programmes that has stuck in my mind is the TV drama

serial *The Lakes* by Jimmy McGovern, broadcast in 1998. He took a known world and yet he peopled it in a way to show the tragedies and the traumas. It was almost verging on melodrama, but in Jimmy's hands he created a completely gripping drama. But that wasn't people in a room talking. Those were big themes. Great things happening. What Alan may have been thinking about is the drama series, the soaps as he would call them. But even here the emotions are vital; it's not just people in a room talking. Everything depends on how well it's done.

BR: Why don't we round off with the crystal ball.

KR: I would like to see more opportunities for single drama on TV. I would like to see more opportunities to take risks so that we don't lose sight of the rawness of drama that has something to say. And that's not just about writing but about the technology and techniques we use. I think we have to change the mix. Living in this country I don't think we have enough stories across a whole multicultural background. There are a lot of very talented black and Asian writers that we haven't seen much of yet on television. That has to change. But other writers just have to take on board the world we live in. It's all about representing that world in a much more interesting and more political way. There's something missing in much of new drama. Maybe the underbelly is getting a bit soft.

BR: So the message is, keep trying.

KR: Yes, develop a tough skin. You only have to listen to any of the greats to know that success does not come easily. And look out for all the different opportunities and don't just think, I only want to write my big feature. Writing is a profession and it's hard work. It's very difficult sitting in a room on your own and having to deliver. When it's going well, any writer will tell you it is a joy; how lucky am I to be paid to do something I love doing. But writers work hard. And they have to work hard to stay in the race.

Interview with Mal Young

As BBC controller of drama series, Mal Young
knows a thing or two about talent spotting
as he reveals to Bob Ritchie

BOB RITCHIE: I think we'd better start by you telling me what your job covers.

MAL YOUNG: It is easier to say what we don't do. I have nothing to do with the single film, the two-, four- or six-part series or the adaptations. My bit is the long-running series. It's what all the channels want because it brings audience loyalty. Because our shows are there on a yearly schedule, our audience can say, 'If it's Saturday night and it's winter, it must be *Casualty*.' Tuesday night is branded as *Holby*. This is what brings the audience to a channel. We've known this for a long time. My department, which is like an in-house independent company, was founded on *Z Cars*, *Softly Softly*, *All Creatures Great and Small* and *Dr Who*. It's a brilliant heritage. My job is to make sure that the BBC, but BBC1 in particular, is fed with new formats so that the appeal is always fresh.

BR: Is there a specific amount of time allocated to continuing series?

MY: No. I am very competitive and I prefer to be told, 'We want your shows because they're good, not because we have to have them.' I think I'd take my eye off the ball very quickly if I had a guarantee of so much transmission time. But I'm fortunate enough to have fourteen titles all on BBC1 and all successful; it's the biggest part of the drama picture.

BR: You also put series on BBC2?

MY: Yes, if required. But we haven't done so for quite some time because they only have four slots a year and they have less money. The main priority in the last four years has been to deliver hits for BBC1. I'm now doing stuff for BBC Choice. We've just green-lit our first piece called *Grease Monkeys* with a brand new Asian writer – quietly exciting, quite different. BBC Choice is a much younger channel and more an experimental channel. But 99 per cent of my output is BBC1. It's a monster that constantly needs feeding and the audience are quite fickle. They won't put up with stuff if it's less than great. But I like that. I'm quite hands-on. I'm always being encouraged to be the head of the department, but I get bored very quickly. I like to write; I like to create shows or work with writers to create them or to script edit them or create characters. So I still write storylines for *Holby* and *Casualty*. It's the exciting bit. I suppose the equivalent of me in the States is the show-runner who is very much running the show but has other creatives working with him and doing the day-to-day and the detail. So *Merseybeats*, Chris Murray and I created that. He's the lead writer but I'll maybe help him with the characters and look at the overall arc of where I want the characters to go from and to. I think that's my main strength, the storylining.

BR: Just as a matter of interest, who came up with the idea for *Merseybeats*?
MY: Well that's a typical way a show is developed. I decided that BBC1 needed a cop show in pre-watershed. We'd successfully launched *Waking The Dead*. *Dalziel and Pascoe* was in its sixth year and doing brilliant business for us. I had *Judge John D*. I had detective-type shows working for me and *In Deep* was working really well, but what I didn't have was the front-line troops.

I'm fascinated by the uniforms. Most cop shows are about the suits and they investigate murders, but actually what touches the viewers more is who's looking after their homes, who's looking after their cars. Fortunately, most people won't come across a murder but many people will be stopped for speeding, have a burglary, have their car broken into, be mugged in the street. *Casualty* and *Holby* are very much of that ilk. They're about everyday stories.

I say to the producers all the time, *'Never* come up with a story where it starts with a doctor saying, "Well I've never seen this disease before."' I hate it. I want stuff where the viewers will relate. I want them to say, 'It's just like that.' The strength of those shows is that the audience identify. So I wanted a cop show they could identify with. And also I said, 'Surely cops are just the same as the rest of us. OK, so they wear a uniform. But they probably break the law. They probably have home lives which are difficult. Society expects them to be better than us but they can't be, they're normal people.' But if I come into work with a headache, the worst I'll do is make a bad judgement on a script. The worst a cop might do is to arrest someone and change their lives because they're in a bad mood. So I said to BBC1, 'I think we should make our own pre-watershed cop show about uniform cops and really touch the audience in a way that they haven't been since *Dixon of Dock Green* and *Z Cars.'*

The thing about *Z Cars*, it had characters. It was character driven. Fancy Smith and all those other names we still remember. It wasn't like *The Bill*. It wasn't about procedure, it was about people sitting in a police car chit-chatting. So I said, 'What if we came up with a character-driven cop show, with the characters all in uniform and no suits in it at all.'

Then I found a writer who understood what I was talking about. Chris Murray, who worked with me on *Doctors* and *Casualty*, knew immediately what I was talking about, and I set him up with the research and away he went. And that's how we start. I set up goal-posts for the writers or producers and say, 'This is what I want you to score.'

BR: How did you get to where you are?
MY: I was art school trained and became a graphic designer, playing in a band spare time as everyone does in Liverpool. Just before I was thirty I decided to give up my day job and try to be a pop star.

Did that for two years playing in bands while filling my daytime by working as a film extra. I suddenly found myself as an extra on lots of TV shows, which was great because I had been a big TV addict since I was a kid. And I realized that all these people were having great fun making television for the likes of me. And I thought, Why do I have to be on the outside looking in; I could be part of this.

I got completely caught up in it. I hated being an extra because you had to leave at the end of the day. I wanted to stay and learn what everyone else was doing. And then I had a small role in a new show called *Brookside* and as luck would have it they were looking for a design assistant and I applied using my art school training and my background as a designer. Suddenly, I found myself on the set of the Grants' house supplying the props and thinking, This is brilliant. It was only a three-week vacancy but when it was over I met Phil Redmond, who ran Mersey TV, who said, 'Oh, you should stay.' And so I stayed twelve years and ended up running the company in partnership with Phil.

I did every job on the way up. That was company philosophy. It wasn't what you'd done but what you wanted to do. So I worked my way up through production and production management. I learned how to write a show. It taught me how to sit in a room with twelve writers and write a show, how to bully them, how to stroke them, how to kick their arses, how to hit deadlines and how to produce scripts and how to work with creative people. I produced *Brookside* for eight years, which is why I get irritated by new people coming up who've been script editors for five minutes and say they want to produce and then they produce for five minutes and think they want to do other things.

In the past people cut their teeth. Jimmy McGovern was on *Brookside* for years before he went off on his own. Kay Mellor wrote a lot of *Coronation Street*s and *Brookside*s before she became Kay Mellor. They perfected their skills. Nowadays there are too many people who write a *Doctors* or a *Casualty* script and think that's it, that they can go off to write their movie. They can't. They haven't lived enough life, they haven't developed their talents.

And then, of course, Channel 4 offered me my own show, so I stayed at Mersey TV and produced *The Beat Goes On*, which was successful, and then suddenly I was getting offers from Greg Dyke who'd just set up Pearson. They had Grundy, *The Bill*, Thames TV and he'd put it all together and he made me head of drama. So I moved to London. I stayed with Pearson a year and turned *The Bill* from half-hours into hours. And then I launched *Family Affairs* for Channel 5. And I did *The Wing and a Prayer*, which was a legal show for Channel 5 which got a BAFTA nomination, so that was exciting. And then a year in, the BBC said, 'Would you like to be head of series?' And I came here.

BR: Are you always looking for new writers?
MY: Yes, yes, yes. New good ones. I always say to them, 'Not all of you will become Alan Bleasdale or Dennis Potter. It's great to aspire but it's not a disaster if you don't become the author of your own piece.' You can have a great time and a great living making some of the most watched TV in this country, by becoming a team writer on *Casualty* or *EastEnders* or *Holby* or *Waking The Dead*, amazing shows that are watched by twenty million. Fantastic. And in America it's seen as a cool thing to be a staff writer. I can help a writer earn a fantastic living.

BR: You think there's a certain amount of snobbery attached to script-writing, that some writers feel that if they can't be Lynda La Plante or Alan Plater, then they don't want to know?
MY: Definitely. They see the biggest sign of success as being celebrated in the writing community. But this denigrates people like Tony Jordan, who is the lead writer on *EastEnders* and is the reason *EastEnders* is going through its best two years ever. We should celebrate those people just as much. It's much harder to write a *Holby* than a one-off play because you have to apply all the rules and turn it round so quickly. It's phenomenal what those writers do. But I also think that popular drama is coming of age. People are starting to buy into it much more. But you are back to the need for new writers; they're the lifeblood. With ninety hours of *Casualty*

and *Holby* a year, with 250 episodes of *Doctors* and *EastEnders* all year round, we've got about 500 hours to fill. And that's just in this department. We always need to renew. And not just with young writers. You might find a nineteen-year-old genius who can write. But more often than not you will find a great talented writer who has lived a life. I worry a little bit about writers who are just constantly coming out of media schools who say, 'I can write.' They probably can, but they haven't lived a life so they've nothing to talk about. They know how to put a script together but they don't know what to say. I always quote the example of Lucy Gannon. She was thirty-eight before she turned professional. By then she had things to say.

BR: How do you encourage writers?
MY: Every way possible from reading and reporting on every unsolicited script that comes into the BBC, to attending writers' workshops and organizing talent searches. We have links into BBC Writers' Room in radio and the Northern Writers' Workshop. We are constantly looking. Everyone's looking. When people say, 'Oh, no one encourages new talent,' that's bollocks. Everyone is. We would be mad not to. But there is no set formula to work to. We have to get to people from diverse backgrounds, not just middle-class, well-educated people who think it would be pleasant to write, better than doing a proper job. I want people who have lived a life and who suddenly think, I'm in my forties and I can write. And they might be able to and we can show them how to go about it.

BR: So what should they do?
MY: Again there is no simple way in. If we had twenty professional writers in here now who work for me they'd all give you a different story about how they got started. And that's quite exciting. I can tell you a success story but I don't want every writer thinking, Oh, that's what you have to do. You have to get yourself known. You have to put yourself about. You don't necessarily need an agent, but that can help if you've got someone to represent you, who knows what everyone is looking for. And then you write and write

and write. The great thing about writing is you don't need any special tools. You need a piece of paper and a pen and a brain. You just write. You enter competitions. You get your friends to comment. You join writers' workshops. Jimmy McGovern just bashed on our door every week to say, 'I want to write, I can do better than you can.' And one week we said, 'OK, prove it.' And he did. You might write for local theatre and get someone from a TV company to come and have a look at your work. You might just write a spec script for a series you believe you want to write for. We probably won't use it because it'll be full of holes but it might prove to us that you can write. It might have a germ of something.

BR: What are the chances of getting into *Casualty* or *EastEnders*?
MY: Straight off, very unlikely because they are very hard shows to do. For *EastEnders* we have a shadow scheme where new writers shadow an old hand but we can't say to viewers, 'This was a trainee writer. Sorry it wasn't very good.' The viewers don't care, they just want quality. So we have to find ways of developing writers on *Doctors*, where it's an easier kind of audience.

BR: Is *Doctors* the only BBC series at the moment that's looking at first-time writers?
MY: Brand new. But BBC Radio uses a lot of new writers. Because they are desperate for people to write radio. And they can learn how to do it without pictures and then be passed over to *Doctors* and learn how to add pictures to it, so that's a good way in. But local theatre leads to radio. And theatre is looked down upon. Everyone says, 'Oh no, I want to be a TV writer.' Well OK, but learn how to write first.

BR: So the medium is not that crucial. The way to begin is simply that, to begin.
MY: Up to a point. The problem with television is that so many think it is easy. They just walk in as if it's their God-given right for me to give them a job. And I say, 'Well, you're not a good enough writer yet. You actually have to be good.' I get an awful lot of stuff

that isn't very good. It's our job to be honest to people and say, 'Thanks, but no thanks,' or, 'Don't give up the day job yet.' Because not everyone can do it. Just like not everyone can be an astronaut or a painter. It is a creative talent that you've either got or you haven't got. We can teach you how to repackage it. We have a thing called first episodes syndrome of a new series. I always say, 'Write your first episode and put it in the bin, because the viewers don't want to see it.' They don't want to see set-up. The viewers are very quick now. They want to get right to the point and have something happen within the first five minutes. Grab the audience, move with it, have consequence, dramatize. We can teach all these things but what we can't teach is the basic creativity. The talent to be able to story-tell. To engage an audience with a great story.

BR: What are the most common pitfalls for new writers?
MY: To write a derivative of what was on TV last year or on at the moment. A couple of years ago everything I was getting was *X Files* meets *This Life*. I would see what they were thinking: That's a success; I'll put those two things together. I get an amazing number of private detective stories. Why? Private detectives stopped being interesting in the 1960s. Private detectives can't detect anything any more. It's boring. They follow someone who might be having an affair for days with no result. But you'd be amazed how many scripts I get about smoky offices above shops. It's just so old-fashioned and so out of date.

So, have a new idea, for God's sake. Example: Pete Lawson developed his talents on *London Bridge*, the Carlton soap, but it was only regional and a few years ago it was cancelled. But he showed promise. We picked him up. Every time we tried to give him something to do like a *Casualty* or a *Holby*, he couldn't do it; he was so specific to his own voice he couldn't write someone else's piece. He came to us and he said, 'I want to do this thing about a single mum.' And we weren't sure he had the voice. And he went away and wrote it himself. He didn't ask us for money, he wanted to show that he could do it. So he, off his own bat, wrote a spec script, sixty minutes. He made me read it and I groaned and I thought, The chances of this being great . . .

But it was a page turner. I was gripped; the characters leapt off the page. It was about a single mum who had three kids and each of the kids has a different dad. He'd written it in voice-over. There was a great wank gag by page four and I thought, 'Bloody hell, that's courageous.' It was funny, it was warm, it was contemporary, it said something about today's society and it was different. But he'd written it as a film. And I said, 'Sorry, Pete, but we're not making one-offs. But could you return the characters? Could they come back each week?' And he came back to me with twelve ideas of what they could do next. We got the green light and it's on air tomorrow night with Pauline Quirke. And it's fantastic.

These are the things you hope and pray for every day. But you also get a lot of dross. The common pitfall is to forget that this is to be watched by an audience. A writer thinks, Oh, of course they'll like it because I've written it. And they won't because it's crap. It doesn't relate to anyone. I say, 'Make it so I'll think, Can't wait to get home tonight, there's something I've got to see.' And that's what TV should do. It should make you emote. It should engage you.

BR: Should writers show their work to other people before they send it in?
MY: Yes, but not to people who love them. They'll all go 'Very nice' and be very impressed with a big thick book. You need to get someone working in local theatre, or a lecturer in a drama college or a professional to say if it's any good or not.

BR: What about the good scripts?
MY: It's so trite to say this but, what makes a good book? It's something that I haven't read before. It's engaging and entertaining. How many times have you picked up a book and loved the cover, loved the premise but not got past page five. Loads of times. It's the same with TV scripts. So many writers say, 'Oh, it's great by episode two or three.' And I say, 'Well, I'm afraid I'm not going to get there. If you haven't engaged me in the first ten minutes, I'm off.' When

you pay to go to see theatre or a film, you've decided to give up the next two hours of your life, and for you to walk out takes a lot of effort because you're thinking, What else am I going to do tonight? TV, you've got the quick choice; it's on the end of your fingertip. And you can go to 200 other options or you could switch off and do something else and not feel let down.

BR: So the writer has to grab attention within the first ten minutes?
MY: Yes, but that doesn't mean to say that you have to have an explosion. You have to interest people. The slowest pieces in the world can still intrigue and draw you in.

BR: You said earlier that audiences catch on very quickly. Do you think they have become more sophisticated?
MY: Oh yes, definitely. They're tele-literate. They know the tricks. They get bored very quickly. The younger viewers are exposed to much more going on in the world than in the past, so they pick up on subtleties. You don't have to over-explain things.

BR: Can good writing be taught?
MY: We touched on that earlier. It think it can be honed. You can teach format; you can teach tricks of the trade; you can teach story-telling structure. But dialogue and characterization, I think you either have the talent or not. We can develop that talent and bring it out but it has to be there.

BR: The drama series that we see, how much is that your personal taste?
MY: The drama series is driven by my judgement, not my taste. I have to be the gatekeeper. Someone has to run the department. If you have a committee-driven creative structure you're screwed because you'll never make a decision. Everyone will be very reasonable and go, 'Oh, what do you think?' And suddenly it'll be a mishmash of ideas but not one good one. The way it works here is that BBC1 has appointed me controller of this output and the final arbiter for what we make. It is what I believe BBC1 wants and needs for the BBC1 audience. I don't give the audience what they think

they want. I try to shock them; I try to surprise them, educate them, entertain and inform.

BR: Crystal-gazing. What do you think's going to happen in the next twenty years or so?

MY: The mess with digital TV has been such that I hope it's taught everyone that for the next twenty years people will still want TV in the traditional way coming from the box in the corner. The technology will help us record things, but that's all that's changing. The explosion of new channels means that we have to be better than ever before. It isn't dumbing down. We have to keep our eye on the ball and it makes us work harder. Every single time you look at the hits, it's quality. You see the figures for *EastEnders*, it's a fickle audience. If we don't deliver every single episode as a blistering corker of a quality drama, they go. You're as good as last night's show, and I love that. I think we'll just see drama getting better, another golden age of television. There will be another Dennis Potter, there will be another Alan Bleasdale, there will be another generation of people with something to say.

This Gun That I Have in My Right Hand Is Loaded

Timothy West

When Timothy West tried his hand at creating the worst possible radio play, he was so successful that his catalogue of errors was adopted by the BBC for induction courses. As a teaching aid it is unrivalled. With generous permission of the author, *This Gun That I Have in My Right Hand Is Loaded*, is reproduced here as a classic of misconception.

ANNOUNCER: Midweek Theatre

(*Music and keep under*)

We present John Pullen and Elizabeth Proud as Clive and Laura Barrington, Malcolm Hayes as Heinrich Oppenheimer, Diana Olsson as Gerda, and Dorit Welles as the Barmaid, with John Hollis, Anthony Hall and Fraser Kerr, in 'This Gun That I Have in My Right Hand Is Loaded'.

(*Bring up music then crossfade to traffic noises. Wind backed by ship's sirens, dog barking, hansom cab, echoing footsteps, key chain, door opening, shutting*)

LAURA: (*off*) Who's that?
CLIVE: Who do you think, Laura, my dear? Your husband.
LAURA: (*approaching*) Why, Clive!
RICHARD: Hello, Daddy.

66

CLIVE: Hello, Richard. My, what a big boy you're getting. Let's see, how old are you now?
RICHARD: I'm six, Daddy.
LAURA: Now Daddy's tired, Richard, run along upstairs and I'll call you when it's supper time.
RICHARD: All right, Mummy.

(*Richard runs heavily up wooden stairs*)

LAURA: What's that you've got under your arm, Clive?
CLIVE: It's an evening paper, Laura.

(*Paper noise*)

I've just been reading about the Oppenheimer smuggling case. (*effort noise*) Good gracious, it's nice to sit down after that long train journey from the insurance office in the City.
LAURA: Let me get you a drink, Clive darling.

(*Lengthy pouring, clink*)

CLIVE: Thank you, Laura, my dear.

(*Clink, sip, gulp*)

Aah! Amontillado, eh? Good stuff. What are you having?
LAURA: I think I'll have a whisky, if it's all the same to you.

(*Clink, pouring, syphon*)

CLIVE: Whisky, eh? That's a strange drink for an attractive auburn-haired girl of twenty-nine. Is there . . . anything wrong?
LAURA: No, it's nothing, Clive, I—
CLIVE: Yes?
LAURA: No, really I—
CLIVE: You're my wife, Laura. Whatever it is you can tell me. I'm your husband. Why, we've been married – let me see – eight years, isn't it?
LAURA: Yes, I'm sorry Clive, I . . . I'm being stupid. It's . . . just . . . this.

(Paper noise)

CLIVE: This? Why, what is it Laura?

LAURA: It's . . . it's a letter. I found it this morning in the letter box. The Amsterdam postmark and the strange crest on the back . . . it . . . frightened me. It's addressed to you. Perhaps you'd better open it.

CLIVE: Ah ha.

(Envelope tearing and paper noise)

Oh, dash it, I've left my reading glasses at the office. Read it to me, will you, my dear.

LAURA: Very well.

(Paper noise)

Let's see. 'Dear Mr Barrington. If you would care to meet me in the Lounge Bar of Berridge's Hotel at seven-thirty on Tuesday evening the twenty-first of May, you will hear something to your advantage.

(Crossfade to Oppenheimer's voice and back again immediately)

Please wear a dark red carnation in your buttonhole for identification purposes. Yours faithfully, H. T. Oppenheimer.' Clive! Oppenheimer! Surely that's—

CLIVE: By George, you're right . . . Where's my evening paper?

(Paper noise as before)

Yes! Oppenheimer! He's the man wanted by the police in connection with this smuggling case.

LAURA: Darling, what does it all mean?

CLIVE: Dashed if I know. But I intend to find out. Pass me the Southern Region Suburban Timetable on the sideboard there. Now, where are we—

(Brief paper noise)

Six-fifty-one! Yes, I'll just make it. Lucky we bought those dark red carnations.

(*Flower noise*)

There we are. Well – (*stretching for fade*) – Lounge Bar of Berridge's Hotel, here . . . I . . . come

. . . .

(*Fade*)

(*Fade in pub noises, glasses, chatter, till, darts, shove-halfpenny, honkytonk piano, Knees up Mother Brown etc.*)

HAWKINS: (*middle-aged, cheerful, Londoner*) Evening, Mabel. Busy tonight, isn't it?

BARMAID: It certainly is, Mr Hawkins. I've been on my feet all evening. (*going off*) Now then, you lot, this is a respectable house, this is.

(*Singing and piano fades abruptly to silence*)

FARRELL: (*approaching, middle-aged, cheerful, Londoner*) Evening, George, what are you having?

HAWKINS: No, no, let me.

FARRELL: Come on!

HAWKINS: Well, then, a pint of the usual.

(*Till*)

FARRELL: Two pints of the usual, please, Mabel.

(*Money*)

BARMAID: (*off*) Coming up, Mr Farrell.

HAWKINS: Evening, Norman.

JACKSON: (*middle-aged, cheerful, Londoner*) Hello there, George. What are you having, Bert?

FARRELL: I'm just getting them, Norman.

69

JACKSON: Well, leave me out then, I'm getting one for Charlie
Illingworth. Two halves of the usual, Mabel.
BAINES: (*coming up, middle-aged, cheerful, Londoner*) Evening all.
JACKSON: Hello, Arnold, haven't seen you in ages.

(*Till*)

BARMAID: Your change, Mr Farrell.

(*Money*)

FARRELL: Thanks, Mabel. Where's Charlie gone to? Ah, there you
are. Charlie, you know Arnold Baines, don't you?
ILLING.: (*cheerful, Londoner, middle-aged*) Known the old so-and-so
for ages. What'll you have?
JACKSON: No, I'm getting them, what is it?
BAINES: Oh, I'll just have my usual, thanks.
JACKSON: Who's looking after you, George, old man?

(*Money*)

BARMAID: There's yours, Mr Hawkins.
HAWKINS: Bung ho.

(*Till*)

FARRELL: Cheers, George.
BAINES: Cheers, Norman.
JACKSON: Cheers, Bert.
ILLING.: Cheers, Arnold.

(*Till*)

BAINES: Well, well, look who's coming over.
ILLING.: Isn't that young Clive Barrington from the Providential
Insurance?
BAINES: As happily married a man as ever I saw.
CLIVE: (*approach*) Evening, Arnold. Evening, Bert, Charlie, George.
Evening, Norman.
BARMAID: Evening, Mr Barrington.

FARRELL: Evening, Clive.

BAINES: (*simul*) Long time no see.

JACKSON: Hello Barrington old lad.

ILLING.: How goes it.

HAWKINS: What ho then, mate.

HAWKINS: What are you having?

CLIVE: A whisky, please.

HAWKINS: Any particular brand?

CLIVE: I'll have the one nearest the clock.

HAWKINS: Half a minute. There's a bloke over there can't take his eyes off you, Clive. Over in the corner, see him? Wearing a dark blue single-breasted dinner jacket and tinted spectacles. A foreigner, or my name's not George Hawkins.

CLIVE: Yes, by George, you're right, George. Excuse me.

(*Peak chatter*)

OPPENHEIMER: (*middle-European accent*) So, Herr Barrington, you are here at last. I was becoming impatient.

CLIVE: Well, now I am here, perhaps you would be so good as to explain what the blazes all this is about?

OPPEN.: Certainly, but not here. We will go to my place in Wiltshire where we can talk. My car is outside. Come.

(*Fade on pub background*)

(*Fade up car noise slowing, stopping, engine ticking over*)

Excuse me, Officer.

POLICEMAN: Yes, sir?

OPPEN.: Am I on the right road for Wiltshire?

POLICEMAN: That's right, sir. Straight on, then turn left.

(*Car revs up, moves off. Crossfade to car slowing down on gravel path and stopping. Car door bangs eight times. Footsteps on gravel. Front door creaks open. Distant piano, Moonlight Sonata*)

OPPEN.: Ah, that is my sister playing.

(Piano nearer. The sonata comes to its close. Suspicion of needle noise at the end)

GERDA: Ha! Managed that difficult A flat major chord at last.

OPPEN.: Gerda, my dear, we have a visitor. Herr Clive Barrington from the Providential Insurance Gesellschaft. Herr Barrington, this is my sister Gerda.

GERDA: I am pleased to meet you, Herr Barrington. Has Heinrich told you what we have in mind?

OPPEN.: Nein, not yet, Liebchen. Herr Barrington, first a drink. Champagne, I think, to celebrate.

(Champagne cork, pour, fizz, clink)

CLIVE: Thank you. Now, Mr Oppenheimer, or whatever your name is, don't you think it's time you did some explaining?

OPPEN.: Ja, of course. The stolen diamonds about which your Major Kenwood-Smith has seen fit to call in Scotland Yard—

CLIVE: Major Kenwood-Smith? You mean Major Kenwood-Smith who's head of my department at the Insurance Office?

OPPEN.: Right first time, Herr Barrington. As I was saying, the diamonds are safely in my hands.

CLIVE: What! You mean to tell me—

OPPEN.: One moment, please, let me continue. I intend to return them, but on one condition. Now listen carefully; this . . . is . . . what . . . I . . . want . . . you . . . to . . . do . . .

(Bring up threatening music to divide scenes)

(Fade music behind Oppenheimer)

. . . and I think that is all I need to tell you, my dear Herr. Now I must leave you; I have one or two . . . little matters to attend to. *(on mike)* Auf Wiedersehen.

(Door slams immediately some way off)

GERDA: Won't you sit down, Herr Barrington.

CLIVE: Thank you, Countess.

(Sitting noise)

Look, I don't know how far you're involved in this hellish business, but I would just like to say how exquisitely I thought you played that sonata just now. It happens to be a favourite of mine.

GERDA: Ja? You like my playing, yes?

CLIVE: Beautiful, and yet . . . no, it would be impertinent of me . . .

GERDA: Please.

CLIVE: Well then, if you insist. I thought that in the Andante – the slow movement – your tempo was a little . . . what shall I say?

GERDA: Strict?

CLIVE: Exactly.

GERDA: *(coming in close)* I had no idea you knew so much about music.

CLIVE: Please, Countess, I beg of you. I don't know what kind of a hold that filthy swine your brother has over you, and I don't want to know, but you don't belong here. For Pete's sake, why not leave with me now, before it's too late.

GERDA: Nein, nein, I cannot . . . *(in tears)*

CLIVE: Why, Countess, why?

GERDA: I will tell you. It is better that you should know. It all started a long time ago, when I was a little Fräulein in the tiny village of Bad Obersturmmbannführershof, in the Bavarian Alps . . .

(Fade. Bring up London traffic. Big Ben chimes the hour and then strikes twelve. As it strikes we move out of the traffic, a car stops, squeal of brakes, car doors, footsteps, newsboys, tugs, barrel organ, creaking door, more footsteps down a very long corridor passing offices with typewriters until a small door opens at the end of the passage and we move into a small room on the last stroke of twelve)

POWELL: Ha! Twelve o'clock already. Morning, Sergeant McEwan. Or perhaps I should say 'Good afternoon.'

MCEWAN: *(Scots)* Whichever you like, sir!

73

(*Good-humoured laughter*)

POWELL: As a matter of fact, I've been out on a job already this morning. I bet you just thought I'd overslept, didn't you, Sergeant?

MCEWAN: What, you sir? Hoots, no. Not Detective Inspector 'Bonzo' Powell, VC, who went over the top at Tobruk; one-time Channel swimmer, and one of the toughest and at the same time one of the most popular officers at Scotland Yard here? I should say not. Och.

POWELL: No, I got a line on our old friend Heinrich Oppenheimer, at long last. Our chap at Swanage says Oppenheimer has a private submarine moored nearby – it's my guess he'll try and get the diamonds out of the country tonight.

MCEWAN: Havers! Where will he make for, d'ye ken?

POWELL: I don't know, but it's my guess he'll make straight for Amsterdam. Come on, Sergeant, we're going down to Swanage. And . . . the . . . sooner . . . the . . . better . . .

(*Urgent music. Then fade behind gulls, rowlocks, wash. Studio clock should be particularly noticeable in this scene*)

(*Note: all the Germans in this scene are indistinguishable one from the other, and indeed may all be played by the same actor as Oppenheimer*)

LUDWIG: We are nearly at the submarine now, mein Kommandant.

OPPEN.: Ach. Sehr gut. Tell me once more what you have done with the prisoners, my sister Gerda and that meddling fool Barrington.

LUDWIG: Karl found them attempting to telephone Scotland Yard from the porter's lodge. They have been tied up and taken on board the submarine half an hour ago.

OPPEN.: That is gut. I will teach the fool Englishman to double-cross me. Achtung! Here we are at the submarine. Karl! Heinz! Kurt! Lower a rope ladder.

KARL: Ja, mein Kommandant.

(*Feet on tin tray*)

OPPEN.: It is four o'clock. We will sail immediately.

(*Change to submarine acoustic*)

HEINZ: The diamonds are safely locked in your cabin, mein Kommandant.
OPPEN.: Jawohl. Kurt! Heinz! Karl! Prepare to dive!

(*Diving noises. Klaxon*)

Set a course for Amsterdam.
KURT: Steer east north east eight degrees by north.

(*Cries of jawohl, Achtung, midships, etc*)

OPPEN.: Ludwig!
LUDWIG: Ja, mein Kommandant.
OPPEN.: Take me to the prisoners.
LUDWIG: Ja, mein Kommandant.

(*More feet on tin tray*)

They are in the forward hydroplane compartment.

(*Door opens. Forward hydroplane noises*)

OPPEN.: So, Herr Barrington, we meet again.
CLIVE: You filthy swine, Oppenheimer, you won't get away with this.
OPPEN.: (*becoming slightly manic*) On the contrary, my friend, there is no power on earth that can stop me now. You, I'm afraid, will never reach Amsterdam. There will be an unfortunate . . . accident in the escape hatch.
GERDA: (*a gasp*) Heinrich! You don't mean . . .
OPPEN.: As for you, my dear sister Gerda . . .
CLIVE: Leave the girl out of it, Oppenheimer. She's done nothing to you.

OPPEN.: Charming chivalry, my English friend. But it is to no avail. Come.

CLIVE: All right, you swine, you've asked for it!

(*Blow*)

OPPEN.: Aargh. Himmel! Karl, Kurt!

(*Running footsteps*)

CLIVE: Ah, would you? Then try *this* for size.

(*Blow. Groan*)

If *that's* the way you want it.

(*Blow. Groan*)

KURT: Get him, Hans.
CLIVE: Ah, no you don't. Take *that*.

(*Blow. Groan. A chair falls over*)

GERDA: Look out, Clive. The one with the glasses behind you. He's got a gun.

(*Shot*)

CLIVE: (*winces*)

(*Another chair falls over*)

Phew! Close thing, that.

GERDA: Clive! What happened?
CLIVE: Just my luck; he got me in the arm. Luckily, he caught his foot on that bulkhead coaming; he must have struck his head on that valve group between the depth gauge and the watertight torpedo door.
GERDA: Is he—?
CLIVE: I'm afraid so. Right, now to get this thing surfaced.
GERDA: Do you know how?

CLIVE: It shouldn't be too difficult. Luckily I had a week on subs in RNVR years ago. (*with pain*) This right arm being kaput doesn't help, though. Right, now, just blow . . . the . . . ballast from the main . . . and . . . number four . . . tanks . . . adjust the Hammerschmidt-Brücke stabilizers . . . and up – we – go.

(*Surfacing noises. Sea. The cry of gulls. A few bars of* Desert Island Discs *music. Crossfade to chatter, clink of glasses*)

LAURA: Have another drink, Sergeant.

MCEWAN: Thank you, Mrs Barrington. I'll have a wee drappie.

CLIVE: How about you, Inspector?

POWELL: Don't mind if I do, sir. Charming place you have here, if I may say so; and a charming wife to go with it.

LAURA: (*blushing*) Thank you, Inspector.

CLIVE: Well, I don't mind saying, Inspector, there were one or two moments today when I wondered if I'd ever see either of them again.

LAURA: Tell us, Inspector, exactly when it was you came to realise that Major Kenwood-Smith was behind it all?

POWELL: Well, for a long time it had puzzled us that the safe was blown by a left-handed man – Oppenheimer and his henchmen are all right-handed. Luckily one of our chaps noticed Kenwood-Smith signing a cheque with his *left* hand.

CLIVE: Aha.

POWELL: We asked him a few questions, and he broke down and confessed. Sergeant, you can go on from there.

MCEWAN: Ay, well, the diamonds aboard the submarine turned out to be imitation. Oppenheimer must have been double-crossed at the last minute, and someone in Berridge's Hotel must have performed the switch.

CLIVE: Great Scott, the barmaid!

POWELL: Right, first time, Mr Barrington. We checked in our archives, and she turned out to have a record as long as your arm. She made a dash for it, but in the end she broke down and confessed.

CLIVE: So everything turned out for the best in the end, eh?

POWELL: That's right, sir. And just think, Mrs Barrington, if it hadn't been for young Richard here losing his puppy on Wimbledon Common, none of this might ever have happened.

(*Yapping on disc*)

RICHARD: Down, Lucky, down!

POWELL: Now then, young pup, none of that gnawing at my trouser leg, or I'll have to take you into custody as well!

(*General laughter. Light-hearted rounding-off music and up to finish*)

ANNOUNCER: (*spinning it out – the play has under-run*) You have been listening to 'This Gun That I Have in My Right Hand Is Loaded'.

LISTINGS

Theatre Producers

Actors Touring Company (ATC)
Alford House, Aveline Street, London SE11 5DQ
☎ 020 7735 8311   Fax 020 7735 1031 attn. ATC
Email judith@atc-online.com
Website www.atc-online.com

Artistic Director *Gordon Anderson*
Collaborates with writers on adaptation and/or translation work and
unsolicited mss will be considered in this category as well as new writing. 'We endeavour to read mss but do not have the resources to do so
quickly.' As a small-scale company, all plays must have a cast of six or
less.

Alternative Theatre Company Ltd
Bush Theatre, Shepherds Bush Green, London W12 8QD
☎ 020 7602 3703   Fax 020 7602 7614
Email info@bushtheatre.co.uk

Literary Manager *Nicola Wilson*
FOUNDED 1972. Trading as The Bush Theatre. Produces nine new plays a
year (principally British) including up to three visiting companies also
producing new work: 'we are a writer's theatre'. Previous productions:
Kiss of the Spiderwoman Manuel Puig; *Raping the Gold* Lucy Gannon; *The
Wexford Trilogy* Billy Roche; *Love and Understanding* Joe Penhall; *This

Limetree Bower Conor McPherson; *Discopigs* Enda Walsh; *The Pitchfork Disney* Philip Ridley; *Caravan* Helen Blakeman; *Beautiful Thing* Jonathan Harvey; *Killer Joe* Tracy Letts; *Shang-a-Lang* Catherine Johnson; *Howie the Rookie* Mark O'Rowe. Scripts are read by a team of associates, then discussed with the management, a process which takes about four months. The theatre offers a small number of commissions, recommissions to ensure further drafts on promising plays, and a guarantee against royalties so writers are not financially penalized even though the plays are produced in a small house. Writers should send scripts (full-length plays only) with small sae for acknowledgement and large sae for return of script.

Birmingham Repertory Theatre

Centenary Square, Broad Street, Birmingham B1 2EP
☎ 0121 245 2000   Fax 0121 245 2100
Website www.birmingham-rep.co.uk

Associate Director (Literary) *Ben Payne*
Literary Officer *Caroline Jester*
The Birmingham Repertory Theatre aims to provide a platform for the best work from new writers from both within and beyond the West Midlands region. The Rep is committed to a policy of integrated casting and to the production of new work which reflects the diversity of contemporary experience. The commissioning of new plays takes place across the full range of the theatre's activities: in the Main House, The Door (which is a dedicated new writing space) and on tour to community venues in the region. 'Writers are advised that the Rep is very unlikely to produce an unsolicited script. We usually assess unsolicited submissions on the basis of whether it indicates a writer with whom the theatre may be interested in working. The theatre runs a programme of writers' attachments every year in addition to its commissioning policy and maintains close links with *Stagecoach* (the regional writers' training agency) and the MA in Playwriting Studies at the University of Birmingham.' For more information contact the Literary Officer.

Bootleg Theatre Company

23 Burgess Green, Bishopdown, Salisbury, Wiltshire SP1 3EL
☎ 01722 421476
Email colin@thebootlegtheatrecompany.fsnet.co.uk

Contact *Colin Burden*
FOUNDED 1984. Tries to encompass as wide an audience as possible and
has a tendency towards plays with socially relevant themes. A good bet for
new writing since unsolicited mss are very welcome. 'Our policy is to
produce new and/or rarely seen plays and anything received is given the
most serious consideration.' Actively seeks to obtain grants to commission
new writers for the company. Productions include: *Clubland* Giles, Harris,
Suthers and Mordell; *Hanging Hanratty* Michael Burnham; *The Truth About
Blokes* Trevor Suthers; *Cool Blokes: Decent Suits* Russell Mardell.

Borderline Theatre

Darlington New Church, North Harbour Street, Ayr KA8 8AA
☎ 01292 281010   Fax 01292 263825
Email enquiries@borderlinetheatre.co.uk
Website www.borderlinetheatre.co.uk

Producer *Eddie Jackson*
FOUNDED 1974. Borderline is one of Scotland's leading touring companies.
Committed to new writing, it tours an innovative programme of new plays
and radical adaptations/translations of classic texts in an accessible and
entertaining style. Tours to main-house theatres and small venues throughout Scotland. Productions include the world premieres of *The Angels' Share*
Chris Dolan; *The Prince and the Pilot* Anita Sullivan. Previous writers have
included Dario Fo, Liz Lochhead and John Byrne. Borderline is also committed to commissioning and touring new plays for young people. Please
contact before submitting material.

Bristol Old Vic Theatre Company (Theatre Royal, New Vic Studio and Basement)

Theatre Royal, King Street, Bristol BS1 4ED
☎ 0117 949 3993   Fax 0117 949 3996

Email admin@bristol-old-vic.co.uk
Website www.bristol-old-vic.co.uk

Bristol Old Vic is committed to the commissioning and production of new writing in the Theatre Royal (650 seats). Plays must have enough popular appeal to attract an audience of significant size. In the New Vic Studio (150 seats) up to four plays a year are produced. The theatre will read and report on unsolicited scripts, and asks for a fee of £15 per script to cover the payments to readers. 'We also seek to attract emerging talent to the Basement, a profit-share venue (50 seats) committed to producing one-act plays. Plays for the Basement will be read free of charge although no report can be provided.' In all cases, if return of script is required, please supply sae.

Chester Gateway Theatre Trust Ltd
Hamilton Place, Chester, Cheshire CH1 2BH
☎ 01244 318104   Fax 01244 317277
Email jasminelendry@gateway-theatre.org
Website www.chestergateway.co.uk

Chief Executive *Jasmine Hendry*
FOUNDED 1968. 440-seater main house and 120-seater Manweb Studio. Committed to producing two in-house productions a year and aims to present a varied programme of theatre, dance, music, opera and comedy. The Education and Access Department works in schools and the community, and a writers' group meets fortnightly. Each year the group presents rehearsed readings using professional actors and directors.

Clwyd Theatr Cymru
Mold, Flintshire CH7 1YA
☎ 01352 756331   Fax 01352 701558
Email drama@celtic.co.uk
Website www.clwyd-theatr-cymru.co.uk

Literary Manager *William James* (williamjames@clwyd-theatr-cymru.co.uk)
Clwyd Theatr Cymru produces a season of plays each year performed by a core ensemble, along with tours throughout Wales (in English and Welsh). Plays are a mix of classics, revivals, contemporary drama. Recent

new writing includes: *The Rabbit* Meredydd Barker; *Journey of Mary Kelly* Siân Evans; *Rape of the Fair Country*, *Hosts of Rebecca* and *Song of the Earth* all adapt. Manon Eames; *The Changelings* Gregg Cullen; *Celf* Yasmina Reza, *Damwain a Hap* Dario Fo, both trans. Manon Eames; *Flora's War/Rhyfel Flora*, *Word for Word/Gair am Air* and *The Secret/Y Gyfrinach* Tim Baker. Plays by Welsh writers or with Welsh themes will be considered.

Colchester Mercury Theatre Limited

Balkerne Gate, Colchester, Essex CO1 1PT
☎ 01206 577006   Fax 01206 769607
Email mercury.theatre@virgin.net

Artistic Producer *Gregory Floy*
Associate Director *Adrian Stokes*
Producing theatre with a wide-ranging audience. Unsolicited scripts welcome. The theatre has a free playwright's group for adults with a serious commitment to writing plays.

Contact Theatre Company

Oxford Road, Manchester M15 6JA
☎ 0161 274 3434   Fax 0161 274 0640
Email info@contact-theatre.org.uk

Artistic Director *John E. McGrath*
'In partnership with the BBC, we are investing in innovative approaches to the discovery of new writers – and new kinds of writing – for stage, screen, radio and new media.' In general, Contact works primarily with the 13–30 age group and is particularly interested in materials that relate to the lives and culture of young people. 'We welcome work from writers of all ages. Hearing from a variety of voices, from different cultures and backgrounds, is also important to us. We encourage concise pitches from writers – no more than ten pages – including a summary and some sample pages.'

Crucible Theatre

55 Norfolk Street, Sheffield S1 1DA
☎ 0114 249 5999   Fax 0114 249 6003
Associate Director *Michael Grandage*

Literary Associates *Matthew Byam Shaw, Anna Mackmin*
'Most of the new work we present will be the result of commissions or a
prolonged exchange of ideas and script development with writers in whom
we have expressed an interest. However, we are interested in all new work
and offer a free script reading service for unsolicited scripts. NB We do not
offer readers' reports. Please ring or send sae for full details of script
reading service.'

Cwmni Theatr Gwynedd
Deiniol Road, Bangor, Gwynedd LL57 2TL
☎ 01248 351707   Fax 01248 351915
Email theatr@theatregwynedd.co.uk

Contact *Artistic Director*
FOUNDED 1984. A mainstream company, performing in major theatres on
the Welsh circuit. Welsh-language work only at present. Classic Welsh
plays, translations of European repertoire and new work, including adaptations from novels. New Welsh work always welcome; works in English
considered if appropriate for translation (i.e. dealing with issues relevant
to Wales). 'We are keen to discuss projects with established writers and
offer commissions where possible.'

Derby Playhouse
Eagle Centre, Derby DE1 2NF
☎ 01332 363271   Fax 01332 547200
Website www.derbyplayhouse.co.uk

Chief Executive *Karen Hebden*
Creative Producer *Stephen Edwards*
Derby Playhouse is interested in new work and has produced several
world premieres over the last year. 'We have a discrete commissioning
budget but already have several projects under way. Due to the amount
of scripts we receive, we now ask writers to send a letter accompanied by
a synopsis of the play, a résumé of writing experience and any ten pages
of the script they wish to submit. We will then determine whether we
think it is suitable for the Playhouse, in which case we will ask for a full
script.' Writers are welcome to send details of rehearsed readings and

productions as an alternative means of introducing the theatre to their work.

Druid Theatre Company

Chapel Lane, Galway, Republic of Ireland

☎ 00 353 91 568660   Fax 00 353 91 563109

Email info@druidtheatre.com

Website www.druidtheatre.com

Contact *Literary Manager*

FOUNDED 1975. Based in Galway and playing nationally and internationally, the company operates a major programme for the development of new writing. While focusing on Irish work, the company also accepts unsolicited material from outside Ireland.

Dundee Repertory Theatre

Tay Square, Dundee DD1 1PB

☎ 01382 227684   Fax 01382 228609

Email hglen@dundeereptheatre.co.uk

Website www.dundeereptheatre.co.uk

Contact *Artistic Director*

FOUNDED 1939. Plays to a varied audience. Translations and adaptations of classics, and new local plays. Most new work is commissioned. Interested in contemporary plays in translation and in new Scottish writing. No scripts except by prior arrangement.

Eastern Angles Theatre Company

Sir John Mills Theatre, Gatacre Road, Ipswich, Suffolk IP1 2LQ

☎ 01473 218202   Fax 01473 384999

Email admin@easternangles.co.uk

Website www.easternangles.co.uk

Artistic Director *Ivan Cutting*

General Manager *Jill Streatfeild*

FOUNDED 1982. Plays to a rural audience for the most part. New work only: some commissioned, some devised by the company, some researched documentaries. Unsolicited mss welcome from regional writers. 'We are always keen to develop and produce new writing, especially that which is germane to a rural area.'

Gate Theatre Company Ltd
11 Pembridge Road, London W11 3HQ
☎ 020 7229 5387   Fax 020 7221 6055

Artistic Director *Erica Whyman*
FOUNDED 1979. Plays to a mixed, London-wide audience, depending on production. Aims to produce British premieres of plays which originate from abroad and translations of neglected classics. Most work is with translators. Recent productions: *Ion* Euripides, trans. Stephen Sharkey; *Les Justes* Albert Camus, trans. Gillian Hannah. Positively encourages writers from abroad to send in scripts or translations. Most unsolicited scripts are read but it is extremely unlikely that new British, Irish or North American plays will have any future at the theatre due to emphasis on plays translated from foreign languages. Please address submissions to 'Scripts'.

Graeae Theatre Company
Interchange Studios, Hampstead Town Hall Centre,
213 Haverstock Hill, London NW3 4QP
☎ 020 7681 4755   Fax 020 7681 4756
Email info@graeae.org
Website www.graeae.org
Minicom 020 7267 3167

Artistic Director *Jenny Sealey*
Executive Producer *Roger Nelson*
Europe's premier theatre company of disabled people, the company tours nationally and internationally with innovative theatre productions highlighting both historical and contemporary disabled experience. Graeae also runs Forum Theatre and educational programmes available to schools, youth clubs and day centres nationally, provides vocational training in theatre arts (including playwriting). Unsolicited scripts from disabled writers welcome. New work examining disability issues is commissioned.

Hampstead Theatre

Eton Avenue, London NW3 3EU
☎ 020 7722 9224   Fax 020 7722 3860
Website www.hampstead-theatre.co.uk

Literary Manager *Jeanie O'Hare*
A brand new Hampstead Theatre opened in January 2003. The building is
an intimate space with a flexible stage and an auditorium capable of
expanding to seat 325. The artistic policy continues to be the production of
British and international new plays and the development of important
young writers. 'We are looking for writers who recognize the power of
theatre and who have a story to tell. All plays are read and discussed. We
give feedback to all writers with potential.' Writers produced at Hampstead
include: Michael Frayn, Roy Williams, Shelagh Stephenson, Simon Block,
Philip Ridley, Frank McGuinness, Rona Munro, Brad Fraser and Abi
Morgan.

Harrogate Theatre Company

Oxford Street, Harrogate, North Yorkshire HG1 1QF
☎ 01423 502710   Fax 01423 563205
Email staff.name@harrogatetheatre.demon.co.uk

Artistic Director *Hannah Chissick*
Produces four to five productions a year on the main stage, one of which
may be a new play but is most likely to be commissioned. Annual main
stage youth theatre production may also be commissioned. Over the next
two years it is planned to workshop and read new plays by local writers
and possibly stage them in the studio. Unsolicited scripts from outside
Yorkshire are unlikely to receive a production or workshop. Please write
with a brief synopsis initially.

The Hiss & Boo Company Ltd

1 Nyes Hill, Wineham Lane, Bolney, West Sussex RH17 5SD
Fax 01444 882057
Email hissboo@msn.com
Website www.hissboo.co.uk

Contact *Ian Liston*
Particularly interested in new thrillers, comedy thrillers, comedy and melodrama – must be commercial full-length plays. Also interested in plays/plays with music for children. No one-acts. Previous productions: *The Shakespeare Revue; Come Rain Come Shine; Sleighrider; Beauty and the Beast; An Ideal Husband; Mr Men's Magical Island; Mr Men and the Space Pirates; Nunsense; Corpse!; Groucho: A Life in Revue; See How They Run; Christmas Cat and the Pudding Pirates; Pinocchio* and traditional pantos written by Roy Hudd for the company. 'We are keen on revue-type shows and compilation shows but *not* tribute-type performances.' No unsolicited scripts, no telephone calls. Send synopsis and introductory letter in the first instance.

Hull Truck Theatre Company
Spring Street, Hull HU2 8RW
☎ 01482 224800   Fax 01482 581182

Executive Director *Joanne Gower*
John Godber, of *Teechers, Bouncers, Up 'n' Under* fame, the artistic director of this high-profile northern company since 1984, has very much dominated the scene in the past with his own successful plays. The emphasis is still on new writing but Godber's work continues to be toured extensively. Most new plays are commissioned. Previous productions: *Dead Fish* Gordon Steel; *Off Out* and *Fish and Leather* Gill Adams; *Happy Families* John Godber. The company receives a large number of unsolicited scripts but cannot guarantee a quick response. Bear in mind the artistic policy of Hull Truck, which is 'accessibility and popularity'. In general they are not interested in musicals, or in plays with casts of more than eight.

Stephen Joseph Theatre
Westborough, Scarborough, North Yorkshire YO11 1JW
☎ 01723 370540   Fax 01723 360506

Artistic Director *Alan Ayckbourn*
Literary Manager *Laura Harvey*
A two-auditorium complex housing a 165-seat end stage theatre/cinema (the McCarthy) and a 400-seat theatre-in-the-round (the Round). Positive

policy on new work. For obvious reasons, Alan Ayckbourn's work features quite strongly but a new writing programme ensures plays from other sources are actively encouraged. Also runs a lunchtime season of one-act plays each summer. Writers are advised however that the SJT is very unlikely to produce an unsolicited script; synopses are preferred. Recent commissions and past productions include: *A Listening Heaven* and *Clock-watching* Torben Betts; *Larkin with Women* Ben Brown; *Amaretti Angels* Sarah Phelps; *Something Blue* Gill Adams; *The Star Throwers* Paul Lucas; *Man for Hire* Meredith Oakes; *Safari Party* Tim Firth; *Gameplan, Flatspin, Roleplay* and *House and Garden* Alan Ayckbourn. 'Writers are welcome to send details of rehearsed readings and productions as an alternative means of introducing the theatre to their work.' Submit to *Laura Harvey* enclosing an sae for return of mss.

Bill Kenwright Ltd
BKL House, 106 Harrow Road, London W2 1RR
☎ 020 7446 6200   Fax 020 7446 6222

Contact *Bill Kenwright*
Presents both revivals and new shows for West End and touring theatres. Although new work tends to be by established playwrights, this does not preclude or prejudice new plays from new writers. Scripts should be addressed to Bill Kenwright with a covering letter and sae. 'We have enormous amounts of scripts sent to us although we very rarely produce unsolicited work. Scripts are read systematically. Please do not phone; the return of your script or contact with you will take place in time.'

Komedia
Gardner Street, North Lane, Brighton, East Sussex BN1 1UN
☎ 01273 647101   Fax 01273 647102
Email info@komedia.co.uk
Website www.komedia.co.uk

Contact *David Lavender*
FOUNDED in 1994, Komedia promotes, produces and presents new work. Mss of new plays welcome.

Leicester Haymarket Theatre
Belgrave Gate, Leicester LE1 3YQ
☎ 0116 253 0021   Fax 0116 251 3310
Website www.leicesterhaymarkettheatre.org

Artistic Directors *Paul Kerryson, Kully Thiarai*
Leicester Haymarket Theatre aims for a balanced programme of original and established works. It is a multicultural, racially integrated company with educational projects attached to all productions and areas of work. Forthcoming productions include two new plays, *Unsuitable Girls* Dolly Dhingra and *Bali – The Sacrifice* Girish Karnad. There is also a full studio programme and thriving youth theatre.

Library Theatre Company
St Peter's Square, Manchester M2 5PD
☎ 0161 234 1913   Fax 0161 228 6481
Email ltc@libraries.manchester.gov.uk
Website www.libtheatreco.org.uk

Artistic Director *Chris Honer*
Produces new and contemporary work, as well as occasional classics. No unsolicited mss. Send outline of the nature of the script first. Encourages new writing through the commissioning of new plays and through a programme of rehearsed readings to help writers' development.

Live Theatre Company
7/8 Trinity Chare, Newcastle upon Tyne NE1 3DF
☎ 0191 261 2694   Fax 0191 232 2224
Email info@live.org.uk
Website www.live.org.uk

Artistic Director *Max Roberts*
Executive Director *Jim Beirne*
FOUNDED 1973. Produces shows at its refurbished 200-seat venue, and also tours regionally and nationally. Company policy is to produce work that is rooted in the culture of the region, particularly for those who do not normally get involved in the arts. The company is particularly interested

in promoting new writing. As well as full-scale productions the company organizes workshops, rehearsed readings and other new writing activities. The company also enjoys a close relationship with New Writing North. Productions include: *Buffalo Girls* Karin Young; *Two* Jim Cartwright; *Cabaret* and an ambitious cycle of plays *Twelve Tales of Tyneside* which involved twelve writers; *Falling Together* Tom Hadaway; *Cooking With Elvis* Lee Hall; *Bones* Peter Straughan; *Laughter When We're Dead* Sean O'Brien and *ne1* and *Tales From the Backyard* Alan Plater.

London Bubble Theatre Company
3–5 Elephant Lane, London SE16 4JD
☎ 020 7237 4434   Fax 020 7231 2366
Email peth@londonbubble.org.uk
Website www.londonbubble.org.uk

Artistic Director *Jonathan Petherbridge*
Produces workshops, plays and events for a mixed audience of theatre-goers and non-theatre-goers, wide-ranging in terms of age, culture and class. Previous productions: *Gilgamesh; Sleeping Beauty; Growing People.* Unsolicited mss are received but 'our reading service is extremely limited and there can be a considerable wait before we can give a response'. Commissions approximately one new project a year, often inspired by a promenade site, specific community of interest or workshop group.

Lyric Theatre Hammersmith
King Street, London W6 0QL
☎ 020 8741 0824   Fax 020 8741 5965
Email enquiries@lyric.co.uk
Website www.lyric.co.uk

Artistic Director *Neil Bartlett*
Executive Director *Simon Mellor*
The main theatre stages an eclectic programme of new and revived classics with a particular interest in music theatre. Interested in developing projects with writers, translators and adaptors. The Lyric does not accept unsolicited scripts. Its 110-seat studio focuses on work for children, young people and families.

New Vic Theatre

Etruria Road, Newcastle under Lyme, Staffordshire ST5 0JG
☎ 01782 717954   Fax 01782 712885
Email admin@newvictheatre.org.uk

Artistic Director *Gwenda Hughes*
The New Vic is a purpose-built theatre-in-the-round. Plays to a fairly broad-based audience which tends to vary from one production to another. A high proportion are not regular theatre-goers and new writing has been one of the main ways of contacting new audiences. Synopses preferred to unsolicited scripts.

NITRO

6 Brewery Road, London N7 9NH
☎ 020 7609 1331   Fax 020 7609 1221
Email btc@dircon.co.uk
Website www.nitro.co.uk

Artistic Director *Felix Cross*
FOUNDED 1978. Formerly Black Theatre Co-op. Plays to a mixed audience, approximately 65 per cent female. Usually tours nationally twice a year. 'A music theatre company, we are committed in the first instance to new writing by black British writers and work which relates to the black culture and experience throughout the diaspora.' Unsolicited mss welcome.

Northcott Theatre

Stocker Road, Exeter, Devon EX4 4QB
☎ 01392 223999   Fax 01392 223996
Website www.northcott-theatre.co.uk

Artistic Director *Ben Crocker*
FOUNDED 1967. The Northcott is the south-west's principal subsidized producing theatre, situated on the University of Exeter campus. Describes its audience as 'geographically diverse, with a core audience of AB1s (40–60 age range)'. Continually looking to broaden the base of its audience profile, targeting younger and/or non-mainstream theatre-goers. Aims to develop, promote and produce quality new writing which reflects the life

of the region and addresses the audience it serves. Generally works on a commission basis but occasionally options existing new work. Unsolicited mss welcome. Current turnaround on script reading service is approximately three months and no mss can be returned unless a correct value sae is included with the original submission.

Northern Stage

Newcastle Playhouse, Barras Bridge, Newcastle upon Tyne NE1 7RH
☎ 0191 232 3366   Fax 0191 261 8093
Email directors@northernstage.com
Website www.northernstage.com

Artistic Director *Alan Lyddiard*
Executive Director *Caroline Routh*
A contemporary performance company whose trademarks are a strongly visual and physical style, international influences, appeal to young people and strongly linked programmes of community work. As likely to produce devised work as conventional new writing. Before submitting unsolicited scripts, please contact *Brenda Gray*, PA to the directors.

Nottingham Playhouse

Nottingham Theatre Trust, Wellington Circus, Nottingham NG1 5AF
☎ 0115 947 4361   Fax 0115 947 5759

Artistic Director *Giles Croft*
Aims to make innovation popular and present the best of world theatre, working closely with the communities of Nottingham and Nottinghamshire. Unsolicited mss will be read. It normally takes about six months, however, and 'we have never yet produced an unsolicited script. All our plays have to achieve a minimum of 60 per cent audiences in a 732-seat theatre. We have no studio.'

Nottingham Playhouse Roundabout Theatre in Education

Wellington Circus, Nottingham NG1 5AF
☎ 0115 947 4361   Fax 0115 953 9055
Email andrewb@nottinghamplayhouse.co.uk
Website www.roundabout.org.uk

Contact *Andrew Breakwell*
FOUNDED 1973. Theatre-in-education company of the Nottingham Play-house. Plays to a young audience 5–18 years of age. 'Most of our current work uses existing scripts but we try and commission at least one new play every year. We are committed to the encouragement of new writing as and when resources permit. With other major producers in the east Midlands we share the resources of the literary manager who is based at the Playhouse. See website for philosophy and play details. Please make contact before submitting scripts.'

NTC Touring Theatre Company
The Playhouse, Bondgate Without, Alnwick,
Northumberland NE66 1PQ
☎ 01665 602586   Fax 01665 605837
Email admin@ntc-touringtheatre.co.uk
Website www.ntc-touringtheatre.co.uk

Contact *Gillian Hambleton*
General Manager *Anna Flood*
FOUNDED 1978. Formerly Northumberland Theatre Company. A Northern Arts revenue-funded organization. Predominantly rural, small-scale touring company, playing to village halls and community centres throughout the northern region, the Scottish Borders and country-wide. Productions range from established classics to new work and popular comedies, but must be appropriate to their audience. Unsolicited scripts welcome but are unlikely to be produced. All scripts are read and returned with constructive criticism within six months. Writers whose style is of interest may then be com-missioned. The company encourages new writing and commissions when possible. Financial constraints restrict casting to a *maximum* of five.

Nuffield Theatre
University Road, Southampton, Hampshire SO17 1TR
☎ 023 8031 5500   Fax 023 8031 5511

Artistic Director *Patrick Sandford*
Script Executive *John Burgess*

Well known as a good bet for new playwrights, the Nuffield gets an awful lot of scripts. They do a couple of new main stage plays every season. Previous productions: *Exchange* Yuri Trifonov (trans. Michael Frayn) which transferred to the Vaudeville Theatre; *The Floating Light Bulb* Woody Allen (British premiere); new plays by Claire Luckham: *Dogspot*; *The Dramatic Attitudes of Miss Fanny Kemble*; and Claire Tomalin: *The Winter Wife*. Open-minded about subject and style, producing musicals as well as straight plays. Also opportunities for some small-scale fringe work. Scripts preferred to synopses in the case of writers new to theatre. All will, eventually, be read 'but please be patient. We do not have a large team of paid readers. We read everything ourselves.'

Octagon Theatre Trust Ltd

Howell Croft South, Bolton, Lancashire BL1 1SB
☎ 01204 529407   Fax 01204 380110

Executive Director *John Blackmore*
FOUNDED 1967. The Octagon Theatre has pursued a dynamic policy of commissioning new plays in recent years. These have been by both established writers such as Paul Abbott, Tom Elliott, Henry Livings and Les Smith as well as new and emerging writers through partnerships with organizations such as North West Playwrights and the national new writing company Paines Plough. Whilst there is no prescriptive house style at the Octagon, the theatre is nevertheless keen to encourage the development of writers from the north-west region, telling stories that will resonate with the local audience. The associate director *Sue Reddish* coordinates the new writing initiative at the Octagon and any unsolicited scripts are processed through North West Playwrights.

Orange Tree Theatre

1 Clarence Street, Richmond, Surrey TW9 2SA
☎ 020 8940 0141   Fax 020 8332 0369
Email admin@orange-tree.demon.co.uk
Website www.orangetreetheatre.co.uk

Artistic Director *Sam Walters*
One of those theatre venues just out of London which are good for new

writing, both full-scale productions and rehearsed readings. Productions from September 2001: *Flyin' West* Pearl Cleage; *Whispers Along the Patio* David Cregan; *The Caucasian Chalk Circle* Bertolt Brecht; *Have You Anything To Declare?* Maurice Hennequin and Pierre Veber; *The Three Sisters* Anton Chekhov. Unsolicited mss are read, but patience (and sae) required.

Out of Joint
7 Thane Works, Thane Villas, London N7 7PH
☎ 020 7609 0207   Fax 020 7609 0203
Email ojo@outofjoint.co.uk
Website www.outofjoint.co.uk

Director *Max Stafford-Clark*
Producer *Graham Cowley*
Literary Manager *Jenny Worton*
FOUNDED 1993. Award-winning theatre company with new writing central to its policy. Produces new plays which reflect society and its concerns, placing an emphasis on education activity to attract young audiences. Welcomes unsolicited mss. Productions include: *Blue Heart* Caryl Churchill; *Our Lady of Sligo*, *The Steward of Christendom* and *Hinterland* Sebastian Barry; *Shopping and Fucking* and *Some Explicit Polaroids* Mark Ravenhill; *Rita, Sue and Bob Too* Andrea Dunbar; *A State Affair* Robin Soans; *Sliding with Suzanne* Judy Upton.

Oxford Stage Company
131 High Street, Oxford OX1 4DH
☎ 01865 723238   Fax 01865 790625
Website www.oxfordstage.co.uk

Artistic Director *Dominic Dromgoole*
A middle-scale touring company producing established and new plays. At least one new play or new adaptation a year. Due to forthcoming projects not considering unsolicited scripts at present.

Paines Plough
4th Floor, 43 Aldwych, London WC2B 4DN
☎ 020 7240 4533   Fax 020 7240 4534

Email office@painesplough.com
Website www.painesplough.com

Artistic Director *Vicky Featherstone*
Associate Director *John Tiffany*
Literary Associate *Lucy Morrison*
Tours new plays nationally. Works with writers to develop their skills and voices through workshops, rehearsed readings and playwriting projects. Provides a supportive environment for commissioned writers to push themselves and challenge their craft. Will consider unsolicited material from UK writers (please send sae for return of script).

Palace Theatre, Watford
Clarendon Road, Watford, Hertfordshire WD17 1JZ
☎ 01923 235455   Fax 01923 819664
Email enquiries@watfordtheatre.co.uk
Website www.watfordtheatre.co.uk

Artistic Director *Lawrence Till*
An important part of artistic and cultural policy is the commissioning of new plays and translations. Recent new plays: *Elton John's Glasses* David Farr (1997 Writers' Guild Best Regional Play award); *The Talented Mr Ripley* Phyllis Nagy; *The Dark* Jonathan Holloway; *The Late Middle Classes* Simon Gray (1999 Barclays/TMA Best New Play award); *Morning Glory* Sarah Daniels; *The True-Life Fiction of Mata Hari* Diane Samuels; *Full House* and *The Hairless Diva* (after Ionesco) John Mortimer; *Big Night Out at the Little Palace Theatre* Sandi Toksvig and Dillie Keane.

Perth Repertory Theatre
185 High Street, Perth PH1 5UW
☎ 01738 472700   Fax 01738 624576
Email info@perththeatre.co.uk
Website www.perththeatre.co.uk

Artistic Director *Michael Winter*
General Manager *Paul Hackett*
FOUNDED 1935. Combination of one- to four-weekly repertoire of plays and

musicals, incoming tours and studio productions. Unsolicited mss are read when time permits, but the timetable for return of scripts is lengthy. New plays staged by the company are usually commissioned under the Scottish Arts Council scheme.

Polka Theatre for Children
240 The Broadway, Wimbledon, London SW19 1SB
☎ 020 8545 8320   Fax 020 8545 8365
Email info@polkatheatre.com
Website www.polkatheatre.com

Artistic Director *Vicky Ireland*
Administrator *Stephen Midlane*
FOUNDED in 1967 and moved into its Wimbledon base in 1979. Leading children's theatre committed to commissioning and producing new plays. Programmes are planned two years ahead and at least three new plays are commissioned each year. 'Because of our specialist needs and fixed budgets, all our scripts are commissioned from established writers with whom we work very closely. Writers are selected via recommendation and previous work. We do not perform unsolicited scripts. Potential new writers' work is read and discussed on a regular basis; thus we constantly add to our pool of interesting and interested writers. This department is now headed by a new position, director of new writing.'

Queen's Theatre, Hornchurch
Billet Lane, Hornchurch, Essex RM11 1QT
☎ 01708 456118   Fax 01708 452348
Email info@queens-theatre.co.uk
Website www.queens-theatre.co.uk

Artistic Director *Bob Carlton*
The Queen's Theatre is a 500-seat producing theatre in the London Borough of Havering and within the M25. Established in 1953, the theatre has been located in its present building since 1975 and produces up to nine in-house productions per year, including pantomime. The Queen's has re-established a permanent core company of actor/musicians under the artis-

tic leadership of Bob Carlton. Aims to produce distinctive and accessible performances in an identifiable house style focused upon actor/musician shows but, in addition, embraces straight plays, classics and comedies. 'New play/musical submissions are welcome but should be submitted in treatment and not script form.' Each year there is a large-scale community play commissioned from a local writer culminating in a summer event beside the theatre. A new writers' group has been established, led currently by David Eldridge. Enquiries about joining should be directed to the education manager.

Red Ladder Theatre Company

3 St Peter's Buildings, York Street, Leeds, West Yorkshire LS9 8AJ
☎ 0113 245 5311　Fax 0113 245 5351
Email wendy@redladder.co.uk
Website www.redladder.co.uk

Artistic Director/Literary Manager *Wendy Harris*
Administrator *Janis Smyth*
FOUNDED 1968. Commissioning company touring 2–3 shows a year with a strong commitment to new work and new writers. Aimed at an audience of young people aged 14–25 who have little or no access to theatre. Performances held in youth clubs and similar venues where young people choose to meet. Recent productions: *Hold Ya* Chris O'Connell; *LowDown Highnotes* Andrea Earl. The company is particularly keen to enter into a dialogue with writers with regard to creating new work for young people. Red Ladder is running an attachment scheme, Outwrite In, in partnership with BBC Northern Exposure for writers from or based in Bradford. Email the artistic director for more information at the address above.

Red Shift Theatre Company

TRG2 Trowbray House, 108 Weston Street, London SE1 3QB
☎ 020 7378 9787　Fax 020 7378 9789
Email mail@redshifttheatreco.co.uk
Website www.redshifttheatreco.co.uk

Contact *Jonathan Holloway, Artistic Director*
General Manager *Jess Lammin*
FOUNDED 1982. Small-scale touring company which plays to a theatre-literate audience. Unlikely to produce an unsolicited script as most work is commissioned. Welcomes contact with writers – 'we try to see their work' – and receipt of CVs and treatments. Occasionally runs workshops bringing new scripts, writers and actors together. These can develop links with a reservoir of writers who may feed the company. Interested in new plays with subject matter which is accessible to a broad audience and concerns issues of importance; also new translations and adaptations. 2001–02 productions: *Nicholas Nickleby* and *The Love Child*.

Ridiculusmus
c/o Your Imagination, BAC, Lavender Hill, London SW11 5TN
Email ridiculusmus@yourimagination.org
Website www.ridiculusmus.com

Artistic Directors *Jon Hough, David Woods*
FOUNDED 1992. Touring company which plays to a wide range of audiences. Productions have included adaptations of *Three Men In a Boat; The Third Policeman; At Swim Two Birds* and original work: *The Exhibitionists; Yes, Yes, Yes* and *Say Nothing*. Unsolicited scripts not welcome.

Royal Court Theatre
Sloane Square, London SW1W 8AS
☎ 020 7565 5050   Fax 020 7565 5002 (Literary office)
Website www.royalcourttheatre.com

Literary Manager *Graham Whybrow*
The Royal Court is a leading international theatre producing up to seventeen new plays each year in its 400-seat proscenium theatre and 80-seat studio. In 1956 its first director George Devine set out to find 'hard-hitting, uncompromising writers whose plays are stimulating, provocative and exciting'. This artistic policy helped transform post-war British theatre, with new plays by writers such as John Osborne, Arnold Wesker, John Arden, Samuel Beckett, Edward Bond and David Storey, through to Caryl

Churchill, Jim Cartwright, Kevin Elyot and Timberlake Wertenbaker. Since 1994 it has produced a new generation of writers such as Joe Penhall, Rebecca Prichard, Sarah Kane, Jez Butterworth, Martin McDonagh, Mark Ravenhill, Ayub Khan-Din, Conor McPherson, Roy Williams and many other first-time writers. The Royal Court has programmes for young writers and international writers, and it is always searching for new plays and new playwrights.

Royal Exchange Theatre Company
St Ann's Square, Manchester M2 7DH
☎ 0161 833 9333   Fax 0161 832 0881
Website www.royalexchange.co.uk

Literary Manager *Sarah Frankcom*
FOUNDED 1976. The Royal Exchange has developed a new writing policy which it finds is attracting a younger audience to the theatre. The company has produced new plays by Shelagh Stephenson, Brad Fraser, Simon Burke, Jim Cartwright, Peter Barnes and Alex Finlayson. Also English and foreign classics, modern classics, adaptations and new musicals. The Royal Exchange receives 500–2,000 scripts a year. These are read by Sarah Frankcom and a team of experienced readers. Only a tiny percentage is suitable, but a number of plays are commissioned each year.

Royal Lyceum Theatre Company
Grindlay Street, Edinburgh EH3 9AX
☎ 0131 248 4800   Fax 0131 228 3955

Artistic Director *Mark Thomson*
Administration Manager *Ruth Butterworth*
Administration Director *Sadie McKinlay*
FOUNDED 1965. Repertory theatre which plays to a mixed urban Scottish audience. Produces classic, contemporary and new plays. Would like to stage more new plays, especially Scottish. No full-time literary staff to provide reports on submitted scripts.

Royal National Theatre
South Bank, London SE1 9PX
☎ 020 7452 3333   Fax 020 7452 3350
Website www.nationaltheatre.org.uk

Literary Manager *Jack Bradley*
The majority of the National's new plays come about as a result of direct commission or from existing contacts with playwrights. There is no quota for new work, though so far more than a third of plays presented have been the work of living playwrights. Writers new to the theatre would need to be of exceptional talent to be successful with a script here, though the Royal National Theatre Studio helps a limited number of playwrights, through readings, workshops and discussions. In some cases a new play is presented for a shorter-than-usual run in the Cottesloe Theatre. Scripts considered (send sae).

Royal Shakespeare Company
Dramaturgy, Royal Shakespeare Theatre, Waterside, Stratford upon Avon, Warwickshire CV37 6BB
☎ 01789 412200
Website www.rsc.org.uk

Dramaturg *Paul Sirett*
The RSC is a classical theatre company based in Stratford upon Avon. It has recently transformed itself to create the opportunity for different ensemble companies to work on distinct projects that will open both in Stratford upon Avon and at various venues around London. The company also has an annual residency in Newcastle upon Tyne and tours both nationally and internationally. As well as Shakespeare, English classics and foreign classics in translation, new plays counterpoint the RSC's repertory, especially those which celebrate language. 'The dramaturgy department is proactive rather than reactive and seeks out the plays and playwrights it wishes to commission. It will read all translations of classic foreign works submitted, or of contemporary works where the original writer and/or translator is known. It is unable to read unsolicited work from less established writers. It can only return scripts if an sae is enclosed with submission.'

7:84 Theatre Company Scotland

333 Woodlands Road, Glasgow G3 6NG

☎ 0141 334 6686   Fax 0141 334 3369

Email admin@784theatre.com

Website www.784theatre.com

Artistic Director *Gordon Laird*

FOUNDED 1973. One of Scotland's foremost touring theatre companies committed to producing work that addresses current social, cultural and political issues. Recent productions include commissions by Scottish playwrights such as Peter Arnott *A Little Rain*; Stephen Greenhorn *Dissent*; David Greig *Caledonia Dreaming* and the Scottish premieres of Tony Kushner's *Angels in America* and Athol Fugard's *Valley Song*. 'The company is committed to a new writing policy that encourages and develops writers at every level of experience, to get new voices and strong messages on to the stage.' New writing development has always been central to 7:84's core activity and has included summer schools and the 7:84 Writers' Group. The company continues to be committed to this work and its development. 'Happy to read unsolicited scripts.'

Shared Experience

The Soho Laundry, 9 Dufours Place, London W1F 7SJ

☎ 020 7434 9248   Fax 020 7287 8763

Email admin@setheatre.co.uk

Joint Artistic Directors *Nancy Meckler, Polly Teale*

FOUNDED 1975. Varied audience depending on venue, since this is a touring company. Productions have included: *Anna Karenina, Mill on the Floss* and *War and Peace* all adapt. Helen Edmundson; *The Danube* Maria Irene Fornes; *Desire Under the Elms* Eugene O'Neill; *I Am Yours* Judith Thompson; *The House of Bernarda Alba* trans. Rona Munro; *The Magic Toyshop* adapt. Bryony Lavery. No unsolicited mss. Primarily not a new writing company but 'we are interested in innovative new scripts'.

Sherman Theatre Company
Senghennydd Road, Cardiff CF24 4YE
☎ 029 2064 6901   Fax 029 2064 6902
Website www.shermantheatre.co.uk

Artistic Director *Phil Clark*
FOUNDED 1973. Theatre for young people, with main house and studio. Encourages new writing; has produced eighty-six new plays in the last ten years. Previous productions include a David Wood adaptation of Roald Dahl's *James and the Giant Peach*, plays by Frank Vickery *Pullin the Wool*; Helen Griffin *Flesh and Blood*; Patrick Jones *Everything Must Go*; Terry Deary *Horrible Histories Crackers Christmas*; Mike Kenny *Puff the Magic Dragon*; Brendan Murray *Something Beginning With . . .*; Roald Dahl *The Enormous Crocodile*; Roger Williams *Pop*; Arnold Wesker *Break, My Heart*. The company has presented four seasons of six new plays live on stage and broadcast on BBC Radio Wales, and four series of one-act lunchtime plays on stage and then filmed for HTV Wales. Priority will be given to Wales-based writers.

Show of Strength
74 Chessel Street, Bedminster, Bristol BS3 3DN
☎ 0117 902 0235   Fax 0117 902 0196
Email sheila@showofstrength.freeserve.co.uk

Artistic Director *Sheila Hannon*
FOUNDED 1986. Plays to an informal, younger than average audience. Aims to stage at least one new play each season with a preference for work from Bristol and the south-west. Will read unsolicited scripts but a lack of funding means they are unable to provide written reports. Output: *Blue Murder, So Long Life* and *Nicholodeon* Peter Nichols; *Lags* Ron Hutchinson; *A Busy Day* Fanny Burney. Also rehearsed readings of new work.

Snap People's Theatre Trust
29 Raynham Road, Bishop's Stortford, Hertfordshire CM23 5PE
☎ 01279 461607   Fax 01279 506694
Email info@snaptheatre.co.uk
Website www.snaptheatre.co.uk

Contacts *Andy Graham, Gill Bloomfield*
FOUNDED 1979. Plays to young people (5–11; 12–19), and to the under 25s. Writers should make contact in advance of sending material. New writing is encouraged and should involve, be written for or by young people. 'Projects should reflect the writer's own beliefs, be thought-provoking, challenging and accessible. The writer should be able to work with designers, directors and musicians in the early stages to develop the text and work alongside other disciplines.'

Soho Theatre Company
21 Dean Street, London W1D 3NE
☎ 020 7287 5060   Fax 020 7287 5061
Email writers@sohotheatre.com
Website www.sohotheatre.com

Artistic Director *Abigail Morris*
Dedicated to new writing, the company has an extensive research and development programme consisting of a free script reading service, workshops and readings. Also runs many courses for new writers. The company produces around four plays a year. Previous productions include: *Office* Shan Khan, winner of the 2000 Verity Bargate award; *Angels and Saints* Jessica Townsend, joint winner of the 1998 Peggy Ramsay award; *Jump Mr Malinoff Jump* Toby Whithouse, winner of the 1998 Verity Bargate award; *Gabriel* Moira Buffini, winner of the 1996 LWT award; *Be My Baby* Amanda Whittington; *Kindertransporte* Diane Samuels. Runs the Verity Bargate award, a biennial competition.

Sphinx Theatre Company
25 Short Street, London SE1 8LJ
☎ 020 7401 9993   Fax 020 7401 9995
Email sphinxtheatre@demon.co.uk
Website www.sphinxtheatre.co.uk

Artistic Director *Sue Parrish*
General Manager *Amanda Rigali*
FOUNDED 1973. Tours new plays by women nationally to small and mid-scale venues. Synopses and ideas are welcome.

The Steam Industry
Finborough Theatre, 118 Finborough Road, London SW10 9ED
☎ 020 7244 7439   Fax 020 7835 1853
Website www.steamindustry.co.uk *or*
www.finboroughtheatre.co.uk

Artistic Director *Phil Willmott*
Director, Finborough Theatre *Neil McPherson*
Since June 1994, the Finborough Theatre has been a base for The Steam Industry who produce in and out of the building. Their output is diverse and prolific and includes a high percentage of new writing alongside radical adaptations of classics and musicals. The space is also available for a number of hires per year and the hire fee is sometimes negotiable to encourage innovative work. Unsolicited scripts are no longer welcome. The company has developed new work by writers such as Chris Lee, Anthony Neilson, Naomi Wallace, Conor McPherson, Tony Marchant, Diane Samuels and Mark Ravenhill.

Swansea Little Theatre Ltd
Dylan Thomas Theatre, Maritime Quarter, Gloucester Place, Swansea SA1 1TY
☎ 01792 473238

Secretary *Gwynn Roberts*
A wide variety of plays, from pantomime to the classics. New writing encouraged. New plays considered by the artistic committee.

Talawa Theatre Company Ltd
3rd Floor, 23–5 Great Sutton Street, London EC1V 0DN
☎ 020 7251 6644   Fax 020 7251 5969
Email hq@talawa.com
Website www.talawa.com

Administrator *Suzannah Bedford*
FOUNDED 1985. 'Aims to provide high-quality productions that reflect the significant creative role that black theatre plays within the national and international arena and also to enlarge theatre audiences from the black

community.' Previous productions include all-black performances of *The Importance of Being Earnest* and *Antony and Cleopatra*; plus Jamaican pantomime *Arawak Gold*; *The Gods Are Not to Blame*; *The Road* Wole Soyinka; *Beef, No Chicken* Derek Walcott; *Flying West* Pearl Cleage; *Othello* William Shakespeare. Seeks to provide a platform for new work from up and coming black British writers. Send synopsis in the first instance. Runs a black script development project. Talawa is funded by the London Arts Board (for three years).

Theatre Absolute

57–61 Corporation Street, Coventry CV1 1GQ
☎ 024 7625 7380   Fax 024 7655 0680
Email julia@theatreabsolute.co.uk
Website www.theatreabsolute.co.uk

Artistic Director/Writer *Chris O'Connell*
Producer *Julia Negus*
FOUNDED 1992. An independent theatre company which commissions, produces and tours new plays which are based on a strong narrative text and aimed at audiences aged 15 and upwards. Productions include: *Car*, winner of an Edinburgh Fringe First award 1999 and a *Time Out* live award – Best New Play on the London Fringe 1999; and most recently, *Raw*, winner of a Fringe First award 2001. Alongside the Belgrade Theatre, the company also runs The Writing House, a script development scheme.

Theatre of Comedy Company

210 Shaftesbury Avenue, London WC2H 8DP
☎ 020 7379 3345   Fax 020 7836 8181
Email info@toc.dltentertainment.co.uk

Chief Executive *Richard Porter*
Creative Director *Keith Murray*
FOUNDED 1983 to produce new work as well as classics and revivals. Interested in strong comedy in the widest sense – Chekhov comes under the definition as does farce. Also has a light entertainment division, developing new scripts for television, namely situation comedy and series.

Theatre Royal, Plymouth

Royal Parade, Plymouth, Devon PL1 2TR
☎ 01752 230347   Fax 01752 230499
Email d.prescott@theatreroyal.com
Website www.theatreroyal.com

Artistic Director *Simon Stokes*
Artistic Associate *David Prescott*
Stages small-, mid- and large-scale drama and music theatre. Commissions and produces new plays. Unsolicited scripts with sae are read and responded to. Send one script at a time – by post only.

Theatre Royal Stratford East

Gerry Raffles Square, London E15 1BN
☎ 020 8534 7374   Fax 020 8534 8381
Email jperies@stratfordeast.com
Website www.stratfordeast.com

New Writing Manager *James Peries*
Lively east London theatre, catering for a very mixed audience, both local and London-wide. Produces plays, musicals, youth theatre and local community plays/events, all of which is new work. Special interest in Asian and black British work, and contemporary London/UK stories. New initiatives include developing contemporary British musicals. Unsolicited scripts which are fully completed and have never been produced are welcome. Feedback is given only on scripts that closely meet the artistic remit.

Theatre Royal Windsor

Windsor, Berkshire SL4 1PS
☎ 01753 863444   Fax 01753 831673
Email info@theatreroyalwindsor.co.uk
Website www.theatreroyalwindsor.co.uk

Executive Producer *Bill Kenwright*
Executive Director *Mark Piper*
Plays to a middle-class, West End-type audience. Produces thirteen plays a year and 'would be disappointed to do fewer than two new plays in a year;

always hopes to do half a dozen'. Modern classics, thrillers, comedy and farce. Only interested in scripts along these lines.

Theatre Workshop Edinburgh

34 Hamilton Place, Edinburgh EH3 5AX
☎ 0131 225 7942   Fax 0131 220 0112

Artistic Director *Robert Rae*
First ever professional producing theatre to fully include disabled actors in all its productions. Plays to a young, broad-based audience with many pieces targeted towards particular groups or communities. Output has included *D.A.R.E.* Particularly interested in issues-based work for young people and minority groups. Frequently engages writers for collaborative work and devised projects. Commissions a significant amount of new writing for a wide range of contexts, from large-scale community plays to small-scale professional productions. Favours writers based in Scotland, producing material relevant to a contemporary Scottish audience.

Tiebreak Theatre

Heartsease High School, Marryat Road, Norwich, Norfolk NR7 9DF
☎ 01603 435209   Fax 01603 435184
Email info@tiebreak-theatre.com
Website www.tiebreak-theatre.com

Artistic Director *David Farmer*
FOUNDED 1981. Specializes in high-quality theatre for children and young people, touring schools, youth centres, small-scale theatres, museums and festivals. Productions: *Time and Tide; The Snow Egg; One Dark Night; Suitcase Full of Stories; Flint People; Intake/Outake; Fast Eddy; Breaking the Rules; George Speaks; Frog and Toad; Singing in the Rainforest; The Invisible Boy; My Friend Willy; The Ugly Duckling.* New writing encouraged. Interested in low-budget, small-cast material only. School and educational material of special interest. 'Scripts welcome but please ring first to discuss any potential submission.'

The Torch Theatre
St Peter's Road, Milford Haven, Pembrokeshire SA73 2BU
☎ 01646 694192   Fax 01646 698919
Email info@torchtheatre.co.uk
Website www.torchtheatre.org.uk

Artistic Director *Peter Doran*
FOUNDED 1977. Stages a mixed programme of in-house and middle-scale touring work. Unsolicited scripts will be read and guidance offered but production unlikely due to restricted funding. Please include sae for return of script and notes; mark clearly, 'FAO Peter Doran'. Torch Theatre Company productions include: *Dancing at Lughnasa; Neville's Island; The Woman in Black; Abigail's Party; Taking Steps; Blue Remembered Hills; A Prayer for Wings; Little Shop of Horrors; The Caretaker*, plus annual Christmas musicals.

Traverse Theatre
Cambridge Street, Edinburgh EH1 2ED
☎ 0131 228 3223   Fax 0131 229 8443
Email roxana@traverse.co.uk
Website www.traverse.co.uk

Artistic Director *Philip Howard*
Literary Director *Roxana Silbert*
International Literary Associate *Katherine Mendelsohn*
Literary Development Officer *Hannah Rye*
The Traverse is Scotland's new writing theatre, with a particular commitment to producing new Scottish plays. However, it also has a strong international programme of work in translation and visiting companies. Previous productions: *Gagarin Way* Gregory Burke; *Wiping My Mother's Arse* Iain Heggie; *The Speculator* David Greig; *The Juju Girl* Aileen Ritchie; *Perfect Days* Liz Lochhead. Please address unsolicited scripts to *Roxana Silbert*, literary director.

Tricycle Theatre
269 Kilburn High Road, London NW6 7JR
☎ 020 7372 6611   Fax 020 7328 0795
Website www.tricycle.co.uk

Artistic Director *Nicolas Kent*
FOUNDED 1980. Plays to a very mixed audience, in terms of both culture and class. Previous productions: *Stones in his Pockets* Marie Jones; *The Stephen Lawrence Enquiry – The Colour of Justice* adapt. from the enquiry transcripts Richard Norton-Taylor; *Nuremberg* adapt. from transcripts of the trials Richard Norton-Taylor; *Joe Turner's Come and Gone, The Piano Lesson* and *Two Trains Runnin'* all August Wilson; *Kat and the Kings* David Kramer. New writing welcome from women and ethnic minorities (particularly black, Asian and Irish). Looks for a strong narrative drive with popular appeal, not 'studio' plays. Fee £12 per script. Supplies written reader's reports. Can only return scripts if postage coupons or sae are enclosed with original submission.

Tron Theatre Company
63 Trongate, Glasgow G1 5HB
☎ 0141 552 3748   Fax 0141 552 6657
Email neil@tron.co.uk
Website www.tron.co.uk

Administrative Director *Neil Murray*
FOUNDED 1981. Plays to a broad cross-section of Glasgow and beyond, including international tours. Recent productions: *Our Bad Magnet* Douglas Maxwell; *Further Than the Furthest Thing* Zinnie Harris (co-production with the Royal National Theatre). Interested in ambitious plays by UK and international writers. No unsolicited mss.

Unicorn Theatre for Children
St Mark's Studios, Chillingworth Road, London N7 8QJ
☎ 020 7700 0702   Fax 020 7700 3870
Email admin@unicorntheatre.com
Website www.unicorntheatre.com

Artistic Director *Tony Graham*
Literary Manager *Carl Miller*
FOUNDED 1947, was resident at the Arts Theatre from 1967 until April 1999. Produces new plays at the Pleasance Theatre in north London, Regent

Park's Open Air Theatre, and tours both nationally and internationally. Plays to children, aged 4–12, their teachers and families. Recent work: *Pinocchio* Michael Rosen; *Red, Red Shoes* Charles Way; *1001 Nights* Shahrukh Husein. 2002: *Peter Rabbit* adapt. Adrian Mitchell; *Great Expectations* adapt. John Clifford; *Merlin the Magnificent* adapt. Stuart Paterson. Moving to Unicorn Children's Centre with two theatres on Bankside in central London, to open 2004. Does not produce unsolicited scripts but works with commissioned writers. Those interested in working with the company should send details of relevant previous work and why they would like to write for Unicorn.

Warehouse Theatre

62 Dingwall Road, Croydon CRO 2NF
☎ 020 8681 1257   Fax 020 8688 6699
Email warehous@dircon.co.uk
Website www.warehousetheatre.co.uk

Artistic Director *Ted Craig*
South London's new writing theatre (adjacent to East Croydon railway station) seats 100–20 and produces up to six new plays a year. Also co-produces with, and hosts, selected touring companies who share the theatre's commitment to new work. Continually building upon a tradition of discovering and nurturing new writers, with activities including a monthly writers' workshop and the annual International Playwriting Festival. Also hosts youth theatre workshops and Saturday morning children's theatre. Previous productions: *Iona Rain* Peter Moffat; *Fat Janet is Dead* Simon Smith; (both past winners of the International Playwriting Festival) *The Shagaround* Maggie Neville; *Coming Up* James Martin Charlton and M. G. 'Monk' Lewis; *The Castle Spectre* ed. Phil Willmott; *Dick Barton Special Agent; Dick Barton and the Curse of the Pharaoh's Tomb* and *Dick Barton: The Tango of Terror* Phil Willmott. Unsolicited scripts welcome but it is more advisable to submit plays through the theatre's International Playwriting Festival (see page 247).

West Yorkshire Playhouse

Playhouse Square, Leeds, West Yorkshire LS2 7UP
☎ 0113 213 7800   Fax 0113 213 7250
Email alex.chisholm@wyp.org.uk
Website www.wyp.org.uk

Literary Manager *Alex Chisholm*
Committed to working with new writing originating from or set in the
Yorkshire and Humberside region. New writing from outside the region is
programmed usually where writer or company is already known to the
theatre. The Playhouse runs workshops, courses and writers' events including Thursday Night Live, an open platform held at the theatre for local
writers and performers. For more information contact the literary manager
on 0113 213 7286 or email to address above. Scripts should be submitted
with sae for return.

Whirligig Theatre

14 Belvedere Drive, Wimbledon, London SW19 7BY
☎ 020 8947 1732   Fax 020 8879 7648
Email whirligig-theatre@virgin.net

Contact *David Wood*
One play a year in major theatre venues, usually a musical for primary
school audiences and weekend family groups. Interested in scripts which
exploit the theatrical nature of children's tastes. Previous productions: *The
See-Saw Tree; The Selfish Shellfish; The Gingerbread Man; The Old Man of
Lochnagar; The Ideal Gnome Expedition; Save the Human; Dreams of Anne Frank;
Babe, the Sheep-Pig.*

White Bear Theatre Club

138 Kennington Park Road, London SE11 4DJ
Administration: 3 Dante Road, Kennington, London SE11 4RB
☎ 020 7793 9193   Fax 020 7793 9193

Contact *Michael Kingsbury*
Administrator *Julia Parr*
FOUNDED 1988. Output primarily new work for audiences aged 20–35.

Unsolicited scripts welcome, particularly new work with a keen eye on contemporary issues, though not agitprop. *Absolution* by Robert Sherwood was nominated by the Writers' Guild for Best Fringe Play and *Spin* by the same author was the *Time Out* Critics' Choice in 2000. The theatre received the *Time Out* award for Best Fringe Venue in 2001 and a Peter Brook award for best up-and-coming venue. The Writers' Guild, sponsored by the Mackintosh Foundation, leads writer workshops and readings throughout the year.

Film, Television and Video Production Companies

Abstract Images
117 Willoughby House, Barbican, London EC2Y 8BL
☎ 020 7638 5123
Email productions@abstract-images.co.uk

Contact *Howard Ross*
Television documentary and drama programming. Also theatre productions. Output: *Balm in Gilead* (drama); *Road* (drama); *Bent* (drama); *God: For & Against* (documentary); *This Is a Man* (drama/doc). Encourages new writers; send synopsis in the first instance.

Alomo Productions
1 Stephen Street, London W1T 1AL
☎ 020 7691 6531   Fax 020 7691 6081

Alomo is a FremantleMedia company. Major producer of television drama and comedy. Output: *Starting Out; Dirty Work; Goodnight Sweetheart; Birds of a Feather; Love Hurts; The New Statesman; Grown Ups; Unfinished Business; Cry Wolf.* New writers encouraged.

Anglo/Fortunato Films Ltd
170 Popes Lane, London W5 4NJ
☎ 020 8932 7676   Fax 020 8932 7491

Contact *Luciano Celentino*
Film, television and video producer/director of action comedy and psych-thriller drama. No unsolicited mss.

Antelope (UK) Ltd
The Highgate Business Centre, 33 Greenwood Place, London
NW5 1LD
☎ 020 7428 3920   Fax 020 7428 3921
Email antelope@antelope.co.uk
Website www.antelope.co.uk

Managing Director *Mick Csáky*
Head of Production *Justin Johnson*
Film, television and video productions for drama, documentary and corporate material. Output: *Cyberspace* (ITV); *Brunch* (Ch5); *The Pier* (weekly arts and entertainment programme); *Placido Domingo* (ITV); *Baden Powell – The Boy Man; Howard Hughes – The Naked Emperor* (Ch4 'Secret Lives' series); *Hiroshima*. No unsolicited mss – 'we are not reading any new material at present'.

Arena Films Ltd
2 Pelham Road, London SW19 1SX
☎ 020 8543 3990   Fax 020 8540 3992

Producer *David Conroy*
Film and TV drama.

Arlington Productions Ltd
Pinewood Studios, Iver Heath, Buckinghamshire SL0 ONH
☎ 01753 651700   Fax 01753 656050

Television producer. Specializes in popular international drama, with occasional forays into other areas. 'We have an enviable reputation for encouraging new writers but only accept unsolicited submissions via agents.'

The Ashford Entertainment Corporation Ltd
182 Brighton Road, Coulsdon, Surrey CR5 2NF
☎ 020 8645 0667   Fax 020 8763 2558
Email info@ashford-entertainment.co.uk
Website www.ashford-entertainment.co.uk

Managing Director *Frazer Ashford*
Head of Production *Georgina Huxstep*
FOUNDED in 1996 by award-winning film and TV producer Frazer Ashford whose credits include *Great Little Trains* (Mainline Television for Westcountry/Ch4, starring the late Willie Rushton); *Street Life* and *Make Yourself at Home* (both for WTV). Produces theatrical films and television – drama, lifestyle and documentaries. Happy to receive ideas for documentaries but submit a one-page synopsis only in the first instance, enclosing sae. 'Be patient, allow up to four weeks for a reply. Be precise with the idea; specific details rather than vague thoughts. Attach a back-up sheet with credentials and supporting evidence, i.e., can you ensure that your idea is feasible?'

Black Coral Productions Ltd
2nd Floor, 241 High Street, London E17 7BH
☎ 020 8520 2830   Fax 020 8520 2358
Email bcp@coralmedia.co.uk
Website www.m4media.net

Contacts *Lazell Daley, Marcia Miller*
Producer of drama and documentary film and television. Committed to the development of new writing with a particular interest in short and feature-length dramas. Offers a script consultancy service for which a fee is payable. Runs courses.

Blackwatch Productions Ltd
752–6 Argyle Street, Anderston, Glasgow G3 8UJ
☎ 0141 222 2640/2641   Fax 0141 222 2646
Email info@blackwatchtv.com

Company Director *Nicola Black*
Director *Paul Gallagher*

Research & Development Officer *Heidi Proven*
Production Manager *Amanda Keown*
Film, television, video producer of drama and documentary programmes.
Output includes *Designer Vaginas; Bonebreakers; Luv Bytes;* and *Can We Can We Carry On, Girls?* for Ch4. Also coordinates *Mesh*, animation scheme.
Does not welcome unsolicited mss.

Blue Heaven Productions Ltd
116 Great Portland Street, London W1W 6PJ
☎ 020 7436 5552   Fax 020 7436 0888

Contact *Christine Benson*
Film and television drama and occasional documentary. Output: *The Ruth Rendell Mysteries; Crime Story: Dear Roy, Love Gillian; Ready When You Are/ Screen Challenge* (three series for Meridian Regional); *The Man who Made Husbands Jealous* (Anglia Television Entertainment/Blue Heaven). Scripts considered but treatments or ideas preferred in the first instance. New writing encouraged.

Bronco Films Ltd
The Producers Centre, 61 Holland Street, Glasgow G2 4NJ
☎ 0141 287 6817   Fax 0141 287 6815
Email broncofilm@btinternet.com
Website www.broncofilms.co.uk

Contact *Peter Broughan*
Film, television and video drama. Output includes *Rob Roy* (feature film) and *Young Person's Guide to Becoming a Rock Star* (TV series). No unsolicited mss.

Carlton Productions
35–8 Portman Square, London W1H 6NU
☎ 020 7486 6688   Fax 020 7486 1132
Website www.carltontv.com

Managing Director/Director of Programmes *Steve Hewlett*
Director of Drama & Co-production *Jonathan Powell*
Makers of independently produced TV drama for ITV. Output: *Crossroads;*

The Vice; Bertie and Elizabeth; The Hunt; Pollyanna; Dirty Tricks; Blue Dove; Plain Jane; Peak Practice; Cadfael. 'We try to use new writers on established long-running series.' Scripts from experienced writers and agents only.

Carnival (Films & Theatre) Ltd
12 Raddington Road, Ladbroke Grove, London W10 5TG
☎ 020 8968 0968   Fax 020 8968 0155
Email info@carnival-films.co.uk
Website www.carnival-films.co.uk

Contact *Brian Eastman*
Film, TV and theatre producer. Film: *The Mill on the Floss* (BBC); *Firelight* (Hollywood Pictures/Wind Dancer Productions); *Up on the Roof* (Rank/ Granada); *Shadowlands* (Savoy/Spelling); *In Hitler's Shadow* (Home Box Office); *Under Suspicion* (Columbia/Rank/LWT). Television: *As If* (Ch4/ Columbia); *Lucy Sullivan is Getting Married* (ITV); *The Tenth Kingdom* (Sky/ NBC); *Agatha Christie's Poirot* (ITV/LWT/A&E); *Every Woman Knows a Secret* and *Oktober* (ITV Network Centre); *The Fragile Heart* (Ch4); *Crime Traveller* (BBC); *Bugs 1–4* (BBC); *Anna Lee* (LWT); *All Or Nothing At All* (LWT); *Head Over Heels* (Carlton); *Jeeves and Wooster I–IV* (Granada); *Traffik* (Ch4); *Forever Green 1–3* (LWT); *Porterhouse Blue* (Ch4); *Blott on the Landscape* (BBC). Theatre: *What a Performance; Juno and the Paycock; Murder is Easy; Misery; Ghost Train; Map of the Heart; Shadowlands; Up on the Roof.*

Celador
39 Long Acre, London WC2E 9LG
☎ 020 7240 8101   Fax 020 7845 6977
Email tvhits@celador.co.uk
Website celador.co.uk

Head of Entertainment *Colman Hutchinson*
Creative Head of Films *Steve Knight*
Producer of TV and radio comedy and light entertainment. Output: *Who Wants to be a Millionaire; Winning Lines; Commercial Breakdown; Britain's Brainiest . . . ; All About Me.* 'We are interested in original non-derivative sitcom scripts and entertainment formats. Some broadcast experience

would be helpful. As a relatively small company our script reading capacity is limited.'

Celtic Films Ltd
21 Grafton Street, London W1S 4EV
☎ 020 7409 2080   Fax 020 7409 2383
Email celticfilms@aol.com

Contact *Stuart Sutherland*
Film and television drama producer. Output includes fourteen feature-length *Sharpe* TV films for Carlton and *A Life for a Life – The True Story of Stefan Kiszko* TV film for ITV. Supports new writing and welcomes unsolicited mss.

Chameleon Television Ltd
Television House, 104 Kirkstall Road, Leeds, West Yorkshire LS3 1JS
☎ 0113 244 4486   Fax 0113 243 1267
Email allen@chameleontv.com

Contacts *Allen Jewhurst, Kevin Sim, Anna Hall, Simon Wells*
Film and television drama and documentary producer. Output includes *The Reckoning* (USA/Ch4); *Dunblane* (ITV); *Foul Play* (Ch5); *St Hildas* and *Rules of the Game* (both for Ch4); *Divorces From Hell*, *New Voices* and *Shipman* (all for ITV). Scripts not welcome unless via agents but new writing is encouraged.

Chatsworth Television Ltd
97–9 Dean Street, London W1D 3TE
☎ 020 7734 4302   Fax 020 7437 3301
Email television@chatsworth-tv.co.uk
Website www.chatsworth-tv.co.uk

Managing Director *Malcolm Heyworth*
Drama, factual and entertainment television producer. Interested in contemporary and factually based series.

Cinema Verity Productions Ltd

11 Addison Avenue, London W11 4QS

☎ 020 7460 2777   Fax 020 7371 3329

Contact *Verity Lambert*

Leading television drama producer whose credits include *She's Out* Lynda la Plante; *Class Act* Michael Aitkens; *May to December* (BBC series); *Running Late* Simon Gray (Screen 1); *The Cazalets* adapt. of *The Cazalet Chronicle* Elizabeth Jane Howard (BBC). No unsolicited mss.

Collingwood & Convergence Productions Ltd

10–14 Crown Street, Acton, London W3 8SB

☎ 020 8993 3666   Fax 020 8993 9595

Email info@crownstreet.co.uk

Producers *Christopher O'Hare, Terence Clegg, Tony Collingwood*
Head of Development *Helen Stroud*

Film and TV. Convergence Productions produces live action, drama documentaries; Tony Collingwood Productions specializes in children's animation. Convergence: *Theo* (film drama series); *Plastic Fantastic* (UK cosmetic surgery techniques, Ch5); *David Starkey's Henry VIII* (Ch4 historical documentary). Collingwood: *RARG* (award-winning animated film); *Captain Zed and the Zee Zone* (ITV); *Daisy-Head Mayzie* (Dr Seuss animated series for Turner Network and Hanna-Barbera); *Animal Stories* (animated poems, ITV network); *Eddy and the Bear* (CITV). Unsolicited mss not welcome 'as a general rule as we do not have the capacity to process the sheer weight of submissions this creates. We therefore tend to review material from individuals recommended to us through personal contact with agents or other industry professionals. We like to encourage new writing and have worked with new writers but our ability to do so is limited by our capacity for development. We can usually only consider taking on one project each year, as development/finance takes several years to put in place.'

Company of Wolves

19–23 Wells Street, London W1P 3FP

☎ 020 7344 8090   Fax 020 7344 8091

Email cofwolves@aol.com

Contact *Stephen Woolley*
Leading feature film producer. Output has included *End Of the Affair;
Butcher Boy; Interview With the Vampire; Michael Collins; Crying Game; Mona
Lisa; Company of Wolves*. Forthcoming productions: *The Actors* (comedy set
in Dublin); *The Borgias; Double Down* (thriller starring Nick Nolte). No
unsolicited material.

Cromdale Films Ltd
12 St Paul's Road, London N1 2QN
☎ 020 7226 0178

Contact *Ian Lloyd*
Film, video and TV: drama and documentary. Output: *The Face of Darkness*
(feature film); *Drift to Dawn* (rock music drama); *The Overdue Treatment*
(documentary); *Russia, The Last Red Summer* (documentary). Initial phone
call advised before submission of scripts.

Dakota Films Ltd
4 Junction Mews, London W2 1PN
☎ 020 7706 9407   Fax 020 7402 6111
Email info@dakota-films.demon.co.uk

Managing Director *Jonathan Olsberg*
Film and television drama. Feature films include: *Me Without You; Janice
Beard 45wpm; Let Him Have It; Othello*. Currently developing a slate of films,
including John Sayles' *Fade to Black* and John Duigan's *Head in the Clouds*,
and a number of projects by new writers. Interested in working with new
talent but does not consider unsolicited material.

Devlin Morris Productions Ltd
97b West Bow, Edinburgh EH1 2JP
☎ 0131 226 7728   Fax 0131 226 6668
Email contact@devlinmorris-prod.sol.co.uk

Contacts *Morris Paton, Vivien Devlin*
Independent media production house encompassing international arts and

travel writing as well as a range of drama, radio, film and television projects.

DMS Films Ltd
369 Burnt Oak Broadway, Edgware, Middlesex HA8 5XZ
☎ 020 8951 6060   Fax 020 8951 6050
Email danny@argonaut.com

Producer *Daniel San*
Film drama producer. Output includes *Understanding Jane; Hard Edge; Strangers*. Welcomes unsolicited screenplays; send synopsis or outline in first instance.

Double-Band Films
Crescent Arts Centre, 2–4 University Road, Belfast BT7 1NH
☎ 028 9024 3331   Fax 028 9023 6980
Email info@doublebandfilms.com
Website www.doublebandfilms.com

Contacts *Michael Hewitt, Dermot Lavery*
Documentary and drama programmes for film and television. Specialized in documentary production for the past twelve years. Output: *George Best's Body; Escobar's Own Goal; Maradona: Kicking the Habit* (all for Ch4); *Still Life* (short drama film). Currently working on a documentary about English and Argentinean football for Channel 4.

The Drama House Ltd
Coach Road Cottage, Little Saxham, Suffolk IP29 5LE
☎ 01284 810521   Fax 01284 811425
Email jack@dramahouse.co.uk
Website www.dramahouse.co.uk

Contact *Jack Emery*
Film and television producer. Output: *Inquisition* (Ch5); *Little White Lies* (BBC1); *Breaking the Code* (BBC1); *Witness Against Hitler* (BBC1); *Suffer the Little Children* (BBC2). Send two-page synopsis only. All synopses read and returned if accompanied by sae. Interested especially in new writers.

Ealing Films Ltd
Beaumont House, 8 Beaumont Road, Poole, Dorset BH13 7JJ
☎ 01202 706379   Fax 01202 706944

Managing Director *Eben Foggitt*
Head of Development *Anita Simpkins*
Film and television drama producer.

Ecosse Films
12 Quayside Lodge, Watermeadow Lane, London SW6 2UZ
☎ 020 7371 0290   Fax 020 7736 3436
Email info@ecossefilms.com
Website www.ecossefilms.com

Contact *Josie Atkins*
Producer of feature films and television drama such as *Charlotte Gray*; *Mrs Brown* and *Monarch of the Glen*. Submissions through agents only; no unsolicited scripts.

Edinburgh Film Productions
Traquair House, Innerleithen, Peeblesshire EH44 6PP
☎ 01896 831188

Contact *R. Crichton*
Film, TV drama and documentary. Output: *Sara*; *Moonacre*; *Torch*; *Silent Mouse*; *The Curious Case of Santa Claus*; *The Stamp of Greatness*. No unsolicited scripts at present.

Elstree (Production) Co. Ltd
Shepperton Studios, Studios Road, Shepperton, Middlesex TW17 0QD
☎ 01932 592680/1   Fax 01932 592682
Website www.elsprod.com

Contact *Greg Smith*
Produces feature films, TV drama and theatre. Output: *Othello* (BBC); *Great Expectations* (Disney Channel); *Porgy and Bess* (with Trevor Nunn); *Old Curiosity Shop* (Disney Channel/RHI); *London Suite* (NBC/Hallmark); *Ani-*

mal Farm and *David Copperfield* (both for Hallmark/TNT). Co-owner of Circus Films with Trevor Nunn for feature film projects.

Festival Film and Television Ltd
Festival House, Tranquil Passage, Blackheath, London SE3 0BJ
☎ 020 8297 9999   Fax 020 8297 1155
Email raymarshall@festivalfilm.com

Contact *Ray Marshall*
Specializes in television drama. In the last ten years has produced fifteen Catherine Cookson mini-series for ITV, the latest of which was *A Dinner of Herbs*. Looking primarily for commercial TV projects, feature films (no horror or violence) and children's/family drama. Prefers submissions through an agent. Unsolicited work must be professionally presented or it will be returned unread.

Film and General Productions Ltd
4 Bradbrook House, Studio Place, London SW1X 8EL
☎ 020 7235 4495   Fax 020 7245 9853

Contacts *Clive Parsons, Davina Belling*
Film and television drama. Feature films include *True Blue* and *Tea with Mussolini*. Also *Seesaw* (ITV drama); *The Greatest Store in the World* (family drama, BBC); *The Queen's Nose* (children's series, BBC). Interested in considering new writing but subject to prior telephone conversation.

The Firedog Motion Picture Corporation Ltd
182 Brighton Road, Coulsdon, Surrey CR5 2NF
☎ 020 8660 8663   Fax 020 8763 2558
Email info@firedogfilms.co.uk
Website www.firedogfilms.co.uk

Managing Director *Frazer Ashford*
Head of Production *Georgina Huxstep*
Member of the Ashford Entertainment Group. 'Happy to see film/drama ideas.' In the first instance, authors should send a one-page synopsis, their writing CV and a brief history/submission history of the project to date.

Flick Media
15 Golden Square, London W1F 9JG
☎ 020 7734 7979   Fax 020 7287 9495
Website www.flickmedia.co.uk

Contact *Esther Knight*
Producer of film drama, including *Conspiracy of Silence* (feature film). No unsolicited scripts.

Focus Films Ltd
The Rotunda Studios, Rear of 116–18 Finchley Road, London
NW3 5HT
☎ 020 7435 9004   Fax 020 7431 3562
Email focus@pupix.demon.co.uk

Contacts *David Pupkewitz, Malcolm Kohll* (Head of Development)
Film producer. Output: *The Book of Eve* (Canadian drama); *Julia's Ghost* (German co-production); *The 51st State* (feature film); *Secret Society* (comedy drama feature film); *Crimetime* (feature thriller); *Diary of a Sane Man*; *Othello*. Projects in development include *Mutant*; *90 Minutes*; *Barry*. No unsolicited scripts.

Full Moon Productions
rue Fenelon, Salignac Eyvigues, Dordogne 24590, France
☎ 00 33 553 29 94 06   Fax 00 33 553 29 94 06
Email fullmoonproductions@worldonline.fr
Website www.salignacfoundation.com

Contact *Barry C. Paton, BSc.*
Production and logistics management in France. 'We are keen to explore new and innovative drama production for broadcast and/or film. Our script advisors can assess projects. No unsolicited scripts initially, please.' Initial contact should be by letter or email. Also runs training courses in video production and screenwriting.

Gabriela Productions Ltd

51 Goldsmith Avenue, London w3 6HR
☎ 020 8993 3158   Fax 020 8993 8216
Email only4contact@yahoo.com

Contact *W. Starecki*
Film and television drama and documentary productions, including *Blooming Youth* and *Dog Eat Dog* for Ch4 and *Spider's Web* for Polish TV. Welcomes unsolicited mss.

GMT Productions Ltd

The Old Courthouse, 26A Church Street, Bishop's Stortford,
Hertfordshire CM23 2LY
☎ 01279 501622   Fax 01279 501644
Email patrick.wallis@virgin.net

Contacts *Patrick Wallis, Barney Broom*
Film, television and video: drama, documentary, corporate and commercials. No unsolicited mss.

Granada Film

4th Floor, 48 Leicester Square, London WC2H 7FB
☎ 020 7389 8555   Fax 020 7930 8499

Head of Film *Pippa Cross*
Films and TV films. Output: *The Hole*; *Bloody Sunday*; *House of Mirth*; *Longitude*; *My Left Foot*; *Jack and Sarah*; *Girls Night*. No unsolicited scripts. Supportive of new writing but often hard to offer real help as Granada develop mainstream commercial projects which usually require some status in talent areas.

Greenwich Films Ltd

Studio 2B1, The Old Seager Distillery, Brookmill Road, London
SE8 4JT
☎ 020 8694 2211   Fax 020 8694 2971

Contact *Liza Brown, Development Dept.*
Film, television and video: drama. 'We welcome new writers, though as a small outfit we prefer to meet them through personal contacts as we do not have the resources to deal with too many enquiries. No unsolicited mss, just outlines, please.'

Hammerwood Film Productions

110 Trafalgar Road, Portslade, East Sussex BN41 1GS
☎ 01273 277333   Fax 01273 705451
Email filmangels@freenetname.co.uk
Website www.filmangel.co.uk

Contacts *Ralph Harvey, Petra Ginman*
Film, video and TV drama. Output: *Boadicea – Queen of Death* (film co-production with Pan-European Film Productions and Mirabilis Films); *Boadicea – A Celtic Tragedy* (TV series). In pre-production: *Road to Nirvana* (Ealing-style comedy); *The Black Egg* (witchcraft in 17th-century England); *The Ghosthunter; A Symphony of Spies* (true stories of WW2 espionage and resistance required). 'Authors are recommended to access www.filmangel.co.uk (see page 257).'

Hartswood Films Ltd

Twickenham Studios, The Barons, St Margarets, Middlesex
TW1 2AW
☎ 020 8607 8736   Fax 020 8607 8744
Email films.tv@hartswoodfilms.co.uk

Contact *Elaine Cameron*
Film and TV production for drama, comedy and documentary. Output: *Men Behaving Badly* (BBC); *Is It Legal?* (Ch4); *Wonderful You* (ITV); *Border Café* (BBC1); *Coupling* (BBC).

Hat Trick Productions Ltd

10 Livonia Street, London W1F 8AF
☎ 020 7434 2451   Fax 020 7287 9791
Website www.hattrick.com

Contact *Denise O'Donoghue*
Television programmes. Output includes *Clive Anderson All Talk; Small Potatoes; The Wilsons; The Peter Principle; Whatever You Want; Confessions; Drop the Dead Donkey; Father Ted; Game On; Have I Got News For You; If I Ruled the World; Room 101; Whose Line Is It Anyway?; Clive Anderson Talks Back; Dicing with Debt.* The company's drama output includes: *A Very Open Prison; Boyz Unlimited; Crossing the Floor; Eleven Men Against Eleven; Gobble; Lord of Misrule; Mr White Goes to Westminster; Underworld; Sex 'n' Death.* Films: *The Suicidal Dog; Sleeping Dictionary; Bloody Sunday.*

Healthcare Productions Ltd

Unit 1.04 Bridge House, Three Mills, Three Mill Lane, London
E3 3DU
☎ 020 8980 9444   Fax 020 8980 1901
Email penny@healthcareproductions.co.uk
Website www.healthcareproductions.co.uk

Contact *Penny Webb*
Television and video: documentary and drama. Produces training and educational material, in text, video and CD-ROM, mostly health-related, social care issues, law and marriage.

Heritage Theatre Ltd

8 Clanricarde Gardens, London W2 4NA
☎ 020 7243 2750   Fax 020 7792 8584
Email rm@heritagetheatre.com
Website www.heritagetheatre.com

Contact *Robert Marshall*
Video recordings of successful stage plays, sold to the public in VHS and DVD format. 'It is possible to negotiate agreements before the production is staged.'

Hourglass Pictures Ltd
117 Merton Road, Wimbledon, London sw19 1ED
☎ 020 8540 8786   Fax 020 8542 6598
Email pictures@hourglass.co.uk
Website www.hourglass.co.uk

Director *Martin Chilcott*
Film and video: documentary, drama and commercials. Output includes television science documentaries and educational programming. Also health and social issues for the World Health Organization and product information for pharmaceutical companies. Open to new writing.

Ideal Image Ltd
Cherrywood House, Crawley Down Road, Felbridge,
Surrey RH19 2PP
☎ 01342 300566   Fax 01342 312566

Contact *Alan Frost*
Producer of documentary and drama for film, video, TV and corporate clients. Output: *The Pipeline; Beating the Market.* No unsolicited scripts.

Imari Entertainment Ltd
PO Box 158, Beaconsfield, Buckinghamshire HP9 1AY
☎ 01494 677147   Fax 01494 677147
Email info@imari-entertainment.com

Contacts *Jonathan Fowke, David Farey*
TV and video producer, covering all areas of drama and documentary. Also partner company, Imari Multimedia.

Isolde Films Ltd
28 Narrow Street, London E14 8DQ
☎ 020 7702 8700   Fax 020 7702 8701

Contacts *Tony Palmer, Michela Antonello*
Film and TV: drama and documentary. Output: *Wagner; Menuhin; Maria Callas; Testimony; In From the Cold; Pushkin; England, My England* (by John

Osborne); *Kipling*. Unsolicited material is read, but please send a written outline first.

JAM Pictures and Jane Walmsley Productions
8 Hanover Street, London W1S 1YE
☎ 020 7290 2676   Fax 020 7290 2677
Email producers@jampix.com

Contacts *Jane Walmsley, Michael Braham*
JAM Pictures was FOUNDED in 1996 to produce drama for film, TV and stage. Projects include: *Son of Pocahontas* (TV film, ABC); *Breakthrough* (feature co-production with Viacom Productions, Inc.); *One More Kiss* (feature, directed by Vadim Jean); *Bad Blood* (UK theatre tour); *Chalet Girls* (ITV sitcom). Jane Walmsley Productions, formed in 1985 by TV producer, writer and broadcaster, Jane Walmsley, has completed award-winning documentaries and features such as *Hot House People* (Ch4). No unsolicited mss. 'Letters can be sent to us, asking if we wish to see mss; we are very interested in quality material.'

Kudos Productions Limited
65 Great Portland Street, London W1W 7LW
☎ 020 7580 8686   Fax 020 7580 8787
Email reception@kudosproductions.co.uk

Head of Development *Claire Parker*
Head of Drama *Jane Featherstone*
Film and television: drama and documentaries such as *Among Giants* (feature); *The Magician's House* and *Spooks* (BBC1 series) and *Psychos* (Ch4 series); *Confidence Lab* (BBC2 series). No unsolicited mss.

Lagan Pictures Ltd
21 Tullaghbrow, Tullaghgarley, Ballymena, Co Antrim BT42 2LY
☎ 028 2563 9479/077 9852 8797   Fax 028 2563 9479

Producer/Director *Stephen Butcher*
Film, video and TV: drama, documentary and corporate. Output: *A Force Under Fire* (Ulster TV). In development: *Into the Bright Light of Day* (drama-

doc); *The £10 Float* (feature film); *The Centre* (drama series). 'We are always interested in hearing from writers originating from or based in Northern Ireland or anyone with, preferably unstereotypical, projects relevant to Northern Ireland. We do not have the resources to deal with unsolicited mss, so please write with a brief treatment/synopsis in the first instance.'

Landseer Film and Television Productions Ltd

140 Royal College Street, London NW1 0TA
☎ 020 7485 7333   Fax 020 7485 7573
Email mail@landseerfilms.com
Website www.landseerfilms.com

Directors *Derek Bailey, Ken Howard*
Film and video production: documentary, drama, music and arts. Output: *Should Accidentally Fall* (BBC/Arts Council); *Nobody's Fool* ('South Bank Show' on Danny Kaye for LWT); *Swinger* (BBC2/Arts Council); *Auld Lang Syne* and *Retying the Knot – The Incredible String Band* (both for BBC Scotland); *Benjamin Zander* ('The Works', BBC2); *Zeffirelli* ('South Bank Show', LWT); *Death of a Legend – Frank Sinatra* ('South Bank Show' special); *Petula Clark*; *Bing Crosby* (both 'South Bank Show'); *Routes of Rock* (Carlton); *See You in Court* (BBC); *Nureyev Unzipped*; *Gounod's Faust*; *The Judas Tree*; *Ballet Boyz*; *4Dance*; *Bourne to Dance* (all for Ch4).

Lilyville Screen Entertainment Ltd

7 Lilyville Road, London SW6 5DP
☎ 020 7371 5940   Fax 020 7736 9431
Email tonycash@msn.com

Contact *Tony Cash*
Drama and documentaries for TV. Output: *Poetry in Motion* (series for Ch4); *Ben Elton*; *Vanessa Redgrave* (both 'South Bank Show'); *Musique Enquête* (drama-based French language series, Ch4); *Landscape and Memory* (arts documentary series for the BBC); Jonathan Miller's production of the *St Matthew Passion* for the BBC; major documentary on the BeeGees for the 'South Bank Show'. Scripts with obvious application to TV may be considered. Interested in new writing for documentary programmes.

Lucida Productions

Lucida Studios, 14 Havelock Walk, London SE23 3HG
☎ 020 8699 5070

Contact *Paul Joyce*
Television and cinema: arts, adventure, current affairs, documentary, drama
and music. Output has included: *Motion and Emotion: The Films of Wim
Wenders; Dirk Bogarde – By Myself; Sam Peckinpah – Man of Iron; Kris Kristof-
ferson – Pilgrim; Wild One: Marlon Brando; Stanley Kubrick: 'The Invisible Man';
2001: the Making of a Myth* (Ch4). Currently in development for documentary
and drama projects.

LWT United Productions

London Television Centre, Upper Ground, London SE1 9LT
☎ 020 7620 1620

Controller of Drama *Michele Buck*
Television drama. Output: *London's Burning; Night and Day; Hornblower;
Walking on the Moon* Martin Sadofski (drama-doc); *Touching Evil; Where the
Heart Is.*

Malone Gill Productions Ltd

27 Campden Hill Road, London W8 7DX
☎ 020 7937 0557   Fax 020 7376 1727
Email malonegill@cs.com

Contact *Georgina Denison*
Mainly documentary but also some drama. Output includes *The Face of
Russia* (PBS); *Vermeer* ('South Bank Show'); *Highlanders* (ITV); *Storm Chasers;
Nature Perfected; The Feast of Christmas* (all for Ch4); *The Buried Mirror:
Reflections on Spain and the New World* Carlos Fuentes (BBC2/Discovery
Channel). Approach by letter with proposal in the first instance.

Maverick Television
The Custard Factory, Gibb Street, Birmingham B9 4AA
☎ 0121 771 1812   Fax 0121 771 1550
Email maverick@mavericktv.co.uk
Website www.mavericktv.co.uk

Contact *Clare Welch*
FOUNDED 1994. High-quality and innovative DVC programming in both documentary and drama. Expanding into light entertainment and more popular drama. Output includes *Trade Secrets* (BBC2); *Picture This: Accidental Hero* (BBC2); *Motherless Daughters*; *Highland Bollywood*; *Black Bag*; *Health Alert*; *My Teenage Menopause*; *Embarrassing Illnesses*; *Vee-TV*; *Home From Home* (all for Ch4); *Long Haul* (Scottish Screen/STV); *Learning to Love the Grey* (BBC/OU).

Maya Vision International Ltd
43 New Oxford Street, London WC1A 1BH
☎ 020 7836 1113   Fax 020 7836 5169
Website www.mayavisionint.com

Contact *John Cranmer*
Film and TV: drama and documentary. Output: *Saddam's Killing Fields* (for 'Viewpoint', Central TV); *3 Steps to Heaven*; *A Bit of Scarlet* (feature films for BFI/Ch4); *A Place in the Sun*; *North of Vortex* (drama for Ch4/Arts Council); *The Real History Show* (Ch4); *In the Footsteps of Alexander the Great* (BBC2 documentary); *Hitler's Search for the Holy Grail* (Ch4 documentary); *Conquistadors* (BBC2 documentary). No unsolicited material; commissions only.

Mersey Television Company Ltd
Campus Manor, Childwall Abbey Road, Liverpool L16 0JP
☎ 0151 722 9122   Fax 0151 722 1969
Website www.merseytv.com

Chairman *Prof. Phil Redmond*
The best known of the independents in the north of England. Makers of television drama. Output: *Brookside*; *Hollyoaks* (both for Ch4).

Mission Pictures
23 Golden Square, London W1F 9JP
☎ 020 7734 6303   Fax 020 7734 6202
Email info@missionpictures.net

Contacts *Katie Goodson, Ed Rubin*
Feature films, including *Welcome to Sarajevo; Thunderpants; Gridlock'd; The Debt Collector; Splendor; A Texas Funeral; Some Voices; Very Annie-Mary.* Likes to encourage young talent but cannot consider unsolicited mss.

MW Entertainments Ltd
48 Dean Street, London W1D 5BF
☎ 020 7734 7707   Fax 020 7734 7727
Email development@michaelwhite.co.uk

Contact *Michael White*
High-output company whose credits include *Widow's Peak; White Mischief; Nuns on the Run* (co-production with HandMade Films Ltd); *The Comic Strip* series. Also theatre projects, including *Notre-Dame de Paris; Fame; Me and Mamie O'Rourke; She Loves Me; Crazy for You.* Contributions are passed by Michael White to a script reader for consideration.

Newgate Company
13 Dafford Street, Larkhall, Bath, Somerset BA1 6SW
☎ 01225 318335

Contact *Jo Anderson*
A commonwealth of established actors, directors and playwrights, Newgate originally concerned itself solely with theatre writing (at the Bush, Stratford, Roundhouse, etc.). However, in the course of development, several productions fed into a list of ongoing drama for BBC TV/Ch4. Looking to develop this co-production strand for film, television and radio projects with other 'indies'.

Northlight Productions Ltd
The Media Village, Grampian Television, Queen's Cross, Aberdeen
AB15 4XJ
☎ 01224 646460   Fax 01224 646450
Email tv@northlight.co.uk
Website www.northlight.co.uk

Contact *Robert Sproul-Cran*
Film, video and TV: drama, documentary and corporate work. Output ranges from high-end corporate fund-raising videos to *Thicker Than Water*, a drama series currently in development; *Equinox: Lethal Seas* (documentary on whirlpools for Ch4/Discovery); two schools' series for Ch4 including *Chez Mimi*, a five-part drama sitcom in French. Scripts welcome. Has links with EAVE (European Audio-Visual Entrepreneurs) and media.

Open Road Films
The Studio, 37 Redington Road, London NW3 7QY
☎ 020 7813 4333   Fax 020 7916 9172
Email openroadfilms@blueyonder.co.uk

Development Executive *Sophie Prideaux*
Producer *Andrew Holmes*
Company formed by Holmes Associates to produce low- to medium-budget British feature films. Output: *Chunky Monkey*; *Ashes and Sand*. Four projects in development. Unsolicited drama/film scripts will be considered but may take some time for response.

Outcast Production
1 Lewin Road, London SW14 8DW
☎ 020 8878 9486
Email xisle@bluecarrots.com

Contact *Andreas Wisniewski*
Low-budget feature films. No unsolicited mss; send synopsis or treatment only. 'We are actively searching for and encouraging new writing.'

Barry Palin Associates Ltd
Unit 10 Princeton Court, 55 Felsham Road, London SW15 1AZ
☎ 020 8394 5660　Fax 020 8785 0440
Email mail@barrypalinassociates.com

Contact *Barry Palin*
Film, video and TV production for drama, documentary, commercials and corporate material. Output: *Harmfulness of Tobacco* Anton Chekhov short story – BAFTA Best Short Film award winner (Ch4); Corporate: Philip Morris, York International, Republic Bank of New York.

Panther Pictures Ltd
3rd Floor, 16 Golden Square, London W1F 9JQ
☎ 07976 256 610　Fax 020 7734 8858
Website www.pantherpictures.co.uk

Contact *Robert Sutton*
Feature films, including *Inside/Out*, a US/UK/Canada/France co-production.

Parallax Pictures Ltd
7 Denmark Street, London WC2H 8LS
☎ 020 7836 1478　Fax 020 7497 8062
Website www.parallaxpictures.co.uk

Contact *Sally Hibbin*
Feature films/television drama. Output: *Riff-Raff; Bad Behaviour; Raining Stones; Ladybird, Ladybird; I.D.; Land and Freedom; The Englishman Who Went up a Hill But Came Down a Mountain; Bliss; Jump the Gun; Carla's Song; The Governess; My Name Is Joe; Stand and Deliver; Dockers; Hold Back the Night; Bread and Roses; Princesa; The Navigators; Sweet Sixteen; Innocence.*

Passion Pictures
25–7 Riding House Street, London W1W 7DU
☎ 020 7323 9933　Fax 020 7323 9030
Email info@passion-pictures.com

Managing Director *Andrew Ruhemann*
Documentary and drama includes: *One Day in September* (Academy Award winner for best feature documentary, 2000); also commercials and music videos: Carphone Warehouse, Mini, Aero, Gorillaz, Coldplay and Robbie Williams. Unsolicited mss welcome.

PBF Motion Pictures
The Little Pickenhanger, Tuckey Grove, Ripley, Surrey GU23 6JG
☎01483 225179   Fax 01483 224118
Email peter@pbf.co.uk

Contact *Peter B. Fairbrass*
Film, video and TV: drama, documentary, commercials and corporate. Also televized chess series and chess videos. No scripts; send one-page synopsis only in the first instance. 'Good scripts which relate to current projects will be followed up, otherwise not, as PBF do not have the time to reply to proposals which do not interest them. Only good writing stands a chance.'

Penumbra Productions Ltd
80 Brondesbury Road, London NW6 6RX
☎020 7328 4550   Fax 020 7328 3844
Email nazpenumbra@compuserve.com

Contact *H.O. Nazareth*
Film, video, TV and radio: drama and social issues documentaries. Output includes *Fugitive Pieces* (Radio 3 play); *Stories My Country Told Me* (BBC2, 'Arena'); *Repomen* (Ch4, 'Cutting Edge'). Send synopses only, preferably by e-mail. Keen to assist in the development of new writing but only interested in social issue-based material.

Picture Palace Films Ltd
13 Egbert Street, London NW1 8LJ
☎020 7586 8763   Fax 020 7586 9048
Email info@picturepalace.com
Website www.picturepalace.com

Contacts *Malcolm Craddock, Katherine Hedderly*
FOUNDED 1971. Leading independent producer of film and TV drama. Output: *Rebel Heart* (BBC1); *Extremely Dangerous* and *A Life for A Life* (both for ITV); *Sharpe's Rifles* (14 films for Carlton TV); *Little Napoleons* (comedy drama, Ch4); *The Orchid House* (drama serial, Ch4); *Tandoori Nights*; *4 Minutes*; *When Love Dies* (all for Ch4); *Ping Pong* (feature film); *Acid House* (Picture Palace North). Material will only be considered if submitted through an agent.

Plantagenet Films Limited
Ard-Daraich Studio B, Ardgour, Nr Fort William, Inverness-shire PH33 7AB
☎ 01855 841384   Fax 01855 841384
Email plantagenetfilms@aol.com

Contact *Norrie Maclaren*
Film and television: documentary and drama programming such as *Dig* (gardening series for Ch4); various 'Dispatches' for Ch4 and 'Omnibus' for BBC. Keen to encourage and promote new writing; unsolicited mss welcome.

Platinum Film & TV Production Ltd
1b Murray Street, London NW1 9RE
☎ 020 7916 9091   Fax 020 7916 5238
Email inquiries@platinumtv.co.uk

Contact *Terry Kelleher*
Television documentaries, including drama-documentary. Output: *South Africa's Black Economy* (Ch4); *Murder at the Farm* (Thames TV); *The Biggest Robbery in the World* (major investigative true-crime drama-doc for Carlton TV); *Dead Line* (original drama by Chilean exiled Ariel Dorfman for Ch4). Scripts and format treatments welcome.

Portobello Pictures
64A Princedale Road, London W11 4NL
☎ 020 7379 5566   Fax 020 7379 5599

Contact *Eric Abraham*
Film drama, including Jan Sverak's *Dark Blue World*; *Kolya*; Jez Butterworth's *Birthday Girl*; *Mojo*; Tim Roth's *The War Zone*; BBC1's *Dalziel and Pascoe* (series 1–3).

Renaissance Films
34–5 Berwick Street, London W1F 8RP
☎ 020 7287 5190   Fax 020 7287 5191
Website www.renaissance-films.com

Co-Managing Directors *Stephen Evans, Angus Finney*
Director of Development *Caroline Wood*
Feature films: *The Luzhin Defense*; *The Wings of the Dove*; *The Madness of King George* (as Close Call Films); *Twelfth Night*; *Much Ado About Nothing*; *Peter's Friends*; *Henry V*. No unsolicited mss.

Richmond Films & Television Ltd
PO Box 33154, London NW3 4AZ
☎ 020 7722 6464   Fax 020 7722 6232
Email mail@richmondfilms.com

Contact *Development Executive*
Film and TV: drama and comedy. Output: *Press Gang*; *The Lodge*; *The Office*; *Wavelength*; *Privates*. 'No unsolicited scripts. We will accept two pages only consisting of a brief treatment of your project (either screenplay or TV series) which includes its genre and its demographics. Please tell us also where the project has been submitted previously and what response you have had. Your two pages will not be returned.'

RS Productions
47 Laet Street, Newcastle upon Tyne NE29 6NN
☎ 0191 259 1184/07710 064632 (Mobile)   Fax 0191 259 1184
Email enquiries@rsproductions.co.uk
Website www.rsproductions.co.uk

Contact *Mark Lavender*
Feature films, television and new media: drama series/serials and singles.

Targeting TV documentaries and series. Working with established and new talent. Submissions: one- or two-page outline, synopsis or treatment.

Sands Films
119 Rotherhithe Street, London SE16 4NF
☎ 020 7231 2209   Fax 020 7231 2119
Website www.sandsfilms.co.uk

Contacts *Christine Edzard, Olivier Stockman*
Film and TV drama. Output: *Little Dorrit; The Fool; As You Like It; A Dangerous Man; The Long Day Closes; A Passage to India; The Nutcracker; Seven Years in Tibet; The Children's Midsummer Night's Dream.* No unsolicited scripts.

Scala Productions Ltd
15 Frith Street, London W1D 4RE
☎ 020 7734 7060   Fax 020 7437 3248
Email scalaprods@aol.com

Contacts *Nik Powell*
Production company set up by ex-Palace Productions Nik Powell and Stephen Woolley, who have an impressive list of credits including *Company of Wolves; Absolute Beginners; Mona Lisa; Scandal; Crying Game; Backbeat; Neon Bible; 24:7; Little Voice; Divorcing Jack; Welcome to Woop Woop; The Lost Son; Fanny and Elvis; The Last September; Wild About Harry; Last Orders; A Christmas Carol – The Movie; Black and White.* In development: *Leopold Bloom; Boswell for the Defence; The Night We Called It a Day; I'll Sleep When I'm Dead; A Passionate Woman; A Single Shot; Haroun and the Sea of Stories; Level; St Agnes' Stand; Johnny Bollywood; One Love; English Passengers; He Kills Coppers.*

Screen First Ltd
The Studios, Funnells Farm, Down Street, Nutley,
East Sussex TN22 3LG
☎ 01825 712034   Fax 01825 713511
Email info@screenfirst.co.uk

Contacts *M. Thomas, P. Madden*
Television dramas, documentaries, arts and animation programmes. Developing major drama series, feature films, animated specials and series. No unsolicited scripts.

Screen Ventures Ltd
49 Goodge Street, London W1T 1TE
☎ 020 7580 7448
Email sales@screenventures.com

Contacts *Christopher Mould, Naima Mould*
Film and TV sales and production: documentary, music videos and drama. Output: *Life and Limb* (health documentary, Discovery Health Channel); *Pavement Aristocrats* (SABC); *Woodstock Diary; Vanessa Redgrave* (LWT 'South Bank Show'); *Mojo Working; Burma: Dying for Democracy* (Ch4); *Genet* (LWT 'South Bank Show'); *Dani Dares* (Ch4 series on strong women); *Pagad* (Ch4 news report).

September Films Ltd
Glen House, 22 Glenthorne Road, London W6 0NG
☎ 020 8563 9393   Fax 020 8741 7214
Email september@septemberfilms.com
Website www.septemberfilms.com

Head of Production *Elaine Day*
Head of Drama and Film Development *Nadine Mellor*
Factual entertainment and documentary specialists expanding further into television drama and film. Feature film Output includes *Breathtaking; House of America; Solomon and Gaenor.*

Sianco Cyf
7 Ffordd Segontiwm, Caernarfon, Gwynedd LL55 2LL
☎ 01286 673436/07831 726111 (Mobile)   Fax 01286 677616
Email sianco@treannedd.demon.co.uk

Contact *Siân Teifi*
Children's, youth and education programmes and children's drama.

Skyline Productions

10 Scotland Street, Edinburgh EH3 6PS
☎ 0131 557 4580   Fax 0131 556 4377
Email leslie@skyline.uk.com

Producer/Writer *Leslie Hills*
Film and television drama and documentary. Encourages new writers but telephone first before sending material.

SMG & Ginger TV Productions Ltd

116 New Oxford Street, London WC1A 1HH
☎ 020 7663 2300
Website www.ginger.com

Also: SMG TV Productions (Glasgow)
200 Renfield Street, Glasgow G2 3PR
☎ 0141 300 3000

Managing Director *Jagdip Jagpal*
Head of Drama *Erina Rayner, Eric Coulter* (Glasgow)
Executive Producer for Drama *Judy Counihan*
Head of Development and Children's *Elizabeth Partyka*
Head of Factual Programming *John Farren, Helen Alexander* (Glasgow)
SMG (Scottish Media Group) TV Productions Ltd, which incorporates Ginger Television, makes programmes for the national television networks, including ITV, Channel 4 and Sky. Specializes in drama, factual entertainment and children's programming. Output includes *Taggart*; *Rebus*; *Take Me*; *TFI Friday*; *Remembering Lockerbie*; *The Priory*; *How2*.

Spellbound Productions Ltd

90 Cowdenbeath Path, Islington, London N1 0LG
☎ 020 7713 8066   Fax 020 7713 8067
Email phspellbound@hotmail.com

Contact *Paul Harris*
Specializes in feature films for cinema and drama for television. Keen to

support and encourage new writing. Material will only be considered if in correct screenplay format and accompanied by sae.

Spice Factory (UK) Ltd

81 The Promenade, Brighton, East Sussex BN10 8LS

☎ 01273 585275   Fax 01273 585304

Email info@spicefactory.co.uk

Contacts *Lucy Shuttleworth, Emily Kyriakides*

FOUNDED 1995. Film producers. Output: *Pilgrim* (starring Ray Liotta); *Sabotage* (David Suchet, Stephen Fry); *Anazupta* (Lena Headey, Jason Fleming); *Mr In-Between* (Andrew Howard); *Plots With a View* (Christopher Walken, Brenda Blethyn, Alfred Molina, Lee Evans). 'Treatment and/or synopsis for feature-length films. Please enclose sae.'

Standish Films

320 Woodhouse Lane, Wigan, Lancashire WN6 7TD

☎ 077193 75575

Email mail@sirco.co.uk

Website www.sirco.co.uk

Contact *Rosemary Allen*

Film, video and TV: documentary, drama, commercials and corporate, including dramatized training videos. Currently looking for feature film scripts with Anglo/American/European themes. 'Interested in supporting and encouraging new talent and experienced writers looking for new and imaginative ways to express their ideas.' No unsolicited material; send synopses and enquiries via e-mail. Check website for current needs.

Strawberry Productions Ltd

36 Priory Avenue, London W4 1TY

☎ 020 8994 4494   Fax 020 8742 7675

Contact *John Black*

Film, video and TV: drama and documentary; corporate and video publishing.

146

Sweetheart Films

15 Quennel Mansions, Weir Road, London sw12 0NQ
☎ 020 8673 3855

Producer *Karel Bata*
Low-to-medium-budget feature films. No unsolicited mss. 'An introductory letter with, perhaps, a treatment and short extract would receive consideration. We are constantly on the look-out for talent. Tip: study your craft!'

Table Top Productions

1 The Orchard, Chiswick, London w4 1JZ
☎ 020 8742 0507   Fax 020 8742 0507
Email alvin@tabletopproductions.com

Contact *Alvin Rakoff*
TV and film. Output: *Paradise Postponed* (TV mini-series); *A Voyage Round My Father; The First Olympics 1896; Dirty Tricks; A Dance to the Music of Time.* No unsolicited mss. Also Dancetime Ltd.

Talisman Films Ltd

5 Addison Place, London w11 4RJ
☎ 020 7603 7474   Fax 020 7602 7422
Email email@talismanfilms.com

Contact *Richard Jackson*
Drama for film and TV: developing the full range of drama – TV series, serials and single films, as well as theatric features. 'We will only consider material submitted via literary agents.' Interested in supporting and encouraging new writing.

TalkBack Productions

20–1 Newman Street, London w1T 1PG
☎ 020 7861 8000   Fax 020 7861 8001
Email reception@talkback.co.uk

Chief Executive *Peter Fincham*
Managing Director *Sally Debonnaire*
TalkBack Productions is a FremantleMedia company. Specializes in comedy,

comedy drama and drama; also feature lifestyle programmes. Output: *Smith and Jones; Murder Most Horrid; The Day Today; Knowing Me Knowing You with Alan Partridge; I'm Alan Partridge; They Think It's All Over; Never Mind the Buzzcocks; Brass Eye; House Doctor; She's Gotta Have It; Grand Designs; Sword of Honour; In a Land of Plenty; Shooting the Past; 11 o'clock Show; Smack the Pony; Big Train; Los Dos Bros; Your Money or Your Life; Property Ladder; Would Like to Meet.*

Teliesyn

Chapter Arts Centre, Market Road, Canton, Cardiff CF5 1QE
☎ 029 2030 0876   Fax 029 2030 0877
Email tv@teliesyn.demon.co.uk
Website www.teliesyn.co.uk

Contact *Chris Davies*
Film and video: produces drama, documentary, music and social action in English and Welsh. Celtic Film Festival, BAFTA Cymru, Grierson and Indie award winner. Output: *Llafur Cariad* (epic drama, S4C); *How Red Was My Valley* (documentary series on the Labour Party, BBC2W); *Suckerfish* (35mm short); *Navida Nuestra* (Christmas mass from Argentina, S4C); *Subway Cops and the Mole Kings* (Ch4). Will consider unsolicited scripts only if accompanied by synopsis and CV. Encourages new writing wherever possible, in close association with a producer.

Tiger Aspect Productions Ltd

5 Soho Square, London W1D 3QA
☎ 020 7434 0672   Fax 020 7287 1448
Email general@tigeraspect.co.uk
Website www.tigeraspect.co.uk

Contact *Charles Brand*
Television producer for comedy, drama, documentary and entertainment. Output: *Births, Marriages and Deaths; Kid in the Corner; Country House; Gimme Gimme Gimme; Harry Enfield and Chums; Howard Goodall's Big Bangs; Playing the Field* I–III; *Streetmate* I & II; *Let Them Eat Cake; The Vicar of Dibley.* Only considers material submitted via an agent or from writers with a known track record.

Tonfedd Eryri
Hen Ysgol Aberpwll, Y Felinheli, Bangor, Gwynedd LL56 4JS
☎ 01248 671167   Fax 01248 671172
Email swyddfa@ff-eryri.demon.co.uk

Contacts *Hefin Elis, Norman Williams*
Light entertainment, comedy, music and drama.

Touch Productions Ltd
The Malt House Studios, Donhead St Mary, Dorset SP7 9DN
☎ 01747 828030   Fax 01747 828004
Email touch.productions@virgin.net

Contacts *Erica Wolfe-Murray, Malcolm Brinkworth*
Over the past fifteen years has produced 'investigative documentary films, history-based films with a strong contemporary relevance, powerful observational series and innovative films that stretch the form'. Television documentaries such as *Life of a £10 Note*; *Falklands 20th Anniversary*; *OJ – The Untold Story*; *Simon Weston V*; *Siege Doctors* (all for BBC); *The Good Life*; *The Surgery*; *Coast of Dreams*; *A French Affair*; *Watching the Detectives*; *Brown Babies* (all for Ch4); *Fame School*; *Fame School – the Graduates* (both for Meridian). Also has a drama section based on real-life stories, and unsolicited mss are welcome.

UBA Ltd
21 Alderville Road, London SW6 2EE
☎ 01984 623619   Fax 01984 623733
Email shawjshaw@aol.com *or* petershaw@btinternet.com

Contacts *Peter Shaw, Joanna Shaw*
Feature films and TV for an international market. Output: *Windprints*; *The Lonely Passion of Judith Hearne* (co-production with HandMade Films Ltd); *Taffin*; *Castaway*; *Turtle Diary*; *Sweeney Todd*; *Keep the Aspidistra Flying*. In development: *Kinder Garden*; *Rebel Magic*; *No Man's Land*. Prepared to commission new writing whether adapted from another medium or based on a short outline/treatment. Concerned with the quality of the script

(*Turtle Diary* was written by Harold Pinter) and breadth of appeal. 'Exploitation material' not welcome.

UK Film and TV Production Company Plc
3 Colville Place, London W1T 2BH
☎ 020 7255 1650

Contact *Henrietta Fudakowski*
Film and television. Currently looking for feature film or TV drama scripts, with a preference for stories with humour. Return postage and list of credits essential. Please phone before submitting material.

Vanson Productions
PO Box 16926, London SW18 3ZP
☎ 020 8874 4241   Fax 020 8874 3600
Email vansonproductions@btinternet.com

Contact *Yvette Vanson*
Twenty years as documentary producer, then films and drama. Output: *The Murder of Stephen Lawrence* Paul Greengrass (a film with Granada for ITV – BAFTA 2000 Best Single Drama); *Doomwatch* John Howlett and Ian McDonald (science drama with Working Title Films for Ch5). Films in development: *Guts and Glitter* Jo Leigh; *Algeria* Greg Dinner. Latest venture: co-partner in Zephaniah Films with Benjamin Zephaniah in *Face*, six-part children's drama, and *Refugee Boy*, children's feature, both based on Zephaniah's novels. Please ring before sending anything on spec.

Brian Waddell Productions Ltd
Strand Studios, 5/7 Shore Road, Holywood, Co. Down BT8 9HX
☎ 028 9042 7646   Fax 028 9042 7922
Email strand@bwpltv.co.uk

Contacts *Brian Waddell*
Producer of a wide range of television programmes on leisure activities, the arts, music, children's, comedy, travel/adventure and documentaries. Currently developing several film and drama projects.

Wall to Wall
8–9 Spring Place, London NW5 3ER
☎ 020 7485 7424   Fax 020 7267 5292
Website www.walltowall.co.uk

Chief Executive *Alex Graham*
Factual and drama programming. Output includes *A Rather English Marriage*; *Glasgow Kiss*; *Sex, Chips and Rock 'n' Roll*; *The 1940s House*; *Body Story*; *Neanderthal*. Drama ideas welcomed through established agents.

Walsh Bros. Limited
4 The Heights, London SE7 8JH
☎ 020 8858 5870/8854 5557   Fax 020 8858 6870
Email walshbros@lycosmail.com

Producer/Director *John Walsh*
Producer/Head of Finance *David Walsh, ACA*
Producer/Head of Development *Maura Walsh*
Award-winning producer of drama documentaries and feature films. Output: *Monarch* (feature film on the events on the eve of the death of King Henry VIII); *Trex* (factual series shooting in China, Mexico, Vancouver and Alaska); *Nu Model Armi* (documentary); *TUEX2* (shot in Romania, India, Iceland and Louisiana); *Boyz and Girlz*; (documentary series); *Cowboyz and Cowgirlz* (US sequel to the first hit series); *Ray Harryhausen* (profile of the work of Hollywood special-effects legend); *The Comedy Store* (behind-the-scenes view of the birthplace of alternative comedy); *The Sceptic and The Psychic*; *The Sleeper*; *A State of Mind* (film dramas).

Warner Sisters Film & TV Ltd
The Cottage, Pall Mall Deposit, 124 Barlby Road, London W10 6BL
☎ 020 8960 3550   Fax 020 8960 3880
Email sisters@warnercine.com

Chief Executives *Lavinia Warner, Jane Wellesley, Dorothy Viljoen*
FOUNDED 1984. Drama and comedy. TV and feature films. Output includes *Selling Hitler*; *Rides*; *Life's a Gas*; *She-Play*; *A Village Affair*; *Dangerous Lady*; *Dressing for Breakfast*; *The Spy that Caught a Cold*; *The Bite*; *Jilting Joe*; *The*

Jump; Lady Audley's Secret; Do or Die. Developing a wide range of projects including *The Letters* (feature film).

Windrush Productions Ltd
7 Woodlands Road, Moseley, Birmingham B13 4EH
☎ 0121 449 6439/07977 059378 (Mobile)   Fax 0121 449 6439
Email beboyyaa@hotmail.com

Contacts *Pogus Caesar, Shawn Caesar*
Television documentaries, including a multicultural series for Carlton TV (*Xpress and Respect*); *The A-Force* (BBC); *I'm Black in Britain* (Central TV); *Drumbeat* (Carlton). Also produces *Windrush E. Smith Show* (comedy) and Pogus Caesar's *Off the Hook* for BBC Radio Pebble Mill. Produces pop promos/corporate videos for a range of clients. Encourages new writing, especially from the regions. 'We try to seek scripts from writers interested in developing new black fiction/comedy.'

Working Title Films Ltd
Oxford House, 76 Oxford Street, London W1D 1BS
☎ 020 7307 3000   Fax 020 7307 3001/2/3

Co-Chairmen (Films) *Tim Bevan, Eric Fellner*
Head of Development (Films) *Debra Hayward*
Development Executive (Films) *Chris Clark*
Television *Simon Wright*
Feature films, TV drama; also family/children's entertainment and TV comedy. Films: *Bridget Jones's Diary; Captain Corelli's Mandolin; Ali G in da House; Notting Hill; Elizabeth; Plunkett and Macleane; The Borrowers; The Matchmaker; Fargo; Dead Man Walking; French Kiss; Four Weddings and a Funeral; The Hudsucker Proxy; The Tall Guy; Wish You Were Here; My Beautiful Laundrette.* Television: *More Tales of the City; The Borrowers* I & II; *Armistead Maupin's Tales of the City; News Hounds; Randall and Hopkirk Deceased; Doomwatch.* No unsolicited mss at present, but keen to encourage new writing nevertheless via new writers' scheme – contact *Dan Shepherd.*

Wortman Productions UK
48 Chiswick Staithe, London w4 3TP
☎ 020 8994 8886/07976 805976 (Mobile)
Email nevillewortman@beeb.net

Producer *Neville Wortman*
Co-producers with Polestar Pictures Ltd. Feature film and TV production
for drama, documentary, commercials and corporate. Output: *House in the
Country* John Julius Norwich (ITV series); *Tribute to Ellington* (jazz special);
Lost Ships (maritime historical drama series – Discovery Channel); *Criminal
Chronicles* (Russian crime series – BBCTV/Court TV co-production). In prep-
aration: *Samuel's Last Summer* (feature film). Open to new writing, preferably
through agents; single page outline, some pages of dialogue; sae for reply.

W.O.W. Productions
12 Rutland Park Gardens, London NW2 4RG
☎ 020 8451 7922
Email wow@dircon.co.uk

Contacts *Carl Schonfeld, Dom Rotheroe*
Film and television drama and documentary programming. Output includes:
A Sarajevo Diary (documentary); *My Brother Tom* (feature).

Zenith Entertainment Ltd
43–5 Dorset Street, London w1U 7NA
☎ 020 7224 2440   Fax 020 7224 3194
Email general@zenith-entertainment.co.uk

Head of Drama Development *Judith Hackett*
Feature films and TV drama. Films: Todd Haynes' *Velvet Goldmine*; *Wisdom
of Crocodiles*; Nicole Holofcener's *Walking and Talking*. Television: *Hamish
Macbeth*; *Rhodes*; *Bodyguards*; *The Uninvited*; *Bomber*; *2000 Acres of Sky*. No
unsolicited scripts.

Television and Radio

BBC Television and Radio

The structure of the BBC includes four programming divisions: Drama, Entertainment and Children's; Factual and Learning; News; and Sport. Music Production is part of BBC Radio but also produces classical music programmes for television. A New Media division develops the BBC's interactive television and online activities.

Director-General *Greg Dyke*

Television

BBC Television Centre, Wood Lane, London W12 7RJ
☎ 020 8743 8000

Director, Television *Jana Bennett*
Controller, BBC1 *Lorraine Heggessey*
Controller, BBC2 *Jane Root*

Digital television:
Controller, BBC Three *Stuart Murphy*
Controller, BBC Four *Roly Keating*
BBC Three was launched in February 2003, replacing BBC Choice. Broadcasts a wide range of entertainment aimed at a 25–34-year-old audience with programmes such as *Liquid News* – headline stories from the world

of showbusiness. BBC Four, launched in March 2002, is devoted solely to the arts. Programmes include *Readers and Writers*, a weekly book programme.

Radio

Broadcasting House, Portland Place, London W1A 1AA
☎ 020 7580 4468

Director of Radio and Music *Jenny Abramsky*
Controller, Radio 1 *Andy Parfitt*
Controller, Radio 2 *James Moir*
Controller, Radio 3 *Roger Wright*
Controller, Radio 4 *Helen Boaden*
Controller, Radio 5 Live *Bob Shennan*

Digital radio:
BBC 1Xtra
BBC Five Live Sports Extra
BBC 6 Music
BBC 7 (comedy, drama and books)
BBC Asian Network

Drama, entertainment and children's division

Director *Alan Yentob*

BBC Writers' Room finds and champions writers across all BBC platforms, running targeted schemes and workshops linked directly to production. It accepts and assesses unsolicited scripts for film, single TV dramas, comedy and radio drama. It also runs *northern exposure*, which focuses on new writing in the north of England, channelled through theatres in Liverpool, Manchester, Bradford, Leeds and Newcastle. To be considered for one of the schemes run by the Writers' Room, send a sample full-length drama script to: BBC Writers' Room, 1 Mortimer Street, London W1T 3JA. For guidelines on unsolicited scripts log on to www.bbc.co.uk/writersroom or send a large sae to *Jessica Dromgoole*, New Writing Coordinator, BBC Drama, Entertainment and CBBC at the Mortimer Street address above. (For online information and advice, see the section on the BBC Writers' Room on pages 44–5.)

Drama

Controller, Drama Commissioning *Jane Tranter*
Controller of Drama Series *Mal Young*
Head of Films *David Thompson*
Head of Development, Serials *Sarah Brown*
Head of Development, Serials *Serena Cullen*
Head of Development, Films *Tracey Scoffield*
Creative Director, New Writing *Kate Rowland*
Head of Radio Drama *Gordon House*
Executive Producer *Jeremy Mortimer*
Executive Producer *David Hunter*
Executive Producer (Manchester) *Sue Roberts*
Executive Producer (Birmingham)/Editor, The Archers *Vanessa Whitburn*
Executive Producer (World Service Drama) *Marion Nancarrow*

Entertainment

Acting Head of Light Entertainment, Television *Jonathan Glazier*
Head of Comedy Entertainment, Television *Jon Plowman*
Producer *Bill Dare*
Editor, Radio Entertainment *John Pidgeon*
Programmes produced range from *Shooting Stars* and *Jonathan Creek* on television to *Just a Minute*, *I'm Sorry I Haven't a Clue* and *The News Quiz* on Radio 4. Virtually every comic talent in Britain got their first break writing one-liners for topical comedy weeklies. For information on those programmes requiring non-commissioned submissions, join the mailing list for *Writer's Newsletter*. Contact: claire.bartlett@bbc.co.uk

CBBC (children's)

Controller, CBBC *J. Nigel Pickard*
Head of Programmes *Dorothy Prior*
Head of Acquisitions *Theresa Plummer-Andrews*
Executive Producer, CBBC Drama *Elaine Sperber*
Head of Entertainment *Chris Bellinger*
Head of CBBC News/Executive Producer, Exchange *Roy Milani*
Head of CBBC Factual *Jeremy Daldry*
Editor, *Blue Peter* *Steve Hocking*
Executive Producer, CBBC Pre-school *Clare Elstow*
Executive Producer, CBBC Education *Sue Nott*
Creative Director, Children's Programmes, Scotland *Claire Mundell*

BBC Talent
Website www.bbc.co.uk/talent

The BBC's search for new talent covers a wide range of areas including TV and radio producers, presenters, filmmakers, sitcom and comedy writers. Access the website for further information.

BBC World Service
PO Box 76, Bush House, Strand, London WC2B 4PH
☎ 020 7240 3456   Fax 020 7557 1900
Website www.bbc.co.uk/worldservice

Director *Mark Byford*
Director, English Networks and News, BBCWS *Phil Harding*
The World Service broadcasts in English and forty-two other languages. The English service is round the clock, with news and current affairs as the main component. With over 150 million listeners, excluding countries where research is not possible, it reaches a bigger audience than its five closest competitors combined. The World Service is increasingly available throughout the world on local FM stations, via satellite and online as well as through short-wave frequencies. Coverage includes world business, politics, people/events/opinions, development issues, the international scene, developments in science and technology, sport,

religion, music, drama, the arts. BBC World Service broadcasting is financed by a grant-in-aid voted by Parliament amounting to £173.2 million for 2002/03.

BBC regions

BBC Northern Ireland

Broadcasting House, Ormeau Avenue, Belfast BT2 8HQ
☎ 028 9033 8000
Website www.bbc.co.uk/northernireland

Controller *Anna Carragher*
Head of Broadcasting *Tim Cooke*
Head of News and Current Affairs *Andrew Colman*
Editor, News Gathering *Michael Cairns*
Editor, Television News *Angelina Fusco*
Editor, Radio News *Kathleen Carragher*
Head of Drama *Robert Cooper*
Head of Entertainment, Events and Sport *Mike Edgar*
Editor, Entertainment *Alex Johnston*
Head of Factual and Learning *Bruce Batten*
Editor, Learning *Kieran Hegarty*
Editor, Radio Factual *Susan Lovell*
Editor, Television Factual *Deirdre Devlin*
Managing Director, Foyle *Ana Leddy*
Head of Programme Operations *Stephen Beckett*
Regular television programmes include *Newsline 6.30* and a wide range of documentary, popular factual and entertainment. BBC NI is a prime producer of radio and television drama for the network. Radio stations: BBC Radio Foyle and BBC Radio Ulster.

BBC Scotland

Broadcasting House, Queen Margaret Drive, Glasgow G12 8DG
☎ 0141 338 2000
Website www.bbc.co.uk/scotland

Controller *John McCormick*
Controller, Network Development, Nations and Regions *Colin Cameron*
Head of Drama, Television *Barbara McKissack*
Head of Drama, Radio *Patrick Rayner*
Head of Comedy and Entertainment *Mike Bolland*
Head of Factual Programmes *Andrea Miller*
Executive Editor New Media *Julie Adair*
Head of Programmes, Scotland *Ken MacQuarrie*
Head of Radio *Maggie Cunningham*
Head of Gaelic *Donalda MacKinnon*
Commissioning Editor, Television *Ewan Angus*
Headquarters of BBC Scotland with centres in Aberdeen, Dundee, Edinburgh and Inverness. Regular programmes include *Reporting Scotland*; *Sportscene* on television and *Good Morning Scotland*; *Fred Macaulay* on radio.

Aberdeen
Broadcasting House, Beechgrove Terrace, Aberdeen AB9 2ZT
☎ 01224 625233

Head of North *Andrew Jones*
News, plus some features, including the regular *Beechgrove Garden*. Second TV centre, also with regular radio broadcasting.

Dundee
Nethergate Centre, 66 Nethergate, Dundee DD1 4ER
☎ 01382 202481
News base only; contributors' studio.

Edinburgh
The Tun, Holyrood Road, Edinburgh EH8 8JF
☎ 0131 557 5677

Senior Producer, Arts and Features *Jane Fowler*
News, current affairs, arts and features.

Inverness
7 Culduthel Road, Inverness 1V2 4AD
☎ 01463 720720

Editor *Ishbel MacLennan*
News features for Radio Scotland.

Radio Nan Gaidheal
Rosebank, Church Street, Stornoway, Isle of Lewis PA87 2LS
☎ 01851 705000

Editor *Marion MacKinnon*
The Gaelic radio service serving most of Scotland.

BBC Wales
Broadcasting House Llandaff, Cardiff CF5 2YQ
☎ 029 2032 2000   Fax 029 2055 2973
Website www.bbc.co.uk/wales

Controller *Menna Richards*
Head of Programmes (Welsh Language) *Keith Jones*
Head of Programmes (English Language) *Clare Hudson*
Head of News and Current Affairs *Aled Eurig*
Head of Drama *Matthew Robinson*
Series Editor, *Pobol y Cwm* *Bethan Jones*
Headquarters of BBC Wales, with regional centres in Bangor, Aberystwyth, Carmarthen, Wrexham and Swansea. BBC Wales television produces up to twelve hours of English-language programmes a week, twelve hours in Welsh for transmission on S4C and an increasing number of hours on network services. Regular programmes include *Wales Today; Newyddion* (Welsh-language daily news); *Wales on Saturday; Pobol y Cwm* (Welsh-language soap) on television and *Good Morning Wales; Good Evening Wales; Post Cyntaf; Post Prynhawn* on radio.

Bangor
Broadcasting House, Meirion Road, Bangor, Gwynedd LL57 2BY
☎ 01248 370880   Fax 01248 351443
Head of Centre *Marian Wyn Jones*

BBC local radio

BBC Radio Cumbria
Annetwell Street, Carlisle, Cumbria CA3 8BB
☎ 01228 592444   Fax 01228 511195
Email radio.cumbria@bbc.co.uk
Website www.bbc.co.uk/cumbria

Editor *Nigel Dyson*
Occasional opportunities for plays and short stories are advertised on-air.

BBC Hereford and Worcester
Hylton Road, Worcester WR2 5WW
☎ 01905 748485   Fax 01905 748006
Email bbchw@bbc.co.uk
Website www.bbc.co.uk/herefordworcester

Also at: 43 Broad Street, Hereford HR4 9HH
☎ 01432 355252   Fax 01432 356446

Managing Editor *James Coghill*
Has an interest in writers and writing with local connections.

Independent Television

Anglia Television
Anglia House, Norwich, Norfolk NR1 3JG
☎ 01603 615151   Fax 01603 761245
Email angliatv@angliatv.co.uk
Website www.angliatv.co.uk

Managing Director *Graham Creelman*
Controller of Programmes *Neil Thompson*
Anglia Television is a major producer of programmes for the ITV network, including *Trisha* (Trisha Goddard's chat show) and major documentaries. Network drama is produced by Anglia's parent company, Granada.

Border Television plc
Television Centre, Durranhill, Carlisle, Cumbria CA1 3NT
☎ 01228 525101   Fax 01228 541384
Website www.border-tv.com

Deputy Chairman *James Graham, OBE*
Controller of Programmes *Neil Robinson*
Border's programming concentrates on documentaries rather than drama. Most scripts are supplied in-house but occasionally there are commissions. Apart from notes, writers should not submit written work until their ideas have been fully discussed.

Carlton Television
Website www.carlton.com

Chief Executive, Carlton Channels *Clive Jones*
Director of Programmes, Carlton Productions *Steve Hewlett*
Carlton Television holds four of the fifteen regional ITV licences: Carlton – the weekday broadcaster for the London region; Carlton Central Region – covering the east, west and south Midlands; Carlton West Country Region, HTV Wales and HTV West – covering Wales and the west of England. Network drama includes *Crossroads; The Vice; Dead Gorgeous; Forty Something.* (See also Carlton Productions under Film, TV and Video Production Companies on page 120–1.)

Carlton Broadcasting, London Region
101 St Martin's Lane, London WC2N 4RF
☎ 020 7240 4000   Fax 020 7240 4171

Managing Director, Broadcasting *Colin Stanbridge*

Carlton Broadcasting, Carlton Central Region

Gas Street, Birmingham B1 2JT

☎ 0121 643 9898   Fax 0121 634 4240

Website www.carlton.com/central

Managing Director, Broadcasting *Ian Squires*

Regular regional programmes include *Central Weekend; Asian Eye.*

Carlton Broadcasting, Carlton West Country Region

Langage Science Park, Western Wood Way, Plymouth,
Devon PL7 5BQ

☎ 01752 333333   Fax 01752 333444

Website www.carlton.com/westcountry

Managing Director *Mark Haskell*
Director of Programmes *Jane McCloskey*

Came on air in January 1993. News, current affairs, documentary and religious programming.

HTV Wales

The TV Centre, Culverhouse Cross, Cardiff CF5 6XJ

☎ 029 2059 0590   Fax 029 2059 7183

Website www.htvwales.co.uk

Controller/Director of Programmes *Elis Owen*

HTV West

Television Centre, Bath Road, Bristol BS4 3HG

☎ 0117 972 2722   Fax 0117 972 2400

Website www.htvwest.co.uk

Managing Director *Jeremy Payne*
Controller, HTV West and Director of Regional Programmes *Sandra Jones*

Channel 4

124 Horseferry Road, London SW1P 2TX

☎ 020 7396 4444   Fax 020 7306 8356

Website www.channel4.com

Director of Programmes *Tim Gardam*
Head of Film *Paul Webster*
Head of Entertainment *Danielle Lux*

Commissioning editors
Independent Film and Video *Adam Barker*
Head of Drama and Animation *Tessa Ross*
Head of Comedy *Caroline Leddy*
Documentaries *Peter Dale*
Multicultural Programmes *Yasmin Anwar*
Controller of Acquisition *June Dromgoole*
Channel 4 started broadcasting as a national channel in November 1982. It enjoys unique status as the world's only major public service broadcaster funded entirely by its own commercial activities. All programmes are commissioned from independent production companies and are broadcast across the whole of the UK except those parts of Wales covered by S4C. Its FilmFour channel, launched in November 1998, is a premium pay-TV channel featuring modern independent cinema. A second digital channel, E4, was launched in January 2001, broadcasting a range of programmes similar to Channel 4.

Channel 5

22 Long Acre, London WC2E 9LY
☎ 020 7550 5555   Fax 020 7550 5554
Website www.channel5.co.uk

CEO *Jane Lighting*
Director of Programmes *Kevin Lygo*
Controller of Children's and Religious Programmes *Nick Wilson*
Senior Programme Controller *Chris Shaw*
Controller of Drama Programmes *Corinne Hollingworth*
Channel 5 Broadcasting Ltd won the franchise for Britain's third commercial terrestrial television station in 1995 and came on air at the end of March 1997. Regular programmes include *Family Affairs* (Monday to Friday soap opera); *Open House* (Gloria Hunniford's daytime magazine show), plus documentaries, drama, films, children's programmes, sport and entertainment.

Channel Television

Television Centre, La Pouquelaye, St Helier, Jersey, Channel Islands JE1 3ZD
☎ 01534 816816   Fax 01534 816817

Also at: Television House, Bulwer Avenue, St Sampsons, Guernsey GY2 4LA
☎ 01481 241888   Fax 01481 241878
Website www.channeltv.co.uk

Managing Director *Michael Lucas*
Director of Programmes *Karen Rankine*
Channel Television is the ITV broadcaster to the Channel Islands, serving 143,000 residents, most of whom live on the main islands, Jersey, Guernsey, Alderney and Sark. The station has a weekly reach of more than 94 per cent with local programmes (in the region of five and a half hours each week) at the heart of its service.

GMTV

The London Television Centre, Upper Ground, London SE1 9TT
☎ 020 7827 7000   Fax 020 7827 7249
Email talk2us@gmtv.co.uk
Website www.gmtv.co.uk

Managing Director *Paul Corley*
Director of Programmes *Peter McHugh*
Managing Editor *John Scammell*
Winner of the national breakfast television franchise. Jointly owned by Scottish Media Group, Carlton Communications, Walt Disney Company and Granada Group. GMTV took over from TV-AM on 1 January 1993, with live programming from 6.00 a.m. to 9.25 a.m. Regular news headlines, current affairs, topical features, showbiz and lifestyle, sports and business, quizzes and competitions, travel and weather reports. Launched its digital service, GMTV2, in January 1999, with daily broadcasts from 6.00 a.m. to 9.25 a.m. News reports, travel, health and lifestyle features, some simulcast with GMTV1. Children's programming on Saturdays.

Grampian Television Limited
Craigshaw Business Park, West Tullos, Aberdeen AB12 3QH
☎ 01224 848848   Fax 01224 848800
Website www.grampiantv.co.uk

Managing Director *Derrick Thomson*
Extensive regional news and reports including farming, fishing and sports, interviews and leisure features, various light entertainment, Gaelic and religious programmes, and live coverage of the Scottish political, economic and industrial scene. Serves the area from Fife to Shetland. Regular programmes include *North Tonight* and *The People Show*.

Granada Television
Quay Street, Manchester M60 9EA
☎ 0161 832 7211   Fax 0161 953 0283
Website www.granadamedia.com

Director of Programmes *John Whiston*
Director of Production *Claire Poyser*
Controller of Regional Programmes *Kieron Collins*
Controller of Drama *Carolyn Reynolds*
Controller of Current Affairs and Features *Jeff Anderson*
Opportunities for freelance writers are not great but mss from professional writers will be considered. All mss should be addressed to the head of scripts. Regular programmes include *Coronation Street; Tonight*.

LWT (London Weekend Television)
The London Television Centre, Upper Ground, London SE1 9LT
☎ 020 7620 1620
Website www.itv.com/lwt

Chairman *Charles Allen*
Managing Director *Lindsay Charlton*
Director of Production *Tamara Howe*
Controller of Entertainment and Comedy *Bob Massie*
Controller of Drama *Michele Buck*
Controller of Arts *Melvyn Bragg*

Makers of current affairs, entertainment and drama series such as *Blind Date*; *Surprise Surprise*; *Where the Heart Is*; *Night and Day*; *London's Burning*; also *The South Bank Show*; *Jonathan Dimbleby*. Provides a large proportion of ITV's drama and light entertainment, and also for BSkyB and Channel 4.

Meridian Broadcasting
Television Centre, Southampton, Hampshire SO14 0PZ
☎ 023 8022 2555   Fax 023 8033 5050
Email viewerliaison@meridiantv.com
Website www.meridiantv.com

Managing Director *Lindsay Charlton*
Controller of Regional Programmes *Mark Southgate*
Meridian's studios in Southampton provide a base for network and regional productions. Regular regional programmes include the award-winning news service, *Meridian Tonight*; also *Countryways*; *Grass Roots*.

S4C
Parc Ty Glas, Llanishen, Cardiff CF14 5DU
☎ 029 2074 7444   Fax 029 2075 4444
Email s4c@s4c.co.uk
Website www.s4c.co.uk

Chief Executive *Huw Jones*
Director of Programmes *Huw Eirug*
The Welsh channel, established by the Broadcasting Act 1980, is responsible for a schedule of Welsh- and English-language programmes on the fourth channel in Wales. Known as S4C, the analogue service is made up of about thirty-four hours per week of Welsh-language programmes and more than eighty-five hours of English-language output from Channel 4. S4C digital broadcasts in Welsh exclusively for eighty hours per week. Ten hours a week of the Welsh programmes are provided by the BBC; the remainder are purchased from HTV and independent producers. Drama, comedy and documentary are all parts of S4C's programming.

Scottish Television Ltd
200 Renfield Street, Glasgow G2 3PR
☎ 0141 300 3000   Fax 0141 300 3030
Website www.stv.co.uk

Managing Director, Scottish TV *Sandy Ross*
Head of Features and Entertainment *Agnes Wilkie*
Head of Drama *Eric Coulter*
Scottish Television produces sixteen and a half hours of television a week
for the central Scotland region. This is made up of news, current affairs
and sport, and a wide-ranging portfolio of other programmes ranging from
entertainment, documentary and religion to regional drama such as *High
Road* and *New Found Land*. Scottish Television also produces a wide range
of programming such as drama for other broadcasters including the ITV
Network. The company is always interested in new ideas and proposals.

Tyne Tees Television
Television Centre, Newcastle upon Tyne NE1 2AL
☎ 0191 261 0181   Fax 0191 261 2302
Email tyne.tees@granadamedia.com
Website www.tynetees.tv

Managing Director *Margaret Fay*
Controller of Programmes *Graeme Thompson*
Head of New Media *Malcolm Wright*
Programming covers religion, politics, news and current affairs, regional
documentaries, business, entertainment, sport and arts. Regular pro-
grammes include *North East Tonight with Mike Neville* and *Around the House*
(politics). In 2003, Tyne Tees screen a series of eight new regional dramas –
Hot House – showcasing North East writers and directors.

UTV (Ulster Television)
Havelock House, Ormeau Road, Belfast BT7 1EB
☎ 028 9032 8122   Fax 029 9024 6695
Website www.u.tv

Director of Television *Alan Bremner*
Regular programmes on news and current affairs, politics, sport, education, music, light entertainment, arts, health and local culture.

Yorkshire Television
The Television Centre, Leeds, West Yorkshire LS3 1JS
☎ 0113 243 8283   Fax 0113 244 5107
London office: Global House, 96–108 Great Suffolk Street, London
SE1 OBE
☎ 020 7578 4304   Fax 020 7578 4320
Website www.granadamedia.com

Chairman *Charles Allen*
Managing Director *David Croft*
Director of Programmes, Yorkshire Tyne Tees Productions *John Whiston*
Controller of Drama, Yorkshire Tyne Tees Productions *Keith Richardson*
Controller of Drama, YTV *Carolyn Reynolds*
Controller of Comedy Drama and Drama Features *David Reynolds*
Part of Granada Media Group. Drama series, situation comedies, film productions and long-running series like *Emmerdale* and *Heartbeat*. Always looking for strong writing in these areas, but prefers to find it through an agent. Documentary/current affairs material tends to be supplied by producers; opportunities in these areas are rare but adaptations of published work as a documentary subject are considered. In theory, opportunity exists within series, episode material. Best approach is through a good agent.

UK Literary Agents

* = Member of the Association of Authors' Agents

The Agency (London) Ltd*

24 Pottery Lane, Holland Park, London W11 4LZ
☎ 020 7727 1346   Fax 020 7727 9037
Email info@theagency.co.uk

Contacts *Stephen Durbridge, Leah Schmidt, Sebastian Born, Julia Kreitman, Bethan Evans, Hilary Delamere, Katie Haines, Ligeia Marsh*
FOUNDED 1995. Handles children's fiction, TV, film, theatre, radio scripts. No adult fiction or non-fiction. No reading fee.

Commission: home 10%; US by arrangement.

Darley Anderson Literary, TV & Film Agency*

Estelle House, 11 Eustace Road, London SW6 1JB
☎ 020 7385 6652   Fax 020 7386 5571
Email enquiries@darleyanderson.com

Contacts *Darley Anderson* (thrillers), *Kerith Biggs* (crime/foreign rights), *Elizabeth Wright* (women's fiction/love stories/tear-jerkers), *Carrie Neilson* (TV/film, children's books)
Run by an ex-publisher who has a knack for spotting talent and is a tough negotiator. Handles commercial fiction and non-fiction; children's fiction; also selected scripts for film and TV. No academic books or poetry. Special interests: all types of thrillers and young male fiction, all types of American

Brie Burkeman*

14 Neville Court, Abbey Road, London NW8 9DD
☎ 0709 223 9113   Fax 0709 223 9111
Email brie.burkeman@mail.com

Contact *Brie Burkeman*
FOUNDED 2000. Handles commercial and literary full-length fiction and non-fiction. Film, TV, theatre scripts. No academic, poetry, short stories, musicals or short films. No reading fee but return postage essential. Unsolicited email attachments will be deleted without opening. Also independent film and TV consultant to literary agents.

Commission: home 15%; overseas 20%.

Capel & Land Ltd*

29 Wardour Street, London W1D 6PS
☎ 020 7734 2414   Fax 020 7734 8101
Email robert@capelland.co.uk

Contact *Georgina Capel*
FOUNDED 2000. Handles fiction and non-fiction. Also film, TV, theatre and radio scripts. No children's or illustrated books. Send sample chapters and synopsis with covering letter in the first instance. No reading fee.

Clients: Kunal Basu, Julie Burchill, Andrew Greig, Henry Porter, Andrew Roberts, Louis Theroux, Lucy Wadham.

Commission: home, US and translation 15%.

Casarotto Ramsay and Associates Ltd

National House, 60–6 Wardour Street, London W1V 3HP
☎ 020 7287 4450   Fax 020 7287 9128
Email agents@casarotto.uk.com
Website www.casarotto.uk.com

Contacts *Jenne Casarotto, Tracey Hyde, Charlotte Kelly, Jodi Shields, Chris Cope, Elinor Burns* (film/TV/radio); *Tom Erhardt, Mel Kenyon* (stage);
(Books handled by Lutyens and Rubinstein)

Took over the agency responsibilities of Margaret Ramsay Ltd in 1992, incorporating a strong client list with names like Alan Ayckbourn, Caryl Churchill, Willy Russell and Muriel Spark. Handles scripts for TV, theatre, film and radio. No unsolicited material without preliminary letter.

Clients: J. G. Ballard, Edward Bond, Simon Callow, David Hare, Terry Jones, Neil Jordan, Willy Russell.

Commission: home 10%; US and translation 20%.

Overseas associates: worldwide.

Jonathan Clowes Ltd*
19 Iron Bridge House, Bridge Approach, London NW1 8BD
☎ 020 7722 7674   Fax 020 7722 7677

Contacts *Ann Evans, Chloe Loyd, Lisa Whadcock*
FOUNDED 1960. Pronounced 'clewes'. Now one of the biggest fish in the pond, and not really for the untried unless a true high-flyer. Fiction and non-fiction, plus scripts. No textbooks or children's. Special interests: situation comedy, film and television rights. No unsolicited mss; authors come by recommendation or by successful follow-ups to preliminary letters.

Clients: David Bellamy, Len Deighton, Elizabeth Jane Howard, Doris Lessing, David Nobbs, Gillian White and the estate of Kingsley Amis.

Commission: home and US 15%; translation 19%.

Overseas associates: Andrew Nurnberg Associates; Sane Töregard Agency.

Elspeth Cochrane Personal Management
14/2 Second Floor, South Bank Commercial Centre, 140 Battersea Park Road, London SW11 4NB
☎ 020 7622 0314   Fax 020 7622 5815
Email info@ecpma.com
Website www.ecpma.com

Contact *Elspeth Cochrane*
FOUNDED 1960. Handles fiction, non-fiction, biographies, screenplays. Subjects have included Richard Burton, Marlon Brando, Sean Connery, Clint Eastwood, Lord Olivier. Also scripts for all media, with special interest in drama. No unsolicited mss. Preliminary letter, synopsis and sae is essential in the first instance.

Clients: Royce Ryton, Robert Tanitch.

Commission: 12.5% ('but this can change; the percentage is negotiable, as is the sum paid to the writer').

Rosica Colin Ltd
1 Clareville Grove Mews, London SW7 5AH
☎ 020 7370 1080   Fax 020 7244 6441

Contact *Joanna Marston*
FOUNDED 1949. Handles all full-length mss, plus theatre, film, television and sound broadcasting but few new writers being accepted. Preliminary letter with return postage essential; writers should outline their writing credits and whether their mss have previously been submitted elsewhere. May take 3–4 months to consider full mss; synopsis preferred in the first instance. No reading fee.

Commission: home 10%; US 15%; translation 20%.

Curtis Brown Group Ltd*
Haymarket House, 28/29 Haymarket, London SW1Y 4SP
☎ 020 7396 6600   Fax 020 7396 0110
Email cb@curtisbrown.co.uk

Also at: 37 Queensferry Street, Edinburgh EH2 4QS
☎ 0131 225 1286/1288   Fax 0131 225 1290

Chairman *Paul Scherer*
Group Managing Director *Jonathan Lloyd*
Directors *Mark Collingbourne* (Finance), *Fiona Inglis* (MD, Australia)
Books, London *Jonathan Lloyd, Anna Davis, Jonny Geller, Hannah Griffiths,*

Ali Gunn, Camilla Hornby, Anthea Morton-Saner, Peter Robinson, Vivienne Schuster, Mike Shaw, Elizabeth Stevens
Books, Edinburgh *Giles Gordon*
Foreign Rights *Diana Mackay, Carol Jackson, Kate Cooper*
Film/TV/Theatre *Nick Marston* (MD, Media Division), *Ben Hall, Philip Patterson*
Presenters *Sue Freathy, Julian Beynon*
Long-established literary agency, whose first sales were made in 1899. Merged with John Farquharson, forming the Curtis Brown Group Ltd in 1989. Also represents directors, designers and presenters. Handles a wide range of subjects including fiction, general non-fiction, children's books and associated rights (including multimedia) as well as film, theatre, TV and radio scripts. Outline for non-fiction and short synopsis for fiction with two or three sample chapters and autobiographical note. No reading fee. Return postage essential.

Commission: home 10%; US and translation 20%.

Overseas associates: in Australia, Canada and the US.

Judy Daish Associates Ltd

2 St Charles Place, London W10 6EG
☎ 020 8964 8811   Fax 020 8964 8966

Contacts *Judy Daish, Sara Stroud, Tracey Elliston*
FOUNDED 1978. Theatrical literary agent. Handles scripts for film, TV, theatre and radio. No books. Preliminary letter essential. No unsolicited mss.

The Dench Arnold Agency

24 D'Arblay Street, London W1F 8EH
☎ 020 7437 4551   Fax 020 7439 1355
Website www.den008charnold.co.uk

Contacts *Elizabeth Dench, Michelle Arnold*
FOUNDED 1972. Handles scripts for TV and film. Unsolicited mss will be read, but a letter with sample of work and CV (plus sae) is preferred.

Clients: Peter Chelsom.

Commission: home 10–15%.

Overseas associates: William Morris/Sanford Gross and C.A.A., Los Angeles.

Laurence Fitch Ltd
Mezzanine, Quadrant House, 80–2 Regent Street, London W1B 5AU
☎ 020 7734 9911
Email information@laurencefitch.com
Website www.laurencefitch.com

Contact *Brendan Davis*
FOUNDED 1952, incorporating the London Play Company (1922) and in association with Film Rights Ltd (1932). Handles children's and horror books, scripts for theatre, film, TV and radio only. No unsolicited mss. Send synopsis with sample scene(s) in the first instance. No reading fee.

Clients: Carlo Ardito, Hindi Brooks, John Chapman and Ray Cooney, John Graham, Glyn Robbins, Gene Stone, the estate of Dodie Smith, Edward Taylor.

Commission: UK 10%; overseas 15%.

Overseas associates: worldwide.

Jill Foster Ltd
9 Barb Mews, Brook Green, London W6 7PA
☎ 020 7602 1263   Fax 020 7602 9336
Email agents@jflagency.com

Contacts *Jill Foster, Alison Finch, Simon Williamson*
FOUNDED 1976. Handles scripts for TV, drama and comedy. No fiction, short stories or poetry. No unsolicited mss; approach by letter in the first instance. No approaches by email. No reading fee.

Clients: Ian Brown, Nick Doughty, Jan Etherington and Gavin Petrie, Phil Ford, Rob Gittins, Jenny Lecoat, Peter Tilbury, Susan Wilkins.

Commission: home 12.5%; books, US and translation 15%.

French's
78 Loudoun Road, London NW8 0NA
☎ 020 7483 4269   Fax 020 7722 0754

Contact *Mark Taylor*
FOUNDED 1973. Handles fiction and non-fiction; and scripts for all media, especially novels and screenplays. No religious or medical books. No unsolicited mss. 'For unpublished authors we offer a reading service at £70 per ms, exclusive of postage.' Interested authors should write in the first instance.

Commission: home 10%.

Futerman, Rose & Associates*
Heston Court Business Estate, 19 Camp Road, Wimbledon, London SW19 4UW
☎ 020 8947 0188   Fax 020 8286 4861
Email guy@futermanrose.co.uk
Website www.futermanrose.co.uk

Contacts *Guy Rose, Alexandra Groom, Christopher Oxford*
FOUNDED 1984. Handles scripts for film, TV and theatre. Commercial fiction and non-fiction with film potential, biography and show business. No unsolicited mss. Send preliminary letter with a brief résumé, detailed synopsis and sae.

Clients: Alexandra Connor, Frank Dickens, Martin Dillon, Iain Duncan Smith, Royston Ellis, Charles Fourie, Russell Warren Howe, Sue Lenier, John McVicar, Angela Meredith, Valerie Grosvenor Myer, Yvonne Ridley, Gordon Thomas, Simon Woodham.

Commission: literature: 12.5–17.5%; drama/screenplays: 15–20%.

Overseas associates: worldwide.

Eric Glass Ltd
25 Ladbroke Crescent, London W11 1PS
☎ 020 7229 9500   Fax 020 7229 6220
Email eglassltd@aol.com

Contact *Janet Glass*
FOUNDED 1934. Handles fiction, non-fiction and scripts for publication or production in all media. No poetry, short stories or children's works. No unsolicited mss. No reading fee.

Clients: Marc Camoletti, Charles Dyer and the estates of Rodney Ackland, Jean Cocteau, Philip King, Robin Maugham, Beverley Nichols, Jack Popplewell, Jean-Paul Sartre, Arthur Schnitzler.

Commission: home 15%; US and translation 20%.

Overseas associates: in the US, Australia, France, Germany, Greece, Holland, Italy, Japan, Poland, Scandinavia, South Africa, Spain.

The Rod Hall Agency Ltd
3 Charlotte Mews, London W1T 4DZ
☎ 020 7637 0706   Fax 020 7637 0807
Email office@rodhallagency.com
Website www.rodhallagency.com

Contacts *Rod Hall, Clare Barker, Charlotte Mann*
FOUNDED 1997. Handles drama for film, TV and theatre. Does not represent writers of episodes for TV series where the format is provided but represents originators of series.

Clients: Simon Beaufoy (*The Full Monty*), Jeremy Brock (*Mrs Brown*), Lee Hall (*Billy Elliot*), Liz Lochhead (*Perfect Days*), Martin McDonagh (*The Beauty Queen of Leenane*). Introductory letter required with brief description of the work to be considered together with CV. No reading fee.

Commission: home 10%; US 15%; translation 20%.

Valerie Hoskins Associates
20 Charlotte Street, London W1T 2NA
☎ 020 7637 4490   Fax 020 7637 4493
Email vha@vhassociates.co.uk

Contacts *Valerie Hoskins, Rebecca Watson*
FOUNDED 1983. Handles scripts for film, TV and radio. Special interests:

feature films, animation and TV. No unsolicited scripts; preliminary letter of introduction essential. No reading fee.

Commission: home 12.5%; US 20% (maximum).

ICM
Oxford House, 76 Oxford Street, London W1D 1BS
☎ 020 7636 6565   Fax 020 7323 0101

Contacts *Greg Hunt, Cathy King, Hugo Young, Michael McCoy, Sue Rodgers, Jessica Sykes*
FOUNDED 1973. Handles film, TV and theatre scripts. No books. No unsolicited mss. Preliminary letter essential. No reading fee.

Commission: 10%.

Overseas associates: ICM, New York/Los Angeles.

Juvenilia
Avington, Near Winchester, Hampshire SO21 1DB
☎ 01962 779656   Fax 01962 779656
Email juvenilia@clara.co.uk

Contact *Rosemary Bromley*
FOUNDED 1973. Handles young/teen fiction and picture books; non-fiction and scripts for TV and radio. No poetry or short stories unless part of a collection or picture-book material. No unsolicited mss. Send preliminary letter with full details of work and biographical outline in first instance. Preliminary letters unaccompanied by return postage will not be answered. Enquiries by phone, fax or email will not be answered.

Clients: Paul Aston, Elisabeth Beresford, Linda Birch, Denis Bond, Terry Deary, Ann Evans, Gaye Hicyilmaz, Tom Holt, Tony Maddox, Phil Mc-Mylor, Anna Perara, Elizabeth Pewsey, Fran and John Pickering, Saviour Pirotta, Eira Reeves, Kelvin Reynolds, James Riordan, Peter Riley, Susan Rollings, Malcolm Rose, Cathy Simpson, Keith West.

Commission: home 10%; US 15%; translation 20%.

Paul Kiernan
PO Box 120, London SW3 4LU
☎ 020 7352 5562

Contact *Paul Kiernan*
FOUNDED 1990. Handles fiction and non-fiction, including autobiography and biography, plus specialist writers for subjects such as cookery or gardening. Also scripts for TV, film, radio and theatre (but TV and film scripts from book-writing clients only). No unsolicited mss. Preferred approach is by letter or personal introduction. Letters should include synopsis and brief biography. No reading fee.

Clients: K. Banta, Lord Chalfont, Ambassador Walter J. P. Curley, Sir Paul Fox.

Commission: home 15%; US 20%.

L & M (Labour and Management Limited)
Milton House, Milton Street, Waltham Abbey, Essex EN9 1EZ
☎ 01992 711511/614527   Fax 01992 711511

Contact *Tricia Sumner*
FOUNDED 1995. Specializes in literary fiction, theatre, TV, radio and film. Special interests multicultural, gay, feminist and anti-establishment writing. No new authors taken on except by recommendation. No unsolicited mss.

Clients: Marion Baraitser, Kathleen Kiirik Bryson, John R. Gordon, Barry Grossman, Angela Lanyon, Catherine Muschamp, Roland Moore, Jeremy Rayner.

Commission: home 15%; overseas 20–25%.

Bill McLean Personal Management Ltd
23B Deodar Road, London SW15 2NP
☎ 020 8789 8191

Contact *Bill McLean*
FOUNDED 1972. Handles scripts for all media. No books. No unsolicited mss. Phone call or introductory letter essential. No reading fee.

Clients: Dwynwen Berry, Graham Carlisle, Pat Cumper, Jane Galletly, Patrick Jones, Tony Jordan, Bill Lyons, John Maynard, Michael McStay, Les Miller, Ian Rowlands, Jeffrey Segal, Richard Shannon, Ronnie Smith, Barry Thomas, Garry Tyler, Frank Vickery, Laura Watson, Mark Wheatley.

Commission: home 10%.

Andrew Mann Ltd*
1 Old Compton Street, London W1D 5JA
☎ 020 7734 4751   Fax 020 7287 9264
Email manscript@onetel.net.uk

Contacts *Anne Dewe, Tina Betts, Sacha Elliot*
FOUNDED 1975. Handles fiction, general non-fiction and film, TV, theatre, radio scripts. No unsolicited mss. Preliminary letter, synopsis and sae essential. No reading fee.

Commission: home 15%; US and translation 20%.

Various overseas associates.

Manuscript ReSearch
PO Box 33, Bicester, Oxfordshire OX26 4ZZ
☎ 01869 323447   Fax 01869 324 096

Contact *Graham Jenkins*
FOUNDED 1988. Principally handles scripts suitable for film/TV outlets. Will only consider book submissions from established clients. Preferred first approach from new contacts is by letter with brief outline and sae.

Commission: home 10%; overseas 20%.

MBA Literary Agents Ltd*
62 Grafton Way, London W1T 5DW
☎ 020 7387 2076   Fax 020 7387 2042
Email <firstname>@mbalit.co.uk

Contacts *Diana Tyler, John Richard Parker, Meg Davis, Laura Longrigg, David Riding*

FOUNDED 1971. Handles fiction and non-fiction, TV, film, radio and theatre scripts. No unsolicited mss. Works in conjunction with agents in most countries. Also UK representative for Writers House, Inc., the Donald Maass Agency and the JABberwocky Agency.

Clients: Campbell Armstrong, A. L. Barker, estate of Harry Bowling, Jeffrey Caine, Glenn Chandler, Andrew Cowan, Patricia Finney, Maggie Furey, Sue Gee, Joanna Hines, B. S. Johnson estate, Robert Jones, Anne McCaffrey, Paul Magrs, Susan Oudot, Sir Roger Penrose, Anne Perry, Gervase Phinn, Christopher Russell, Jim Shields, Iain Sinclair, Steve Strange, Mark Wallington, Patrick Wilde, Paul Wilson, Valerie Windsor, The Chap Magazine (website).

Commission: home 15%; overseas 20%; theatre/TV/radio 10%; film 10–20%.

William Morris Agency (UK) Ltd*
52/53 Poland Street, London W1F 7LX
☎ 020 7534 6800   Fax 020 7534 6900
Website www.wma.com

Managing Director *Stephanie Cabot*
London office FOUNDED 1965. Worldwide theatrical and literary agency with offices in New York, Beverly Hills and Nashville and associates in Sydney. Handles fiction, general non-fiction, TV and film scripts. Mss for books with preliminary letter and s.a.e. to book department. No reading fee.

Commission: TV 10%; UK books 15%; US books and translation 20%.

The Narrow Road Company
182 Brighton Road, Coulsdon, Surrey CR5 2NF
☎ 020 8763 9895   Fax 020 8763 9329
Email coulsdon@narrowroad.co.uk

Contacts *Richard Ireson, Isabella Summers, James Ireson*
FOUNDED 1986. Part of the Narrow Road Group. Theatrical literary agency. Handles scripts for TV, theatre, film and radio. No novels or poetry. No unsolicited mss; approach by letter with CV. Interested in writers with some experience and original ideas.

Clients: Vanessa Brooks, Steve Gooch, David Halliwell, Brian Marshall, Andy Smith.

PFD*
Drury House, 34–43 Russell Street, London WC2B 5HA
☎ 020 7344 1000   Fax 020 7836 9539/7836 9541
Email postmaster@pfd.co.uk
Website www.pfd.co.uk

Joint Chairmen *Anthony Jones, Tim Corrie*
Managing Director *Anthony Baring*
Books *Caroline Dawnay, Michael Sissons, Pat Kavanagh, Charles Walker, Rosemary Canter, Robert Kirby, Simon Trewin, James Gill*
Serial *Pat Kavanagh, Carol MacArthur*
Film/TV *Anthony Jones, Tim Corrie, Norman North, Charles Walker, Vanessa Jones, St John Donald, Rosemary Scoular, Natasha Galloway, Jago Irwin, Louisa Thompson, Lynda Mamy*
Actors *Maureen Vincent, Ginette Chalmers, Dallas Smith, Lindy King, Ruth Young, Lucy Brazier, Kathryn Fleming*
Theatre *Kenneth Ewing, St John Donald, Nicki Stoddart, Rosie Cobbe*
Children's *Rosemary Canter*
Multimedia *Rosemary Scoular*
FOUNDED 1988 as a result of the merger of A. D. Peters & Co. Ltd and Fraser & Dunlop, and was later joined by the June Hall Literary Agency. Handles all sorts of books including fiction and children's, plus scripts for film, theatre, radio and TV material. Prospective clients should write 'a full letter, with an account of what he/she has done and wants to do and enclose, when possible, a detailed outline and sample chapters'. Screenplays and TV scripts should be addressed to 'Film & Script Dept'. Enclose sae. No reading fee. The Children's Dept accepts unsolicited written material in the form of a covering letter, brief plot summary and one paragraph only of text; submissions from illustrators also welcome.

Clients: Julian Barnes, Alan Bennett, Alain de Botton, A. S. Byatt, estate of C. S. Forester, Nicci Gerrard, Robert Harris, Nick Hornby, Clive James, Russell Miller, estate of Nancy Mitford, John Mortimer, Andrew Motion,

Douglas Reeman, Ruth Rendell, Anthony Sampson, Gerald Seymour, Tom Stoppard, Emma Thompson, Joanna Trollope, estate of Evelyn Waugh.

Commission: home 10%; US and translation 20%.

Real Creatives Worldwide
14 Dean Street, London W1D 3RS
☎ 020 7437 4188
Email realcreatives@aol.com

Contacts *Mark Maco, Malcolm Rasala, Simon Boyes, James Allen, Ian Mennea, Darren Guthrie*
FOUNDED 1984. Specializes in drama, science, technology, factual and entertainment. Represents Hollywood TV/film writers and directors, as well as designers, editors, producers and composers. 'Send letter or email requesting a writer's submission agreement covering libel, defamation, plagiarism, etc.' Reading fee: £25. Has a production arm making motion pictures, television, etc.

Sayle Screen Ltd
11 Jubilee Place, London SW3 3TD
☎ 020 7823 3883   Fax 020 7823 3363
Email info@saylescreen.com
Website www.saylescreen.com

Agents *Jane Villiers, Matthew Bates, Toby Moorcroft, Cathy Kehoe*
Specializes in writers and directors for film and television. Also deals with theatre and radio. Works in association with the Sayle Literary Agency representing film and TV rights in novels and non-fiction.

Clients: Shelagh Delaney, Marc Evans, Margaret Forster, Rob Green, Mark Haddon, Christopher Monger, Paul Morrison, Gitta Sereny, Sue Townsend. No unsolicited material without preliminary letter.

The Sharland Organisation Ltd
The Manor House, Manor Street, Raunds, Northamptonshire
NN9 6JW
☎ 01933 626600   Fax 01933 624860
Email tsoshar@aol.com

Contacts *Mike Sharland, Alice Sharland*
FOUNDED 1988. Specializes in national and international film and TV negotiations. Also negotiates multimedia, interactive TV deals and computer game contracts. Handles scripts for film, TV, radio and theatre; also non-fiction. Markets books for film and handles stage, radio, film and TV rights for authors. No scientific, technical or poetry. No unsolicited mss. Preliminary enquiry by letter or phone essential.

Commission: home 15%; US and translation 20%.

Various overseas associates.

Sheil Land Associates Ltd*
(incorporating Richard Scott Simon Ltd 1971 and Christy Moore Ltd 1912)
43 Doughty Street, London WC1N 2LH
☎ 020 7405 9351   Fax 020 7831 2127
Email info@sheilland.co.uk

Agents, UK and US *Sonia Land, Luigi Bonomi, Vivien Green, Amanda Preston*
Film/Theatrical/TV *John Rush, Roland Baggot*
Foreign *Amelia Cummins, Vanessa Forbes*
FOUNDED 1962. Handles full-length general, commercial and literary fiction and non-fiction, including: social politics, business, history, military history, gardening, thrillers, crime, romance, fantasy, drama, biography, travel, cookery and humour, UK and foreign estates. Also theatre, film, radio and TV scripts. Welcomes approaches from new clients either to start or to develop their careers. Preliminary letter with sae essential. No reading fee.

Clients: Peter Ackroyd, Vineet Bhatia, Melvyn Bragg, Stephanie Calman, Catherine Cookson estate, Anna del Conte, Elizabeth Corley, Seamus

Deane, Alan Drury, Erik Durschmied, Alan Garner, Bonnie Greer, Susan Hill, Richard Holmes, John Humphries, Mark Irving, James Long, Richard Mabey, Colin McDowell, Patrick O'Brian estate, HRH The Prince of Wales, Esther Rantzen, Pam Rhodes, Jean Rhys estate, Richard and Judy, Martin Riley, Colin Shindler, Tom Sharpe, Martin Stephen, Brian Sykes, Jeffrey Tayler, Alan Titchmarsh, Rose Tremain, Phil Vickery, John Wilsher, Toby Young.

Commission: home 15%; US and translation 20%.

Overseas associate: Georges Borchardt, Inc. (Richard Scott Simon). UK representatives for Farrar, Straus & Giroux, Inc. US film and TV representation: CAA, APA and others.

Micheline Steinberg Playwrights
409 Triumph House, 187–91 Regent Street, London W1R 7WF
☎ 020 7287 4383
Email steinplays@aol.com

Contacts *Micheline Steinberg, Ginny Sennett*
FOUNDED 1988. Specializes in plays for stage, TV, radio and film. Best approach by preliminary letter (with sae).

Commission: home 10%; elsewhere 15%.

The Tennyson Agency
10 Cleveland Avenue, Wimbledon Chase, London SW20 9EW
☎ 020 8543 5939   Fax 020 8543 5939
Email agency@tenagy.co.uk
Website www.tenagy.co.uk

Contact *Christopher Oxford, Adam Sheldon*
FOUNDED 2001. Specializes in theatre, radio, television and film scripts. Other material considered on an ad hoc basis; humanities bias. No short stories, children's, poetry, travel, military/historical, academic or sport. No unsolicited material; send introductory letter with résumé and proposal/outline of work. No reading fee.

Clients: Vivienne Allen, Alastair Cording, Iain Grant, Julian Howell, Philip Hurd-Wood, Joanna Leigh, John Ryan, Walter Saunders, Diana Ward.

Commission: home 12.5–15%; US and translation 17.5–20%.

J. M. Thurley Management
30 Cambridge Road, Twickenham, Middlesex TW11 8DR
☎ 020 8977 3176   Fax 020 8943 2678
Email JMThurley@aol.com

Contact *Jon Thurley*
FOUNDED 1976. Handles full-length fiction, non-fiction, TV and films. Particularly interested in strong commercial and literary fiction. Will provide creative and editorial assistance to promising writers. No unsolicited mss; approach by letter in the first instance with synopsis and first three chapters plus return postage. No reading fee.

Commission: home, US and translation 15%.

Cecily Ware Literary Agents
19C John Spencer Square, London N1 2LZ
☎ 020 7359 3787   Fax 020 7226 9828
Email info@cecilyware.com

Contacts *Cecily Ware, Gilly Schuster, Warren Sherman*
FOUNDED 1972. Primarily a film and TV script agency representing work in all areas: drama, children's, series/serials, adaptations, comedies, etc. No unsolicited mss or phone calls. Approach in writing only. No reading fee.

Commission: home 10%; US 10–20% by arrangement.

A. P. Watt Ltd*
20 John Street, London WC1N 2DR
☎ 020 7405 6774   Fax 020 7831 2154
Email apw@apwatt.co.uk
Website www.apwatt.co.uk

Directors *Caradoc King, Linda Shaughnessy, Derek Johns, Georgia Garrett, Nick Harris, Natasha Fairweather, Joanna Frank (Associate)*

FOUNDED 1875. The oldest-established literary agency in the world. Handles full-length typescripts, including children's books, screenplays for film and TV. No poetry, academic or specialist works. No unsolicited mss accepted.

Clients: Trezza Azzopardi, Quentin Blake, Marika Cobbold, Helen Dunmore, Nicholas Evans, Giles Foden, Esther Freud, Janice Galloway, Martin Gilbert, Nadine Gordimer, Linda Grant, Colin and Jacqui Hawkins, Reginald Hill, Michael Holroyd, Michael Ignatieff, Mick Jackson, Philip Kerr, Dick King-Smith, India Knight, John Lanchester, Alison Lurie, Jan Morris, Jill Murphy, Andrew O'Hagan, Susie Orbach, Tony Parsons, Caryl Phillips, Philip Pullman, Jancis Robinson, Jon Ronson, Elaine Showalter, Zadie Smith, Graham Swift, Colm Tóibín, Fiona Walker and the estates of Wodehouse, Graves and Maugham.

Commission: home 10%; US and translation 20%.

Josef Weinberger Plays

12–14 Mortimer Street, London W1T 3JJ
☎ 020 7580 2827   Fax 020 7436 9616
Email general.info@jwmail.co.uk
Website www.josef-weinberger.com

Contact *Michael Callahan*
Formerly Warner Chappell Plays, Josef Weinberger is now both agent and publisher of scripts for the theatre. No unsolicited mss; introductory letter essential. No reading fee.

Clients: Ray Cooney, John Godber, Peter Gordon, Debbie Isitt, Arthur Miller, Sam Shepard, John Steinbeck.

Overseas associates: in the US, Canada, Australia, New Zealand, India, South Africa and Zimbabwe.

Writers' Courses, Circles and Workshops

Courses

England

Buckinghamshire

National Film and Television School
Beaconsfield Studios, Station Road, Beaconsfield, Buckinghamshire
HP9 1LG
☎ 01494 731425   Fax 01494 674 042
Email admin@nftsfilm-tv.ac.uk
Website www.nftsfilm-tv.ac

Intensive, one-year, full-time screenwriting course for people with established writing skills but little or no experience of writing for the screen. One-year, part-time course for people with some screenwriting experience who are ready to focus on feature script development. Completion of both courses, plus short dissertation, is required for the award of an MA. Courses develop an understanding of the practical stages involved in the making of film and television drama. Range of work covers comedy, TV series and serials, short-film, adaptation and narrative. The ability to collaborate successfully is developed through exercises and projects shared with students in other specializations. 'We encourage the formation of working partnerships which will continue after graduation.'

Cheshire

Burton Manor College

Burton Village, Neston, Cheshire CH64 5SJ
☎ 0151 336 5172   Fax 0151 336 6586
Email enquiry@burtonmanor.com
Website www.burtonmanor.org

Wide variety of short courses, residential and non-residential, on writing and literature including: *Writing About Travel; Plays and Players; The Internet for Writing; Writing for Drama.* Easter writing school and literature summer school. Full details in brochure.

Cornwall

The Indian King Arts Centre

Fore Street, Camelford, Cornwall PL32 9PG
☎ 01840 212111
Email info@indianking.co.uk
Website www.indianking.co.uk

Director *Helen Jagger Wood*
FOUNDED in 1994 to offer people from all walks of life the opportunity to explore and develop their creative writing skills with the support of published writers. The annual programme of residential writing courses starts with the annual poetry festival in memory of Jon Silkin, held on the last weekend before Easter, and continues into the autumn. Visiting writers offer two-day courses (Saturday/Sunday) or four-and-a-half-day courses (Monday evening to Friday evening inclusive) in poetry, short and long fiction and drama. The centre offers writing classes, readings and book launches throughout the year on a weekly, fortnightly and monthly basis as well as having a poetry library.

Derbyshire

University of Derby
Student Information Centre, Kedleston Road, Derby DE22 1GB
☎ 01332 622236   Fax 01332 622754
Email J.Bains@derby.ac.uk (prospectus requests only)
Website www.derby.ac.uk

Contact *Graham Parker*
With upwards of 300 students, *Creative Writing* runs twenty-one modules as part of the undergraduate degree programme. These include: *Storytelling; Poetry; Playwriting; Writing for TV and Radio; Screenwriting; The Short Story; Journalism; Writing for Children*. The courses are all led by practising writers.

Devon

Arvon Foundation (See page 194.)

Dartington College of Arts
Totnes, Devon TQ9 6EJ
☎ 01803 862224   Fax 01803 861666
Email registry@dartington.ac.uk
Website www.dartington.ac.uk

BA(Hons.) course in *Performance Writing*: exploratory approach to writing as it relates to performance. The course is part of a performance arts programme which encourages interdisciplinary work with arts management, music, theatre, visual performance. The programme includes a range of elective modules in digital media and emerging art forms which are available to all students. Contact Subject Director, Performance Writing *Rick Allsopp*.

University of Exeter
Exeter, Devon EX4 4QW
☎ 01392 264580
Website www.ex.ac.uk/drama

Contact The Secretary, Drama Department, Thornlea, New North Road, Exeter EX4 4LA
BA(Hons.) in *Drama* with a third-year option in *Playwriting*. M.Phil. and Ph.D. in *Performance Practice* (including *Playwriting*).

Dorset

Bournemouth University
Bournemouth Media School, Poole House, Talbot Campus, Fern Barrow, Poole, Dorset BH12 5BB
☎ 01202 595553   Fax 01202 595530

Programme Administrator *Katrina King*
Three-year, full-time BA(Hons.) course in *Scriptwriting for Film and Television*.

Gloucestershire

Wye Valley Arts Centre
The Coach House, Mork, St Briavel's, Lydney, Gloucestershire GL15 6QH
☎ 01594 530214/01291 689463   Fax 01594 530321
Email wyeart@cwcom.net
Website www.wyeart.cwc.net

Residential courses (Monday to Friday) held at The Coach House, a country house near Tintern Abbey in the Wye Valley, include: *Creative Writing, Writing for Radio; Fiction Workshop*. 'All styles and abilities. Companions and other guests not taking the courses are welcome to stay.'

Hampshire

King Alfred's College
Winchester, Hampshire SO22 4NR
☎ 01962 841515   Fax 01962 842280
Website www.kingalfreds.ac.uk

Three-year degree course in *Drama, Theatre and Television Studies*, including *Writing for Devised Community Theatre* and *Writing for Television Documentary*. Contact the Admissions Office (☎ 01962 827262).

MA course in *Theatre for Development*, a one-year, full-time course with major project overseas or in the UK. MA course in *Writing for Children* available on either a one- or two-year basis. Contact the Admissions Office (☎ 01962 827235).

Greater London

Arvon Foundation
Administration: 2nd Floor, 42A Buckingham Palace Road, London SW1W ORE
☎ 020 7931 7611   Fax 020 7963 0961
Website www.arvonfoundation.org

Totleigh Barton, Sheepwash, Beaworthy, Devon EX21 5S
☎ 01409 231338   Fax 01409 231144
Email t-barton@arvonfoundation.org

Lumb Bank, Heptonstall, Hebden Bridge, West Yorkshire HX7 6DF
☎ 01422 843714   Fax 01422 843714
Email l-bank@arvonfoundation.org

Moniack Mhor, Teavarran, Kiltarlity, Beauly, Inverness-shire IV4 7HT
☎ 01463 741675
Email m-mhor@arvonfoundation.org

President *Terry Hands*
Chairman *Prue Skene, CBE*
National Director *Helen Chaloner*
FOUNDED 1968. Offers people of any age over 16 and any background the opportunity to live and work with professional writers. Four-and-a-half-day residential courses are held throughout the year at Arvon's three centres, covering poetry, fiction, drama, writing for children, songwriting and the performing arts. Bursaries towards the cost of course fees are

available for those on low incomes, the unemployed, students and pensioners. Runs a biennial poetry competition.

The Central School of Speech and Drama
Embassy Theatre, Eton Avenue, London NW3 3HY
☎ 020 7722 8183   Fax 020 7722 4132

Contact *Nick Wood, Writing and Dramaturgy Tutor*
MA in *Advanced Theatre Practice*. One-year, full-time course aimed at providing a grounding in principal areas of professional theatre practice – writing, dramaturgy, directing, performance, puppetry and design – with an emphasis on collaboration between the various strands. 'The writing and dramaturgy strands are particularly suitable for those wishing to work in a lively and stimulating atmosphere creating, with other practitioners, new work for the theatre.' Prospectus available.

The City Literary Institute
Humanities Dept, Stukeley Street, London WC2B 5LJ
☎ 020 7430 0542   Fax 020 7405 3347
Email humanities@citylit.ac.uk

The Writing School offers a wide range of courses from *Ways Into Creative Writing* and *Writing for Children* to *Playwriting* and *Writing Short Stories*. The creative writing classes may be one-day Saturday classes, weekly sessions over one or more terms, or one-week intensive workshops. The department offers information and advice during term time.

City University
Department of Continuing Education, Northampton Square,
London EC1V 0HB
☎ 020 7040 5060
Email conted@city.ac.uk
Website www.city.ac.uk/conted/cfa.htm

Creative writing classes include: *Writer's Workshop*; *Wordshop* (poetry); *Writing Comedy*; *Playwright's Workshop*; *Writing Freelance Articles for Newspa-*

pers;

LISTINGS

pers; *Writing about Travel*; *Creative Writing*; *Fiction: Short and Long*; *Feature Journalism*; *Writing for Children*.

Middlesex University
School of Humanities, White Hart Lane, London N17 8HR
☎ 020 8411 5000   Fax 020 8411 6652
Email tmadmissions@mdx.ac.uk
Website www.mdx.ac.uk

The UK's longest-established writing degree offers a single or joint honours programme in *Writing and Media* (full- or part-time). This modular programme in creative and media writing gives students an opportunity to explore journalism, poetry, prose fiction and dramatic writing for a wide range of genres and audiences. Option for work experience in the media and publishing. Contact Admissions or *Maggie Butt*, programme leader. (Email m.butt@mdx.ac.uk).

MA in *Writing* (full-time, part-time day and evening classes) includes a specialist strand in Asian and black British writing, approaches to the short story and novel; lectures and workshops from established writers. Options in poetry and scriptwriting are awaiting validation. Contact *Sue Gee* ☎ 020 8411 5941 (Email s.gee@mdx.ac.uk).

University of Surrey Roehampton
School of Arts, Roehampton Lane, London SW15 5PU
☎ 020 8392 3230   Fax 020 8392 3289
Website www.roehampton.ac.uk

Three-year BA(Hons.) programmes in *Drama and Theatre Studies* and *Film and Television Studies* include courses on writing for stage and screen.

University of Westminster
School of Communication and Creative Industries, Harrow Campus, Watford Road, Harrow, Middlesex HA1 3TP
☎ 020 7911 5903   Fax 020 7911 5955
Email harrow-admissions@wmin.ac.uk
Website www.wmin.ac.uk

Courses include part-time MAs available in *Journalism Studies; Film and Television Studies.*

Greater Manchester

The Writers Bureau
Sevendale House, 7 Dale Street, Manchester M1 1JB
☎ 0161 228 2362   Fax 0161 236 9440
Email advisory@writersbureau.com
Website www.writersbureau.com

Comprehensive home-study writing course with personal tuition service from professional writers (fee: £249). Fiction, non-fiction, articles, short stories, novels, TV, radio and drama all covered in detail. Trial period, guarantee and no time limits. ODLQC accredited. Quote Ref. EH03. Free enquiry line: 0800 856 2008.

University of Salford
Postgraduate Admissions, Dept. of Arts, Media and Social Sciences, Adelphi Building, Peru Street, Salford M3 6EQ
☎ 0161 295 6027
Email r.humphrey@salford.ac.uk
Website www.smmp.salford.ac.uk

MA in *Television and Radio Scriptwriting*. Two-year, part-time course taught by professional writers and producers. Also offers a number of master classes with leading figures in the radio and television industry.

Merseyside

University of Liverpool
Centre for Continuing Education, 19 Abercromby Square, Liverpool L69 7ZG
☎ 0151 794 6900/6952 (24 hours)   Fax 0151 794 2544
Website www.liv.ac.uk/conted

Head of Creative Arts *Keith Birch*
Courses include: *Introduction to Creative Writing; The Short Story and the*

Novel; Introduction to Writing Poetry; Introduction to Scripting for Radio and Television; Introduction to Writing Journalism; Science Fiction and Fantasy; Travel Writing; Songwriting; Theatre Playwrights Workshop; Scriptwriting: Situation Comedy; Scriptwriting: Film and Television. Most courses are run in the evening over ten or twenty weeks but there are some linked Saturday and weekday courses on offer. Students have the option of accreditation towards a university award in *Creative Writing.* Some of the above courses are also part of the university's part-time flexible degree pathway (Comb. Hons., Arts). No pre-entry qualifications required. Fees vary with concessions for the unwaged and those in receipt of benefit.

Somerset

Bath Spa University College
Newton Park, Bath BA2 9BN
☎ 01225 875875   Fax 01225 875444
Email enquiries@bathspa.ac.uk
Website www.bathspa.ac.uk

Admissions Officer *Clare Brandram Jones*
Postgraduate Diploma/MA in *Creative Writing.* A course for creative writers wanting to develop their work. Teaching is by published writers in the novel, poetry, short stories and scriptwriting. In recent years, several students from this course have received contracts from publishers for novels, awards for poetry and short stories and have had work produced on BBC Radio.

Surrey

Royal Holloway
University of London, Egham Hill, Egham, Surrey TW20 0EX
☎ 01784 443922   Fax 01784 431018
Email drama@rhul.ac.uk

Contacts *Dan Rebellato, David Wiles*
Three-year BA course in *Theatre Studies* during which playwriting can be studied as an option in the second or third year. MA *Theatre (Playwriting),* a one- or two-year (full- or part-time) postgraduate degree.

Sussex

University of Sussex

Centre for Continuing Education, Education Development
Building, Falmer, Brighton, East Sussex BN1 9RG
☎ 01273 678537   Fax 01273 678848
Email y.d.barnes@sussex.ac.uk
Website www.sussex.ac.uk

Contact (for all courses) *Yvonne Barnes*
Postgraduate Diploma in *Dramatic Writing*: the student is treated as a
commissioned writer working in theatre, TV, radio or film with professional directors and actors. Includes workshops, master classes and a
residential weekend. Sixteen months, part-time; convenor: *Richard Crane*.
Certificate in *Creative Writing*: short fiction, novel and poetry for imaginative writers. Two years, part-time; convenors: *Richard Crane, Mark Slater*.

West Midlands

University of Birmingham

School of Education, Selly Oak, Birmingham B29 6LL
☎ 0121 414 3413   Fax 0121 414 8067
Email S.G.Roseten@bham.ac.uk

Certificate of Higher Education in *Creative Writing* – two years, part-time in
Birmingham and Worcester. Day or evening plus occasional classes,
depending on venue, including theory and practice of writing in a wide
range of literary genres. Course brochures are available from the address
above. Please specify which course you are interested in. Progression routes
to Diploma and degree. Students who can demonstrate qualifications/
writing skills equivalent to Certificate level may apply to join the Diploma
in *Creative Writing*. Additional courses are available at the Selly Oak
campus and in Worcestershire.

The University also offers an M.Phil. in *Playwriting Studies* established by
playwright David Edgar in 1989. Contact *April Di Angelis*, course director
at the Department of Drama and Theatre Arts (☎ 0121 414 5790).

Yorkshire

Arvon Foundation (See page 196.)

University of Hull
Scarborough Campus, Filey Road, Scarborough, North Yorkshire
YO11 3AZ
☎ 01723 362392   Fax 01723 370815
Website www.hull.ac.uk

Director of Studies *David Hughes*
BA Single Honours in *Theatre Studies* incorporates *Writing for Performance* and *Writing for Theatre*. Works closely with the Stephen Joseph Theatre and its artistic director Alan Ayckbourn. The theatre sustains a policy for staging new writers. The campus hosts the annual National Student Drama Festival which includes the International Student Playscript Competition (details from the National Information Centre for Student Drama; email nsdf@hull.ac.uk).

Leeds Metropolitan University
H505, City Site, Calverley Street, Leeds, West Yorkshire LS1 3HE
☎ 0113 283 2600 ext 3860
Email s.morton@lmu.ac.uk
Website www.lmu.ac.uk

Administrator *Samantha Morton*
Offers a Postgraduate Certificate/Diploma/MA in *Screenwriting (Fiction)*.

Ireland

Dingle Writing Courses Ltd
Ballyneanig, Ballyferriter, Tralee, Co. Kerry, Republic of Ireland
☎ 00 353 66 9154990   Fax 00 353 66 9154992
Email info@dinglewriting.com
Website www.dinglewriting.com

Directors *Abigail Joffe, Nicholas McLachlan*
A summer and autumn programme of weekend and five-day residential courses for beginners and experienced writers alike. Tutored by professional writers the courses take place in 'an inspirational setting overlooking Inch strand'. The programme includes poetry, fiction, starting to write and writing for theatre as well as special themed courses. Past tutors have included Jennifer Johnston, Paul Durcan, Anne Enright, Paula Meeham, Jim Perrin, Mary O'Malley, Graham Mort and Michael Donaghy. Writing courses for schools are also available. Brochures and further information from programme director *Camilla Dinkel* at the address above.

Scotland

Arvon Foundation (See page 196.)

Wales

University of Glamorgan
Treforest, Pontypridd CF37 1DL
☎ 01443 482551
Website www.glam.ac.uk

Director, The National Centre for Writing *Prof. Tony Curtis, FRSL*
M.Phil. in *Writing* – a two-year part-time degree for writers of fiction and poets. Established 1993. Contact *Prof. Tony Curtis* at the School of Humanities and Social Sciences.

MA in *Scriptwriting (Theatre, TV or Radio)* – a two-year part-time degree for scriptwriters. Contact *Dr Richard J. Hand*. Also, BA *Creative and Professional Writing* – a three-year course for undergraduates. Contact *Dr Matthew Francis*.

University of Wales, Bangor
Department of English, College Road, Bangor LL57 2DG
☎ 01248 382102   Fax 01248 382102
Email els029@bangor.ac.uk

Ph.D. *Creative and Critical Writing*; MA *Creative Studies (Creative Writing)*; BA *English Literature with Creative Writing*; BA *English Language with Creative Writing*; BA *French with Creative Writing*; BA *German with Creative Writing*. Also MA *Creative Studies (Film Practice)*; MA *Creative Studies (Drama Practice)*; MA *Creative Studies (Media Practice)*. The Centre for the Creative and Performing Arts launched the UK national database on creative writing education in universities and colleges and was the location of the first national and international conferences on creative writers on campus. It is the location of the research programme, Creative Writing in Universities.

Writers' Holiday at Caerlon
School Bungalow, Church Road, Pontnewydd, Cwmbran NP44 1AT
☎ 01633 489438
Email writersholiday@lineone.net
Website www.writersholiday.net

Contact *Anne Hobbs*
Annual six-day conference for writers of all standards held in the summer at the University of Wales' Caerlon campus. Courses, lectures, concert and excursion all included in the fee (£324 in 2002). Private, single and en-suite, full board accommodation. Courses in 2002 included *Writing for Publication*, *Writing Poetry*, *Writing Romantic Fiction* and *Writing for the Radio*.

Circles and Workshops

Kops and Ryan Advanced Playwriting Workshops
41B Canfield Gardens, London NW6 3JL
☎ 020 7624 2940/7263 8740

Tutors *Bernard Kops, Tom Ryan*
Three ten-week terms per year beginning in September. Students may join

course any term. Workshops on Tuesday, 7 p.m.–10 p.m. or Thursday, 7 p.m.–10 p.m., or Saturday, 2 p.m.–5 p.m. Small groups. Focus on structure, character, language, meaning and style through written and improvised exercises, readings of scenes from students' current work and readings of full-length plays. Two actors attend each session. Also, instruction in film technique and private tutorials. Call for details.

North West Playwrights (NWP)
18 St Margaret's Chambers, 5 Newton Street, Manchester M1 1HL
☎ 0161 237 1978   Fax 0161 237 1978
Email newplaysnw@hotmail.com
Website www.newplaysnw.com

FOUNDED 1982. Award-winning organization whose aim is to develop and promote new theatre writing. Operates a script reading service, classes and script development scheme and *The Lowdown* newsletter. Services available to writers in the region only. Also disburses grants to support commissions, residencies, etc.

Pier Playwrights
PO Box 141, Brighton, East Sussex BN2 1LZ
☎ 01273 625132
Email admin@pierplaywrights.co.uk
Website www.pierplaywrights.co.uk

Contact *Chris Taylor*
Run by playwrights for playwrights in the south-east region, Pier Playwrights meets regularly to support writers in all drama forms. Workshops by visiting professionals and skill-sharing workshops in particular media such as screenwriting or writing for radio. The monthly newsletter keeps members informed of writing opportunities and in touch with the industry. Subscription: £15 (individual); £5 (unwaged); £30 (company).

Screenwriters' Workshop
Suffolk House, 1–8 Whitfield Place, London W1T 5JU
☎ 020 7387 5511
Email screenoffice@tiscali.co.uk
Website www.lsw.org.uk

Established 1983. Formerly London Screenwriters' Workshop, the SW is open to writers from all over Britain and Europe. The workshop is an educational charity whose aim is to help writers into the film and TV industries. Many high-profile members. Offers a rolling programme of tuition, networking and events including guest speakers and showcasing opportunities. Membership: £40 p.a. Runs *Feedback* – a script reading service with reduced rates for SW members. Contact *R. Wheeler* (Email ritaw@tiscali.co.uk).

Southwest Scriptwriters
☎ 0117 909 5522   Fax 0117 907 3816
Website www.southwest-scriptwriters.co.uk

Secretary *John Colborn*
FOUNDED 1994 to offer encouragement and advice to those writing for stage, screen, radio and TV in the region. The group, which attracts professional writers, enthusiasts and students, meets regularly at the Theatre Royal, Bristol to read aloud and provide critical feedback on members' work, discuss writing technique and exchange market information. Mike Bullen, writer of ITV's *Cold Feet*, acts as honorary president. Subscription: £5 p.a.

Sussex Playwrights' Club
2 Brunswick Mews, Hove, East Sussex BN3 1HD
☎ 01273 730106
Website www.newventure.org.uk

Secretary *Dennis Evans*
FOUNDED 1935. Aims to encourage the writing of plays for stage, radio and TV by giving monthly dramatic readings of members' work by experienced actors, mainly from local drama groups. Gives constructive,

critical suggestions as to how work might be improved, and suggests possible marketing. Membership is not confined to writers but is open to all who are interested in theatre in all its forms, and all members are invited to take part in discussions. Guests are always welcome at a nominal £1. Meetings held at New Venture Theatre, Bedford Place, Brighton, East Sussex. Subscription: £7 p.a. Contact the secretary for details or visit the 'features' page on the website.

Yorkshire Playwrights
3 Trinity Road, Scarborough, North Yorkshire YO11 2TD
☎ 01723 367449   Fax 01723 367449
Email ScarTam@aol.com
Website www.yorkshireplaywrights.com

Administrator *Ian Watson*
FOUNDED 1989 out of an initiative by Jude Kelly and William Weston of the West Yorkshire Playhouse. A group of professional writers of plays for stage, TV and radio whose aims are to encourage the writing and performance of new plays in Yorkshire. Open to any writers living in Yorkshire who are members, preferably, of the Writers' Guild, or the Society of Authors. Contact the administrator for an information sheet.

UK Publishers with Drama Lists

Amber Lane Press Ltd
Cheorl House, Church Street, Charlbury, Oxfordshire OX7 3PR
☎ 01608 810024   Fax 01608 810024
Email jamberlane@aol.com

Chairman *Brian Clark*
Managing Director/Editorial Head *Judith Scott*
FOUNDED 1979 to publish modern play texts. Publishes plays and books on the theatre. About four titles a year. 'Expressly *not* interested in poetry.' No unsolicited mss. Synopses and ideas welcome.

Playwrights include: Samuel Adamson, Carlo Ardito, 'Biyi Bandele, Steven Berkoff, Michael Burrell, Anton Chekhov, Brian Clark, Barry Collins, Keith Dewhurst, Nell Dunn, Charles Dyer, Donald Freed, Maxim Gorky, Richard Harris, Ronald Harwood, Jim Hawkins, Roy Kift, Bob Larby, Tony Marchant, Rosemary Mason, Sean Mathias, Mark Medoff, Julian Mitchell, Fidelis Morgan and Giles Havergal, Mary O'Malley, Caryl Phillips, Alan Plater, Manuel Puig, Thomas W. Robertson, James Saunders, Anthony Shaffer, Martin Sherman, Kunio Shimizu, Roger Stennett, August Strindberg, William Sutcliffe and Russell Labey, Peter Terson, Heidi Thomas, Brian Thompson, John Wain, Hugh Whitemore, Snoo Wilson, David Wood, Sheila Yeger.

A. & C. Black (Publishers) Ltd

Alderman House, 37 Soho Square, London W1D 3QZ
☎ 020 7758 0200   Fax 020 7758 0222
Email enquiries@acblack.com
Website www.acblack.com

Chairman *Nigel Newton*
Managing Director *Jill Coleman*
Publishes new drama in the New Mermaid series
Playwrights include: George Chapman, John Dryden, George Farquhar, John Ford, Ben Jonson, Thomas Middleton.

Marion Boyars Publishers Ltd

24 Lacy Road, London SW15 1NL
☎ 020 8788 9522   Fax 020 8789 8122
Email marion.boyars@talk21.com
Website www.marionboyars.co.uk

Editor *Julia Silk*
Editor, Non-fiction *Ken Hollings*
FOUNDED 1975, formerly Calder and Boyars. Publishes biography and autobiography, fiction, literature and criticism, music, philosophy, psychology, sociology and anthropology, theatre and drama, film and cinema, women's studies.

Playwrights include: Amiri Baraka, Elias Canetti, Seamus Finnegan, Peter Gill, Witold Gombrowicz, Tadeusz Kantor, Charles Marowitz, Peter Redgrove, Tadeusz Rozewicz, Anthony Shaffer, Yevgeny Shvarts, Peter Weiss, Edgar White.

Brown, Son & Ferguson, Ltd

4–10 Darnley Street, Glasgow G41 2SD
☎ 0141 429 1234   Fax 0141 420 1694
Email info@skipper.co.uk
Website www.skipper.co.uk

Chairman/Joint Managing Director *T. Nigel Brown*
FOUNDED 1850. Publishes Scottish one-act/three-act plays.

Playwrights include: Agnes Adam, Bob Adams, C. Stewart Black, George S. Carruthers, Alan Cochrane, Joe Corrie, Norman Donaldson, Dorothy Dunbar, Jack House, Robert Kemp, Howard M. Lockhart, William Maconachie, Angus MacVicar, Alan Richardson, James Scotland, Hal D. Stewart, D. George Waddell, T. M. Watson, Gordon Wright.

Calder Publications Ltd

51 The Cut, London SE1 8LF

☎ 020 7633 0599   Fax 020 7928 5930

Email info@calderpublications.com

Chairman/Managing Director/Editorial Head *John Calder*

Formerly John Calder (Publishers) Ltd. A publishing company which has grown around the tastes and contacts of John Calder, the iconoclast of the literary establishment. The list has a reputation for controversial and opinion-forming publications; Samuel Beckett is perhaps the most prestigious name. The list includes all of Beckett's prose and poetry. Publishes autobiography, biography, drama, literary fiction, literary criticism, music, opera, poetry, politics, sociology, ENO opera guides. No new material accepted.

Authors include: Antonin Artaud, Marguerite Duras, Martin Esslin, Erich Fried, Robert Menasse, Robert Pinget, Luigi Pirandello, Alain Robbe-Grillet, Nathalie Sarraute, L. F. Celine, Eva Figes, Claude Simon, Howard Barker (plays).

Chapman Publishing

4 Broughton Place, Edinburgh EH1 3RX

☎ 0131 557 2207   Fax 0131 556 9565

Email editor@chapman-pub.co.uk

Website www.chapman-pub.co.uk

Managing Editor *Joy Hendry*

Publishes poetry, drama, short stories, books of contemporary importance in twentieth-century Scotland. No unsolicited mss; synopses and ideas for books welcome.

Playwrights include: George Gunn, George Rosie.

Cressrelles Publishing Co. Ltd

10 Station Road Industrial Estate, Colwall, Malvern, Worcestershire WR13 6RN
☎ 01684 540154   Fax 01684 540154
Email simonsmith@cressrelles4drama.fsbusiness.co.uk

Managing Director *Leslie Smith*
Publishes plays and theatre texts under its Kenyon-Deane and J. Garnet Miller Ltd imprint.

Playwrights include: Vera Arlett, M. E. Atkinson, Sam Bate, Derek Benfield, Jean-Jacques Bernard, Peter Blackmore, Stephen Blandford, G. E. Bollans, Antony Booth, Jack Booth, Margaret Bower, Eileen Brandon, Nicholas Corder, Dymphna Cusack, Frederic Daniels, Doris M. Day, Joyce Dennys, William Dinner, Jean Garstang, Don Hill, Kenneth James, Soinbhe Lally, Jack Last, Claudia Leaf, Kay Macaulife, Andrea MacPhail, Kathy Mead, Ros Moruzzi, Edward Murch, John H. Newmeir, Madge Pemberton, Kenneth Pickering, Warren Chetham Strode, John Stuart-Anderson, Barbara van Kampen, John Waterhouse, Keith Williams, Rob Wise, Philip Worner.

Faber & Faber Ltd

3 Queen Square, London WC1N 3AU
☎ 020 7465 0045   Fax 020 7465 0034
Website www.faber.co.uk

Chief Executive *Stephen Page*
Editor: Plays *Peggy Paterson*
Geoffrey Faber FOUNDED the company in the 1920s, with T. S. Eliot as an early recruit to the board. The original list was based on contemporary poetry and plays (the distinguished backlist includes Auden, Eliot and MacNeice). Publishes poetry and drama, children's, fiction, film, music, politics, biography, wine.

Playwrights/screenwriters include: Woody Allen, Samuel Beckett, Alan Bennett, John Boorman, Joel and Ethan Coen, Brian Friel, David Hare, John Hodge, Patrick Marber, Harold Pinter, Tom Stoppard, Martin Scorsese, Quentin Tarantino.

Samuel French Ltd

52 Fitzroy Street, London W1T 5JR
☎ 020 7387 9373   Fax 020 7387 2161
Email theatre@samuelfrench-london.co.uk
Website www.samuelfrench-london.co.uk

Chairman *Charles R. Van Nostrand*
Managing Director *Vivien Goodwin*
FOUNDED 1830 with the object of acquiring acting rights and publishing plays. Publishes plays only. About fifty titles a year. Unsolicited mss considered only after initial submission of synopsis and specimen scene. Such material should be addressed to the Performing Rights Department.

Nick Hern Books

The Glasshouse, 49A Goldhawk Road, London W12 8QP
☎ 020 8749 4953   Fax 020 8735 0250
Email info@nickhernbooks.demon.co.uk
Website www.nickhernbooks.co.uk

Chairman/Managing Director *Nick Hern*
FOUNDED 1988. Publishes books on theatre and film: from how-to and biography to plays and screenplays. About thirty titles a year. No unsolicited playscripts. Synopses, ideas and proposals for other theatre material welcome. Not interested in material unrelated to the theatre or cinema.

Playwrights include: Henry Adam, Aristophanes, Kate Atkinson, Patrick Barlow, Aphra Behn, Simon Bennett, Simon Block, Howard Brenton, Georg Büchner, Mikhail Bulgakov, Calderón, Caryl Churchll, Jean Cocteau, William Congreve, Dominic Cooke, Mike Cullen, Ariel Dorfman, John Dryden, David Edgar, Euripides, Kevin Elyot, George Farquhar, Georges Feydeau, William Gaminara, Julian Garner, Pam Gems, Sue Glover, Nikolai Gogol, Simon Gray, Stephen Greenhorn, David Haig, Chris Hannan, Robert Holman, Henrik Ibsen, Stephen Jeffreys, Marie Jones, Ben Jonson, Ayub Khan Din, Larry Kramer, Tony Kushner, Mike Leigh, Liz Lochhead, Doug Lucie, Owen McCafferty, Conor McPherson, Christopher Marlowe, Aidan Matthews, Arthur Miller, Gary Mitchell, Molière, Kim Morrissey, Rona Munro, Eugene O'Neill, Peter Nichols, Mark O'Rowe, Joe Orton, Stuart Paterson,

Luigi Pirandello, Terence Rattigan, Billy Roche, Diane Samuels, Friedrich Schiller, Richard Brinsley Sheridan, Joshua Sobol, Sophocles, August Strindberg, Jessica Townsend, Michel Tremblay, Enda Walsh, Paul Webb, John Webster, Frank Wedekind, Oscar Wilde, Nicholas Wright, William Wycherley.

Macmillan Publishers Ltd

Pan Macmillan, 20 New Wharf Road, London N1 9RR
☎ 020 7014 6000   Fax 020 7014 6001
Website www.panmacmillan.com

Chief Executive *Richard Charkin*
FOUNDED 1843. Macmillan is one of the largest publishing houses in Britain, publishing approximately 1,400 titles a year.

Screenwriters/playwrights include: Colin Dexter *Morse*; Ayub Khan Din *East is East*; Graham Lineham and A. Matthews *Father Ted*; Lynda La Plante *Prime Suspect*; Minette Walters *The Sculptress*; W. B. Yeats Collected Plays.

Methuen Publishing Ltd

215 Vauxhall Bridge Road, London SW1V 1EJ
☎ 020 7798 1600   Fax 020 7233 9827
Website www.methuen.co.uk

Managing Director *Peter Tummons*
Publishing Director *Max Eilenberg*
FOUNDED 1889. Divisions: General, Drama, Film, Theatre. No unsolicited mss. Prefers to be approached via agents or a letter of enquiry.

Playwrights include: Aeschylus, Jean Anouilh, Aristophanes, 'Biyi Bandele, Clive Barker, Peter Barnes, J. M. Barrie, Sebastian Barry, Alistair Beaton, Dermot Bolger, Robert Bolt, Edward Bond, Bertolt Brecht, Ken Campbell, Richard Cameron, Jim Cartwright, Caryl Churchill, Noël Coward, Sarah Daniels, Nick Darke, Nick Dear, Eduardo de Filippo, Shelagh Delaney, Claire Dowie, Andrea Dunbar, David Edgar, Charlotte Eilenberg, David Eldridge, Euripides, Dario Fo, Michael Frayn, Max Frisch, Sue Glover, John Godber, Paul Godfrey, Nikolai Gogol, Carlo Goldoni, Maxim Gorky, David

Greig, Nick Grosso, John Guare, Lee Hall, Peter Handke, David Hare, Anne Harvey, Jonathan Harvey, Iain Heggie, Robert Holman, Declan Hughes, Terry Johnson, Sarah Kane, Charlotte Keatley, Barrie Keeffe, Bernard Marie Koltes, Howard Korder, Elizabeth Kuti, David Lan, Bryony Lavery, Robert Lepage, Deborah Levy, Doug Lucie, Martin McDonagh, John McGrath, Duncan McLean, Elizabeth Maclennan, Terrence McNally, David Mamet, Patrick Marber, Mustapha Matura, Arthur Miller, Anthony Minghella, Peter Moffatt, Peter Morris, Tom Murphy, Phyllis Nagy, Anthony Neilson, Peter Nichols, Joseph O'Connor, Eugene O'Brien, Joe O'Byrne, Donal O'Kelly, Joe Orton, Philip Osment, Gary Owen, Louise Page, Stewart Parker, Joe Penhall, Luigi Pirandello, Alan Plater, Stephen Poliakoff, David Rabe, Terence Rattigan, Mark Ravenhill, Christina Reid, Philip Ridley, Billy Roche, Willy Russell, Jean-Paul Sartre, Eric-Emmanuel Schmitt, Ntozake Shange, Sam Shepard, Jack Shepherd, Martin Sherman, Robin Soans, Sophocles, Wole Soyinka, David Spencer, Shelagh Stephenson, David Storey, August Strindberg, C. P. Taylor, Sue Townsend, Judy Upton, Michael Vinaver, Timberlake Wertenbaker, Arnold Wesker, Michael Wilcox, Roy Williams, Snoo Wilson, David Wood, Victoria Wood, Irvine Welsh, Michael West, Peter Whelan, Oscar Wilde, Tennessee Williams.

Oberon Books
521 Caledonian Road, London N7 9RH
☎ 020 7607 3637   Fax 020 7607 3629
Email oberon.books@btinternet.com
Website www.oberonbooks.com

Publishing Director *James Hogan*
Managing Director *Charles D. Glanville*
A rapidly expanding company, Oberon publishes play texts (usually in conjunction with a production) and theatre books. Specializes in contemporary plays and translations of European classics. About seventy titles a year. Publishes over 250 writers and translators including: Neil Bartlett, John Barton, Steven Berkoff, Ranjit Bolt, John Bowen, Howard Brenton, Ken Campbell, Andy de la Tour, Dario Fo, Trevor Griffiths, Sir Peter Hall, Christopher Hampton, Giles Havergal, Rolf Hochhuth, Bernard Kops, Ash Kotak, Henry Livings, Frederick Lonsdale, Robert David MacDonald,

Adrian Mitchell, John Mortimer, Stephen Mulrine, Meredith Oakes, John Osborne, Philip Osment, Michael Pennington, David Pownall, Dennis Quilley, David Rudkin, Colin Teevan, Reza de Wet, John Whiting, Tennessee Williams, Charles Wood.

Penguin Group (UK)
A Pearson Company, 80 Strand, London WC2R ORL
☎ 020 7010 3000   Fax 020 7010 6060
Website www.penguin.co.uk

Group Chairman and Chief Executive *John Makinson*
CEO Penguin UK, Dorling Kindersley Ltd *Anthony Forbes Watson*
Managing Director Penguin *Helen Fraser*
Owned by Pearson plc. The world's best-known book brand and for more than sixty years a leading publisher whose adult and children's lists include fiction, non-fiction, poetry, drama, classics, reference and special interest areas. No unsolicited mss.

Playwrights include: Aeschylus, Edward Albee, Aristophanes, Alan Ayckbourn, Georg Büchner, Anton Chekhov, Euripides, Henrik Ibsen, Eugène Ionescu, Ben Jonson, Mike Leigh, Christopher Marlowe, Thomas Middleton, Arthur Miller, Molière, Luigi Pirandello, Plautus, Jean Racine, Friedrich Schiller, Peter Shaffer, William Shakespeare, George Bernard Shaw, Richard Brinsley Sheridan, R. C. Sherriff, Sophocles, August Strindberg, J. M. Synge, Dylan Thomas, Cyril Tourneur, John Webster, Oscar Wilde, Thornton Wilder, Tennessee Williams, David Wood, W. B. Yeats.

Seren
First Floor, 38–40 Nolton Street, Bridgend CF31 3BN
☎ 01656 663018   Fax 01656 649226
Email seren@seren.force9.co.uk
Website www.seren-books.com

Chairman *Cary Archard*
Managing Director *Mick Felton*
Drama *Amy Wack*

FOUNDED 1981 as a specialist poetry publisher but has now moved into general literary publishing with an emphasis on Wales.

Playwrights include: Dannie Abse, Laurence Allan, Lucinda Coxon, Dic Edwards, Greg Cullen, Lucy Gough, Peter Lloyd, Edward Thomas, Gwyn Thomas, Charles Way.

Colin Smythe Ltd

PO Box 6, Gerrards Cross, Buckinghamshire SL9 8XA

☎ 01753 886000   Fax 01753 886469

Email sales@colinsmythe.co.uk

Website www.colinsmythe.co.uk

Managing Director *Colin Smythe*

FOUNDED 1966. Publishes Anglo-Irish literature, drama, criticism and history. No unsolicited mss. Also acts as literary agent for a small list of authors including Terry Pratchett.

Playwrights include: Brendan Behan, Dion Boucicault, Austin Clark, St John Ervine, Lady Gregory, Douglas Hyde, Denis Johnston, Hugh Leonard, Micheál mac Liammóir, Edward Martyn, Rutherford Mayne, M. J. Molloy, George Moore, T. C. Murray, Sean O'Casey, Frank O'Connor, William Phillips, Lennox Robinson, Francis Warner, Oscar Wilde, W. B. Yeats.

Professional Associations and Societies

BAFTA (British Academy of Film and Television Arts)
195 Piccadilly, London W1J 9LN
☎ 020 7734 0022   Fax 020 7437 0473
Website www.bafta.org

FOUNDED 1947. Membership limited to 'those who have made a significant contribution to the industry' over a minimum period of three years. Best known for its annual awards ceremonies, now held separately for film, television, craft, children's programmes and interactive entertainment, the academy runs a full programme of screenings, seminars, master classes, debates, lectures, etc. It also actively supports training and educational projects.

Also, BAFTA Scotland, BAFTA Wales, BAFTA North, BAFTA LA, BAFTA East Coast (USA) run separate programmes and, in the case of Scotland, Wales and the north of England, hold their own awards.

British Film Institute
21 Stephen Street, London W1T 1LN
☎ 020 7255 1444   Fax 020 7436 0439
24-hour *bfi* events line: ☎ 0870 240 4050
Website www.bfi.org.uk

Chair *Joan Bakewell, CBE*
Director *Jon Teckman*

'The *bfi* offers opportunities to experience, enjoy and discover more about the world of film and television.' Its three main departments are: *bfi* Education, comprising the *bfi* National Library, *bfi* Publishing, *Sight and Sound* magazine and *bfi* Education Projects, which encourages life-long learning about the moving image; *bfi* Exhibition, which runs the National Film Theatre on London's South Bank and the annual London Film Festival, and supports local cinemas and film festivals UK-wide; and *bfi* Collections, which preserves the UK's moving image heritage and promotes access to it through a variety of means, including film, video and DVD releases and touring exhibitions. The *bfi* also runs the *bfi* London IMAX® cinema at Waterloo, featuring the UK's largest screen.

Commercial Radio Companies Association

77 Shaftesbury Avenue, London W1D 5DU
☎ 020 7306 2603   Fax 020 7470 0062
Email info@crca.co.uk

Chairman *Lord Eatwell*
Chief Executive *Paul Brown*
The CRCA is the trade body for the independent radio stations. It represents members' interests to government, the Radio Authority, trade unions, copyright organizations and other bodies.

Drama Association of Wales

The Old Library Building, Singleton Road, Splott, Cardiff CF24 2ET
☎ 029 2045 2200   Fax 029 2045 2277
Email aled.daw@virgin.net

Contact *Teresa Hennessy*
Runs a large playscript lending library; holds an annual playwriting competition (see pages 239–40); offers a script reading service (£15 per script) which usually takes three months from receipt of play to issue of reports. From plays submitted to the reading service, selected scripts are considered for publication of a short run (70–200 copies). Writers receive a percentage of the cover price on sales and a percentage of the performance fee.

Independent Television Commission (ITC)

33 Foley Street, London W1W 7TL
☎ 020 7255 3000   Fax 020 7306 7800
Website www.itc.org.uk

Chief Executive *Patricia Hodgson*
The ITC issues licences and regulates commercial television in the UK; maintains standards of the programmes which appear plus advertising and technical quality. Complaints against the service are investigated by the commission which frequently publishes its findings and is empowered to impose penalties on licensees that do not comply with their licence conditions.

Independent Theatre Council

12 The Leathermarket, Weston Street, London SE1 3ER
☎ 020 7403 1727   Fax 020 7403 1745
Email c.jones@itc-arts.org
Website www.itc-arts.org

Contact *Charlotte Jones*
The management association and representative body for small/middle-scale theatres (up to around 450 seats) and touring theatre companies. Negotiates contracts and has established standard agreements with Equity on behalf of all professionals working in the theatre. Negotiations with the WGGB for a contractual agreement covering rights and fee structure for playwrights were concluded in 1991. Terms and conditions were renegotiated and updated in September 1998. Copies of the minimum terms agreement can be obtained from the Writers' Guild. Publishes a booklet, *A Practical Guide for Writers and Companies* (£3.50 plus p&p), giving guidance to writers on how to submit scripts to theatres and guidance to theatres on how to deal with them.

Irish Playwrights and Screenwriters Guild
Irish Writers' Centre, 19 Parnell Square, Dublin 1, Republic of
Ireland
☎ 00 353 1 872 1302   Fax 00 353 1 872 6282
Email moffats@indigo.ie
Website www.writerscentre.ie/IPSG.html

Contact *Sean Moffatt*
FOUNDED in 1969 to safeguard the rights of scriptwriters for radio, stage
and screen. Subscription fees available on request.

ITV Network Ltd
200 Gray's Inn Road, London WC1X 8HF
☎ 020 7843 8000   Fax 020 7843 8158
Website www.itv.com

The ITV Network Ltd, wholly owned by the ITV companies, independently
commissions and schedules the television programmes which are shown
across the ITV network. As the successor to the Independent Television
Association, it also provides a range of services to the ITV companies
where a common approach is required.

New Writing North
7/8 Trinity Chare, Quayside, Newcastle upon Tyne NE1 3DF
☎ 0191 232 9991   Fax 0191 230 1883
Email subtext.nwn@virgin.net
Website www.newwritingnorth.com

Director *Claire Malcolm*
Administrator *John McGagh*
New Writing North is the literature development agency for the Northern
Arts Board and offers many useful services to writers, organizing events,
readings and courses. NWN produces writing guides and has a website
with literary news, events and opportunities. Administers the Northern
Rock Foundation writer award, the New Playwriting Panel (aiding new
drama) and the Northern Writers' awards, which include tailored development packages (mentoring and financial help). NWN has strong links

with the post of Northern Literary Fellow, awarded by Northern Arts. NWN also programmes the Durham Literature Festival.

PACT (Producers Alliance for Cinema and Television)

45 Mortimer Street, London W1W 8HJ
☎ 020 7331 6000   Fax 020 7331 6700
Email enquiries@pact.co.uk
Website www.pact.co.uk

Chief Executive *John McVay*
Information Manager *David Alan Mills*
FOUNDED 1991. PACT is the trade association of the UK independent television and feature film production sector and is a key contact point for foreign producers seeking British co-production, co-finance partners and distributors. Works for producers in the industry at every level and operates a members' regional network throughout the UK with a divisional office in Scotland. Membership services include: a dedicated industrial relations unit; discounted legal advice; a varied calendar of events; business advice; representation at international film and television markets; a comprehensive research programme; various publications: a monthly magazine, an annual members' directory; affiliation with European and international producers' organizations; extensive information and production advice. Lobbies actively with broadcasters, financiers and governments to ensure that the producer's voice is heard and understood in Britain and Europe on all matters affecting the film and television industry.

The Personal Managers' Association Ltd

1 Summer Road, East Molesey, Surrey KT8 9LX
☎ 020 8398 9796   Fax 020 8398 9796
Email info@thepma.com

Co-chairs *Marc Berlin, Tim Corrie, Nicholas Young*
Secretary *Angela Adler*
An association of artists' and dramatists' agents (membership not open to individuals). Monthly meetings for exchange of information and discussion. Maintains a code of conduct and acts as a lobby when necessary. Applicants

LISTINGS

screened. A high proportion of play agents are members of the PMA. Subscription: £250 p.a.

Player–Playwrights

9 Hillfield Park, London N10 3QT
☎ 020 8883 0371
Email P-P@dial.pipex.com

President *Olwen Wymark*
Contact *Peter Thompson* (at the address above)
FOUNDED 1948. A society giving opportunity for writers new to stage, radio and television, as well as others finding difficulty in achieving results, to work with writers established in those media. At weekly meetings (7.45 p.m.–10.00 p.m., Mondays, upstairs at the Horse and Groom, 128 Great Portland Street, London W1), members' scripts are read or performed by actor members and afterwards assessed and dissected in general discussion. Newcomers and new acting members are always welcome. Subscription: £10 (joining fee); £6 p.a. thereafter, plus £1.50 per attendance.

Radio Authority

Holbrook House, 14 Great Queen Street, London WC2B 5DG
☎ 020 7430 2724   Fax 020 7405 7062
Email info@radioauthority.org.uk
Website www.radioauthority.org.uk

The Radio Authority plans frequencies, awards licences, regulates programming and advertising, and plays an active role in the discussion and formulation of policies which affect the independent radio industry and its listeners. The authority also licenses digital radio services. The national commercial digital radio service was launched on 15 November 1999. The number of independent radio stations, now over 250, continues to increase with new licences being advertised on a regular basis.

Royal Television Society

Holborn Hall, 100 Gray's Inn Road, London WC1X 8AL
☎ 020 7430 1000   Fax 020 7430 0924
Email info@rts.org.uk
Website www.rts.org.uk

FOUNDED 1927. Covers all disciplines involved in the television industry. Provides a forum for debate and conferences on technical, social and cultural aspects of the medium. Presents various awards including journalism, programmes, technology, design and commercials. Publishes *Television Magazine* nine times a year for members and subscribers. Subscription: £70 p.a.

Scottish Young Playwrights

Scottish Youth Theatre, 3rd Floor, Forsyth House, 111 Union Street, Glasgow G1 3TA
☎ 0141 221 5127   Fax 0141 221 9123
Email info@scottishyouththeatre.org.
Website www.scottishyouththeatre.org

Artistic Director *Mary McCluskey*
Scottish Youth Theatre is involved in and operates various projects supporting young writers in Scotland. Further details from the address above.

Society of Authors

84 Drayton Gardens, London SW10 9SB
☎ 020 7373 6642   Fax 020 7373 5768
Email info@societyofauthors.org
Website www.societyofauthors.org

General Secretary *Mark Le Fanu*
FOUNDED 1884. The Society of Authors is an independent trade union with some 7,000 members. It advises on negotiations with publishers, broadcasting organizations, theatre managers and film companies; assists with complaints and takes action for breach of contract, copyright infringement, etc. Together with the Writers' Guild, the society has played a major role in advancing the Minimum Terms Agreement for authors. Among the

---

Society's publications are *The Author* (a quarterly journal) and the 'Quick Guides' series to various aspects of writing (all free of charge to members). Other services include vetting of contracts, emergency funds for writers and various special discounts. There are groups within the society for scriptwriters, children's writers and illustrators, educational writers, academic writers, medical writers and translators. Authors under 35 or over 65, not earning a significant income from their writing, may apply for lower subscription rates. Contact the society for a free booklet and copy of *The Author*. Subscription: £70/75 p.a.

The Society of Authors in Scotland
Bonnyton House, Arbirlot, Angus DD11 2PY
☎ 01241 874131   Fax 01241 874131
Email: info@eileenramsay.co.uk
Website www.writersorg.co.uk

Secretary *Eileen Ramsay*
The Scottish branch of the Society of Authors, which organizes business meetings, social and bookshop events throughout Scotland.

The Writers' Guild of Great Britain
15 Britannia Street, London WC1X 9JN
☎ 020 7833 0777   Fax 020 7833 4777
Email admin@writersguild.org.uk
Website www.writersguild.org.uk

General Secretary *Bernie Corbett*
Assistant General Secretaries *Anne Hogben, Christine Paris*
Annual subscription one per cent of that part of the author's income earned in the areas in which the guild operates, with a basic subscription of £125 and a maximum of £1,250.

FOUNDED 1959. The Writers' Guild is the writers' trade union, affiliated to the TUC. It represents writers in film, radio, television, theatre and publishing. The Guild has negotiated agreements on which writers' contracts are based with the BBC, independent television companies, and PACT (the Producers' Alliance for Cinema and Television). Those agreements are regularly renegotiated, both in terms of finance and conditions. In 1997, the Guild membership joined with that of the Theatre Writers' Union to create a new, more powerful union.

In 1979, together with the Theatre Writers' Union, the Guild negotiated the first ever industrial agreement for theatre writers, the TNC Agreement, which covers the Royal National Theatre, the Royal Shakespeare Company and the Royal Court. Further agreements have been negotiated with the Theatrical Management Association, which covers regional theatre, and the Independent Theatre Council, the organization which covers small theatres and the Fringe.

The Guild initiated a campaign over ten years ago which achieved the first ever publishing agreement for writers with the publisher W. H. Allen. Jointly with the Society of Authors, that campaign has continued and most years see new agreements with more publishers. Perhaps the most important breakthrough came with Penguin on 20 July 1990. The Guild now also has agreements covering HarperCollins, Random House Group, Transworld and others.

The Guild regularly provides individual help and advice to members on contracts, conditions of work, and matters which affect a member's life as a professional writer. Members are given the opportunity of meeting at craft meetings, which are held on a regular basis throughout the year. Writers can apply for full membership if they have one piece of written work for which payment has been received under a contract with terms not less than those negotiated by the Guild. Writers who do not qualify for full membership can apply for candidate membership. This is open to all those who wish to be involved in writing but have not yet had work published. The subscription fee for this is £55.

Writernet

Cabin V, Clarendon Buildings, 25 Horsell Road, Highbury, London N5 1XL
☎ 020 7609 7474   Fax 020 7609 7557
Email writernet@btinternet.com
Website www.writernet.org.uk

Executive Director *Jonathan Meth*

Writernet (formerly the New Playwrights Trust) is the national research and development organization for writing for all forms of live and recorded performance. Publishes a range of information pertinent to writers on all aspects of development and production in the form of pamphlets, and a six-weekly journal which also includes articles and interviews on aesthetic and practical issues. Writernet also runs a script reading service and a link service between writers and producers, organizes seminars and conducts research projects. The latter include research into the use of bilingual techniques in playwriting (*Two Tongues*), documentation of training programmes for writers (*Going Black Under the Skin*) and an investigation of the relationship between live art and writing (*Writing Live*). Subscription information available by post or on website.

Arts Councils and Regional Arts Boards

The Arts Council of England
14 Great Peter Street, London SW1P 3NQ
☎ 020 7333 0100/Minicom: 020 7973 6564   Fax 020 7973 6590
Email enquiries@artscouncil.org.uk
Website www.artscouncil.org.uk

Chairman *Gerry Robinson*
Chief Executive *Peter Hewitt*
The Arts Council of England is the national policy body for the arts in England. It develops, sustains and champions the arts. It distributes public money from government and from the National Lottery to artists and arts organizations both directly and through the ten regional arts boards. The Arts Council works independently and at arm's length from government. Information about Arts Council funding programmes is available on the website, by email or by contacting the enquiry line on 020 7973 6517. Information about funding available from the regional arts boards can be found on the website (www.arts.org.uk) or by contacting your regional arts board.

The Irish Arts Council/An Chomhairle Ealaíon
70 Merrion Square, Dublin 2, Republic of Ireland
☎ 00 353 1 6180200   Fax 00 353 1 6761302
Email info@artscouncil.ie
Website www.artscouncil.ie

Literature Officer *Sinéad Mac Aodha*
The Irish Arts Council has programmes under six headings to assist in the area of literature and book promotion: Writers, Literary Organizations, Publishers, Literary Magazines, Participation Programmes, Literary Events and Festivals. It also awards a number of annual bursaries.

The Arts Council of Northern Ireland
MacNeice House, 77 Malone Road, Belfast BT9 6AQ
☎ 028 9038 5200   Fax 028 9066 1715
Website www.artscouncil-ni.org

Literature Arts Officer *John Brown*
Funds book production by established publishers, programmes of readings, literary festivals, writers-in-residence schemes and literary magazines and periodicals. Occasional schools programmes and anthologies of children's writing are produced. Annual awards and bursaries for writers are available. Holds information also on various groups associated with local arts, workshops and courses.

Scottish Arts Council
12 Manor Place, Edinburgh EH3 7DD
☎ 0131 226 6051   Fax 0131 225 9833
Email administrator@scottisharts.org.uk
Website www.scottisharts.org.uk

Chairman *James Boyle*
Acting Director *Graham Berry*
Literature Director *Jenny Brown*
Literature Officers *Gavin Wallace, Jenny Attala*
Literature Secretary *Catherine Allan*
Principal channel for government funding of the arts in Scotland. The Scottish Arts Council (SAC) is funded by the Scottish Executive. It aims to develop and improve knowledge, understanding and practice of the arts, and to increase their accessibility throughout Scotland. It offers around 1,300 grants a year to artists and arts organizations concerned with the visual arts, crafts, dance and mime, drama, literature, music,

festivals and traditional, ethnic and community arts. It is also a distributor of National Lottery funds to the arts in Scotland. SAC's support for Scottish-based writers with a track record of publication includes bursaries, writing and translation fellowships and book awards. Information available includes lists of literary awards, literary magazines, agents and publishers.

The Arts Council of Wales
Museum Place, Cardiff CF10 3NX
☎ 029 2037 6500   Fax 029 2022 1447
Website www.artswales.org.uk/language.htm

Senior Literature Officer *Tony Bianchi*
Senior Officer: Drama *Sandra Wynne*
Funds literary magazines and book production; writers on tour and bursary schemes; Welsh Academy, Welsh Books Council, Hay-on-Wye Literature Festival and Ty Newydd Writers' Centre at Criccieth; also children's literature, annual awards and translation projects. The council aims to develop theatrical experience among Wales-based writers through a variety of schemes, in particular by funding writers on year-long attachments.

English Regional Arts Boards
English Regional Arts Boards are support and development agencies for the arts in the regions. Policies are developed in response to regional demand and to assist new initiatives in areas of perceived need; they may vary from region to region. The RABs are now responsible for the distribution of Arts Council lottery funding for capital and revenue projects under £100,000.

Support for writers
All the Regional Arts Boards offer support for professional creative writers through a range of grants, awards, advice, information and contacts. Interested writers should contact the board in whose region they live.

At the time of writing the current system of RABs is under review and anyone experiencing problems getting in touch with their RAB is advised to contact the Arts Council of England.

East England
Eden House, 48–9 Bateman Street, Cambridge CB2 1LR
☎ 01223 454400   Fax 01223 2421271
Email east@artscouncil.org.uk
Website www.artscouncil.org.uk/aboutus/contact_east.html

Literature Officer *Lucy Sheerman*
Drama Officer *Alan Orme*
Cinema and Broadcast Media Officer *Martin Ayres*
Covers Bedfordshire, Cambridgeshire, Essex, Hertfordshire, Norfolk and Suffolk and the non-metropolitan authorities of Luton, Peterborough, Southend-on-Sea and Thurrock. Policy emphasizes quality and access. Support is given to publishers and literature promoters based in the region, also to projects which develop audiences for literature performances and publishing, including electronic media. Also provides advice on applying for National Lottery funds.

East Midland
St Nicholas Court, 25–27 Castle Gate, Nottingham, NG1 7AR
☎ 01509 218292   Fax 01509 262214
Email eastmidlands@artscouncil.org.uk
Website www.artscouncil.org.uk/aboutus/contact_eastmidlands.html

Literature Officer *Gill Adams*
Drama Officer *Michaela Waldram*
Covers Derbyshire, Leicestershire, Lincolnshire (excluding North and North-East Lincolnshire), Northamptonshire, Nottinghamshire, and the unitary authorities of Derby, Leicester, Nottingham and Rutland. A comprehensive information service for regional writers includes an extensive *Writers' Information Pack*, with details of local groups, workshops, residential writing courses, publishers and publishing information, regional magazines, advice on approaching the media, on unions, courses and grants. Also available is

a directory of writers, primarily to aid people wishing to organize workshops, readings or writer's residencies. Literature grants are given for work on a specific project, although local history and biography are ineligible for support. A list of writers' groups is available, plus contact details for the East Midlands Literature Development Officer network.

London
2 Pear Tree Court, London EC1R 0DS
☎ 020 7608 6100   Fax 020 7670 4100
Email london@artscouncil.org.uk
Website www.artscouncil.org.uk/aboutus/contact_london.html

Literature Administrator *Sarah Sanders*
London Arts is the regional arts board for the capital, covering the thirty-two boroughs and the City of London. Grants are available to support a variety of literature projects, focusing on three main areas: live literature, including storytelling; support for small presses and literary magazines in the publishing of new or under-represented creative writing; bursaries for writers who have published one book and are working on their second work of fiction or poetry. There are two deadlines each year for applications. Contact the Literature Unit for more information and an application form.

North West
Manchester House, 22 Bridge Street, Manchester M3 3AB
☎ 0161 834 6644   Fax 0161 834 6969
Email northwest@artscouncil.org.uk
Website www.artscouncil.org.uk/aboutus/contact_northwest.html

Arts Officer: Literature *Bronwen Williams* (Email bwilliams@nwarts.co.uk)
Arts Officer: Drama *Ian Tabbron* (Email itabbron@nwarts.co.uk)
NWAB covers Cheshire, Cumbria, Lancashire, the metropolitan districts of Bolton, Bury, Knowsley, Liverpool, Manchester, Oldham, Rochdale, St Helens, Salford, Sefton, Stockport, Tameside, Trafford, Wigan and Wirral, and the unitary authorities of Blackburn with Darwen, Blackpool, Halton and Warrington. Offers financial assistance to a great variety of organizations and individuals through a number of schemes, including

writers' bursaries, residencies and placements and the Live Writing scheme. NWAB publishes a directory of local writers' groups, a directory of writers and a range of information covering topics such as performance and publishing. For further details contact the Literature or Drama Departments.

North East
Central Square, Forth Street, Newcastle upon Tyne NE1 3PJ
☎ 0191 255 8500   Fax 0191 230 1020
Email northeast@artscouncil.co.uk
Website www.artscouncil.org.uk/aboutus/contact_northeast.html

Head of Film, Media and Literature *Mark Robinson*
Literature Officer *Kate Griffin*
Covers County Durham, Northumberland, Teesside and Tyne and Wear, and was the first regional arts association in the country to be set up by local authorities. It supports both organizations and writers and aims to stimulate public interest in artistic events. The Northern Writers' awards scheme is operated through New Writing North (see page 218). Northern Arts makes drama awards to producers. Also funds writers' residencies, and has a fund for publications. Contact list of regional groups available.

South West
Bradninch Place, Gandy Street, Exeter, Devon EX4 3LS
☎ 01392 218188   Fax 01392 229229
Email southwest@artscouncil.co.uk
Website www.artscouncil.org.uk/aboutus/contact_southwest.html

Director of Visual Arts and Media *David Drake*
Visual Arts and Media Administrators *Sara Williams, Kate Offord, Lis Spencer*
Covers Cornwall, Devon, Dorset, Gloucestershire, Somerset, Wiltshire and the unitary authorities of Bristol, Bath and North East Somerset, Swindon, Bournemouth, South Gloucestershire, North Somerset, Torbay, Poole and Plymouth. The central themes running through the board's aims are 'promoting quality and developing audiences for new work'. Specific policies aim to support the development and promotion of new writing and

performance work in all areas of contemporary literature and published arts. There is direct investment in small presses and magazine publishers, literary festivals, writer residencies and training, and marketing bursaries for individual writers. There is also a commitment to supporting the development of new writing in the performing arts, and critical writing within the visual arts and media department.

South East

13 St Clement Street, Winchester, Hampshire SO23 9DQ
☎ 01962 855099   Fax 0870 242 1257
Email southeast@artscouncil.org.uk
Website www.artscouncil.org.uk/aboutus/contact_southeast.html

Literature Officer *Keiren Phelan*
Performing Arts Officer *Roger McCann*
Covers Buckinghamshire, East Sussex, Hampshire, Isle of Wight, Kent, Oxfordshire, Surrey, West Sussex; and the unitary authorities of Bracknell Forest, Brighton and Hove, Medway Towns, Milton Keynes, Portsmouth, Reading, Slough, Southampton, West Berkshire, Windsor and Maidenhead, and Wokingham. Grant schemes accessible to all art forms in the areas of new work, presentation of work and venue development. Awards for individuals include training bursaries and writers' awards schemes. The literature programme aims to raise the profile of contemporary literature in the region and encourage creative writing and reading development projects. Priorities include live literature, writers and readers in residence and training bursaries for writers resident in the region. A regular feature on literature appears in the *Arts News* newsletter.

West Midlands

82 Granville Street, Birmingham B1 2LH
☎ 0121 631 3121   Fax 0121 643 7239
Email westmidlands@artscouncil.org.uk
Website www.artscouncil.org.uk/aboutus/contact_westmidlands.html

Literature Officer *Adrian Johnson*
Covers Shropshire, Staffordshire, Warwickshire and Worcestershire; also the metropolitan districts of Birmingham, Coventry, Dudley, Sandwell,

Solihull, Walsall and Wolverhampton, and the non-metropolitan districts of Herefordshire, Stoke-on-Trent, Telford and Wrekin. There are special criteria across the art forms, so contact the Information Office for details of general support funds for the arts, especially Creative Ambition awards for writers (six application dates throughout the year) and other arts lottery schemes, as well as for the Reading (Correspondence Mss Advice) Service. There are contact lists of writers, storytellers, writing groups, etc. WMA supports the regional publication, *Raw Edge Magazine*: contact PO Box 4867, Birmingham B3 3HD; the Virtual Literature Centre for the West Midlands (and beyond) called Lit-net (www.lit-net.org); and the major storytelling and poetry festivals in Shropshire and Ledbury respectively.

Yorkshire Arts

21 Bond Street, Dewsbury, West Yorkshire WF13 1AY
☎ 01924 455555   Fax 01924 466522
Email yorkshire@artscouncil.org.uk
Website www.artscouncil.org.uk/aboutus/contact_yorkshire.html

Literature Officer *Jane Stubbs*
Theatre Development Officer *Maric Hollander*
Literature and Audience Development Administrator *Kelly McMichael*
Covers North Yorkshire, the metropolitan authorities of Barnsley, Bradford, Calderdale, Doncaster, Kirklees, Leeds, Rotherham, Sheffield and Wake-field, and the unitary authorities of East Riding of Yorkshire, Kingston upon Hull, North Lincolnshire, North East Lincolnshire and York. 'Librar-ies, publishing houses, local authorities and the education service all make major contributions to the support of literature. Recognizing the resources these agencies command, Yorkshire Arts actively seeks ways of acting in partnership with them, while at the same time retaining its particular responsibility for the living writer and the promotion of activities currently outside the scope of these agencies.' Funding goes to a range of indepen-dent publishers, festivals and literature development agencies. Yorkshire Arts also offers a range of development funds to support the individual and the promotion and distribution of literature. Holds lists of writers' groups throughout the region and publishes *Write Angles*, a bi-monthly newsletter. Contact *Kelly McMichael* for further information.

Bursaries, Fellowships and Grants

Arts Council Literature Bursaries, Ireland
An Chomhairle Ealaíon (The Irish Arts Council), 70 Merrion Square, Dublin 2, Republic of Ireland
☎ 00 353 1 6180200   Fax 00 353 1 6761302
Email info@artscouncil.ie
Website www.artscouncil.ie

Literature Officer *Sinéad Mac Aodha*
Bursaries in literature awarded to creative writers of fiction, poetry and drama in Irish and English to enable development or completion of specific projects. A limited number of bursaries may also be given to non-fiction projects of a contemporary nature. Open to Irish citizens or residents only.

Awards: Up to €12,000.

Arts Council Theatre Writing Bursaries
Arts Council of England, 14 Great Peter Street, London SW1P 3NQ
☎ 020 7973 6431   Fax 020 7973 6983
Email jemima.lee@artscouncil.org.uk
Website www.artscouncil.org.uk

Contact *Theatre Writing Section*
Intended to provide experienced playwrights with the opportunity to research and develop a play for the theatre independently of financial

pressures and free from the need to write for a particular market. Bursaries are also available for theatre translation projects. Writers must be resident in England.

Award: £5,500.

Arts Council Theatre Writing Commission Award
Arts Council of England, 14 Great Peter Street, London sw1P 3NQ
☎ 020 7973 6431   Fax 020 7973 6983
Email jemima.lee@artscouncil.org.uk
Website www.artscouncil.org.uk

Contact *Theatre Writing Section*
Theatre companies and groups based in England can apply for a grant of up to half the cost of paying a writer a commission or fee to write a new play, to secure the rights to an unperformed play or to rewrite an unperformed play. The theatre company or organization is expected to find at least half the cost of the fee from their own resources. Commissions are also available for theatre translation projects. Further details available from the theatre writing section.

Alfred Bradley Bursary Award
c/o BBC Radio Drama, Room 1119, New Broadcasting House, Oxford Road, Manchester M60 1SJ
☎ 0161 244 4260   Fax 0161 244 4248

Contact *Coordinator*
Established 1992. Biennial award in commemoration of the life and work of the distinguished radio producer Alfred Bradley. Aims to encourage and develop new radio writing talent in the BBC North region. There is a change of focus for each award; previous years have targeted comedy drama, verse drama, etc. Entrants must live or work in the North region. The award is given to help writers to pursue a career in writing for radio. The most recent award was launched in spring 2002, with a deadline for scripts in autumn 2002. Previous winners: Lee Hall, Mandy Precious, Peter Straughan, Pam Leeson.

Award: Up to £6,000 over two years and a BBC Radio Drama commission; the opportunity to develop further ideas with Radio Drama.

EuroPAWS (European Public Awareness of Science) Drama Script Fund
The EuroPAWS Office, OMNI Communications, Chancel House, Neasden Lane, London NW10 2TU
☎ 020 8214 1543   Fax 020 8214 1544

Contacts *Barrie Whatley, Andrew Millington*
Established 1994. Annual award aimed at encouraging television scriptwriters to include science and engineering scenarios in their work. Grants (currently £2,000) are given to selected writers to develop their script ideas into full treatments; prizes are awarded for the best of these treatments. EuroPAWS holds meetings enabling writers to meet scientists and engineers and also offers a contacts service to put writers in one-to-one contact with specialists who can help them develop their ideas.

Pearson Playwrights' Scheme
80 Strand, London WC2R ORL
Website www.pearson.com

Administrator *Jack Andrews, MBE* ☎ 020 8943 8176)
Awards four bursaries to playwrights annually, each worth £5,000. Applicants must be sponsored by a theatre which then submits the play for consideration by a panel. Each award allows the playwright a twelve-month attachment. Applications invited via theatres in October each year.

Peggy Ramsay Foundation
Hanover House, 14 Hanover Square, London W1S 1HP
☎ 020 7667 5000   Fax 020 7667 5100
Email laurence.harbottle@harbottle.com
Website www.peggyramsayfoundation.org

Contact *G. Laurence Harbottle*
FOUNDED in 1992 in accordance with the will of the late Peggy Ramsay, the well-known agent. Grants are made to writers for the stage who have

some experience and who need time and resources to make writing possible. Grants are also made for writing projects by organizations connected with the theatre. The foundation does not support production costs or any project that does not have a direct benefit to playwriting. Writers must have some record of successful writing for the stage.

Grants: Total £150,000 to £200,000 per year.

Scottish Arts Council Writers' Bursaries

Scottish Arts Council, 12 Manor Place, Edinburgh EH3 7DD
☎ 0131 226 6051   Fax 0131 225 9833
Email jenny.brown@scottisharts.org.uk
Website www.sac.org.uk

Contact *Jenny Brown, Head of Literature*
Bursaries to enable published writers of literary work and recognized playwrights to devote more time to their writing. Around twenty bursaries of up to £15,000 awarded annually; deadline for applications in June and December. Application open to writers based in Scotland.

Prizes

Arts Council Children's Award
Arts Council of England, 14 Great Peter Street, London SW1P 3NQ
☎ 020 7973 6431   Fax 020 7973 6983
Email jemima.lee@artscouncil.org.uk
Website www.artscouncil.org.uk

Contact *Theatre Writing Section*
A new annual award for playwrights who write for children. The plays, which must have been produced professionally between 1 July 2002 and 30 June 2003, should be suitable for children up to the age of twelve and be at least forty-five minutes long. The playwright must be resident in England. Closing date for entries: 4 July 2003. Contact the Theatre Writing Section for full details and application form.

Award: £6,000.

Verity Bargate Award
The Soho Theatre Company, 21 Dean Street, London W1D 3NE
☎ 020 7287 5060   Fax 020 7287 5061
Email writers@sohotheatre.com

Contact *Jo Ingham, Literary Officer*
The award was set up to commemorate the late Verity Bargate, co-founder and director of the Soho Theatre Company. This national award is presented biennially for a new and unperformed play (next in 2004). To go on

the mailing list, please email or send sae to *Jo Ingham*. Previous winners include: Shan Khan, Fraser Grace, Lyndon Morgans, Adrian Pagan, Diane Samuels, Judy Upton and Toby Whithouse.

The Cló Iar-Chonnachta Literary Award
Cló Iar-Chonnachta Teo, Indreabhán, Conamara, Co. Galway, Republic of Ireland
☎ 00 353 91 593307   Fax 00 353 91 593362
Website www.cic.ie

Editor *Róisín Ní Mhianànn*
An annual prize for a newly written and unpublished work in the Irish language. The 2003 award will be for the best collection of short stories or long play. The 2001 winner was Pádraig Ó Siadhail for his collection of short stories, *Na Seacht gCineál Meisce*.

Prize: €6,350.

George Devine Award
17A South Villas, London NW1 9BS
☎ 020 7267 9793 (evenings only)

Contact *Christine Smith*
Annual award for a promising new playwright writing for the stage in memory of George Devine, artistic director of the Royal Court Theatre, who died in 1965. The play, which can be of any length, does not need to have been produced. Send two copies of the script, plus outline of work, to Christine Smith. Closing date: March. Information leaflet available from January on receipt of sae.

Prize: £10,000.

Drama Association of Wales Playwriting Competition
The Old Library, Singleton Road, Splott, Cardiff CF24 2ET
☎ 029 2045 2200   Fax 029 2045 2277
Email aled.daw@virgin.net

Contact *Teresa Hennessy*
Annual competition held to promote the writing of one-act plays in English and Welsh of between twenty and forty-five minutes' playing time. The competition format is reviewed annually, looking at different themes, genres and markets. Application forms from the address above.

EuroPAWS (European Public Awareness of Science) Midas Prize
The EuroPAWS Office, OMNI Communications, Chancel House, Neasden Lane, London NW10 2TU
☎ 020 8214 1543   Fax 020 8214 1544

Contacts *Barrie Whatley, Andrew Millington*
Established 1998. Annual prize awarded to the writer and producer of the best television drama, first transmitted in the year up to the end of October, that bears in a significant way on science or engineering. The drama may be a single play or an episode of a series, serial or soap. It need not necessarily be centred on a science or engineering theme, although clearly it can be. The context and quality of the drama and the audience size all weigh alongside the science in making the award. To enter a programme or suggest that a programme should be entered, contact the EuroPAWS office above.

Prize: £5,000.

The Richard Imison Memorial Award
The Society of Authors, 84 Drayton Gardens, London SW10 9SB
☎ 020 7373 6642   Fax 020 7373 5768
Email info@societyofauthors.org

Contact *The Secretary, The Broadcasting Committee*
Annual award established 'to perpetuate the memory of Richard Imison, to acknowledge the encouragement he gave to writers working in the medium of radio, and in memory of the support and friendship he invariably offered writers in general, and radio writers in particular'. Administered by the Society of Authors and generally sponsored by the Peggy Ramsay Foundation, the purpose is 'to encourage new talent and high standards in writing for radio by selecting the radio drama by a writer new to radio

which, in the opinion of the judges, is the best of those submitted'. An adaptation for radio of a piece originally written for the stage, television or film is not eligible. Any radio drama first transmitted in the UK between 1 January and 31 December by a writer or writers new to radio is eligible, provided the work is an original piece for radio and it is the first dramatic work by the writer(s) that has been broadcast. Submission may be made by any party to the production in the form of two copies of an audio cassette (not returnable) accompanied by a nomination form. The 2001 winner was Murray Gold *Electricity*.

Prize: £1,500.

The London Writers Competition
Room 224a, The Town Hall, Wandsworth High Street, London SW18 2PU
☎ 020 8871 8711   Fax 020 8871 8712
Email arts@wandsworth.gov.uk
Website www.wandsworth.gov.uk

Contact *Wandsworth Arts Office*
Arranged by Wandsworth Borough Council in association with Waterstone's. An annual competition, open to all writers of sixteen or over who live, work or study in the Greater London area. Work must not have been published previously. There are three sections: poetry, short story and play.

Prizes: £1,000 for each section, with a first prize of £600. Poetry and story winners are published and the winning play is showcased in a London venue.

Meyer-Whitworth Award
Arts Council of England, 14 Great Peter Street, London SW1P 3NQ
☎ 020 7973 6431   Fax 020 7973 6983
Email jemima.lee@artscouncil.org.uk
Website www.artscouncil.org.uk

Contact *Theatre Writing Section*
In 1908 the movement for a national theatre joined forces with that to create a memorial to William Shakespeare; the result was the Shakespeare Memorial

National Theatre Committee. This award was established to commemorate all those who worked with the SMNT. The award, endowed by residual funds of the SMNT and now transferred to the Royal National Theatre Foundation, is intended to help further the careers of UK playwrights who are not yet established, and to draw contemporary theatre writers to the public's attention. The award is given to the writer whose play most nearly satisfies the following criteria: a play which embodies Geoffrey Whitworth's dictum that 'drama is important in so far as it reveals the truth about the relationships of human beings with each other and the world at large'; a play which shows promise of a developing new talent; a play in which the writing is of individual quality. Nominations are from professional theatre companies. Plays must have been written in the English language and produced professionally in the UK in the twelve months between 1 August 2002 and 31 July 2003. Candidates will have had no more than two of their plays professionally produced. No writer who has won the award previously may reapply and no play that has been submitted previously for the award is eligible. Closing date: 31 August 2003.

Award: £8,000.

The Dennis Potter Screenwriting Award

BBC Broadcasting House, Whiteladies Road, Bristol BS8 2LR
☎ 0117 974 7586
Email BBC2Awards@bbc.co.uk

Editor *Jeremy Howe*

Annual award established in 1995 in memory of the late television playwright to 'nurture and encourage the work of new writers of talent and personal vision'. The winning drama is screened as part of the BBC2 awards programme in November. Submissions should be made through a BBC TV drama producer or an independent production company (no start date confirmed; contact the editor for further information).

Pulitzer Prizes
The Pulitzer Prize Board, 709 Journalism, Columbia University,
New York NY 10027, USA
☎ 001 212 854 3841/2   Fax 001 212 854 3342
Email pulitzer@www.pulitzer.org
Website www.pulitzer.org

Awards for journalism in US newspapers, and for published literature, drama and music by American nationals. Deadlines: 1 February (journalism); 1 March (music); 1 March (drama); 1 July for books published between 1 January–30 June and 1 November for books published 1 July–31 December (literature). Previous winners include: Michael Chabon *The Amazing Adventures of Kavalier & Clay*; Joseph J. Ellis *Founding Brothers: The Revolutionary Generation*; David Levering Lewis *W. E. B. Du Bois: The Fight for Equality and the American Century, 1919–1963*; Stephen Dunn *Different Hours*; Herbert P. Bix *Hirohito and the Making of Modern Japan*.

The Society for Theatre Research Annual Theatre Book Prize
c/o The Theatre Museum, 1e Tavistock Street, London WC2E 7PA
Email e.cottis@btinternet.com
Website www.str.org.uk

Established 1997. Annual award for books, in English, of original research into any aspect of the history and technique of the British theatre. Not restricted to authors of British nationality nor books from British publishers. Books must be first published in English (no translations) during the calendar year. Play texts and those treating drama as literature are not eligible. Publishers submit books directly to the independent judges and should contact the book prize administrator for further details. The 2001 winners were Jim Davis and Victor Emeljanow *Reflecting the Audience: London Theatregoing, 1840–1880*.

Award: £400.

Sunday Times Young Writer of the Year Award

The Society of Authors, 84 Drayton Gardens, London SW10 9SB
☎ 020 7373 6642   Fax 020 7373 5768
Email info@societyofauthors.org

Contact *Awards Secretary*
Established 1991. Annual award given on the strength of the promise shown by a full-length published work of fiction, non-fiction, poetry or drama. Entrants must be British citizens, resident in Britain and under the age of thirty-five. The panel consists of *Sunday Times* journalists and critics. Closing date: 20 December. The work must be by one author, in the English language, and published in Britain. Applications by publishers via the Society of Authors. The 2001 winner was Zadie Smith *White Teeth.*

John Whiting Award

Arts Council of England, 14 Great Peter Street, London SW1P 3NQ
☎ 020 7973 6431   Fax 020 7973 6983
Email jemima.lee@artscouncil.org.uk
Website www.artscouncil.org.uk

Contact *Theatre Writing Section*
FOUNDED 1965. Annual award to commemorate the life and work of the playwright John Whiting (*The Devils, A Penny for a Song*). Any writer who has received during 2002 and 2003: an award through the Arts Council's theatre writing schemes; a commission from a theatre company in receipt of an annual or revenue subsidy from either the Arts Council or a regional arts board; or a premiere production by a theatre company in receipt of annual subsidy is eligible to apply. The play must have been written during 2002 and/or 2003. Awarded to the writer whose play most nearly satisfies the following criteria: a play in which the writing is of special quality; a play of relevance and importance to contemporary life; a play of potential value to the British theatre. No writer who has won the award previously may reapply and no play that has been submitted for the award previously is eligible. Closing date for entries: 9 January 2004.

Prize: £6,000.

Festivals

International Playwriting Festival
Warehouse Theatre, Dingwall Road, Croydon CR0 2NF
☎ 020 8681 1257   Fax 020 8688 6699
Email warehous@dircon.co.uk
Website www.warehousetheatre.co.uk

Festival Administrator *Rose Marie Vernon*
FOUNDED 1985. Annual competition for full-length unperformed plays, judged by a panel of theatre professionals. Finalists given rehearsed readings during the festival week in November. Entries welcome from all parts of the world. Scripts plus two saes (one script-sized) should reach the theatre by the end of June, accompanied by an entry form (available from the theatre). Previous winners produced at the theatre include: Kevin Hood *Beached*; Ellen Fox *Conversations with George Sandburgh After a Solo Flight Across the Atlantic*; Guy Jenkin *Fighting for the Dunghill*; James Martin Charlton *Fat Souls*; Peter Moffat *Iona Rain*; Dino Mahoney *YoYo*; Simon Smith *Fat Janet is Dead*; Dominic McHale *The Resurrectionists*; Philip Edwards *51 Peg*; Roumen Shomov *The Dove*; Maggie Nevill *The Shagaround*; Andrew Shakeshaft *Just Sitting*. Shares plays with its partner festival in Italy, the Premio Candoni Arta Terme.

London New Play Festival
40/7 Altenburg Gardens, London SW11 1JW
☎ 07050 641959   Fax 07050 642929
Website www.lnpf.co.uk

Literary Manager *Julia Parr*
FOUNDED 1989. Annual festival of new plays held in venues around London each September, centring on a short play platform season held in the West End in association with Really Useful Theatres. LNPF specializes in developing and producing new plays, normally working with early career playwrights. As well as the annual festival, LNPF stages education and production programmes throughout the year. Full information can be found on the website. Script submissions should be sent to *Julia Parr* at the address above.

National Association of Writers' Groups (NAWG) Open Festival of Writing
The Arts Centre, Washington, Tyne and Wear NE38 2AB
☎ 0191 416 9751
Email briannawgfestival@yahoo.co.uk
Website www.nawg.co.uk

Festival Administrator *Brian Lister*
FOUNDED 1997. Annual festival held at St Aidan's College, University of Durham in September or October. Three days of creative writing tuition covering poetry, short and long fiction, playwriting, journalism, TV sitcom and many other subjects all led by professional writer-tutors. Thirty-six workshops, thirty-two surgeries plus seminars and fringe events. Saturday gala dinner and awards ceremony. Full- or part-residential weekend, or single workshops only. Open to all, no qualifications or NAWG membership required.

The Round Festival
c/o Word and Action (Dorset), 75 High Street, Wimborne,
Dorset BH21 1HS
☎ 01202 883197   Fax 01202 881061
Email info@roundfestival.org.uk
Website www.roundfestival.org.uk

Contact *Anne Jennings*
FOUNDED 1990. International festival of theatre-in-the-round held in July
offering a variety of workshops and performances celebrating and exploring
the form. Programme includes performances and play reading (including
new plays) in the round.

Royal Court Young Writers' Programme
The Site, Royal Court Theatre, Sloane Square, London SW1W 8AS
☎ 020 7565 5050   Fax 020 7565 5001
Email ywp@royalcourttheatre.com
Website www.royalcourttheatre.com

Associate Director *Ola Animashawun*
Open to young people up to the age of twenty-five. The YWP focuses on
the process of playwriting by running a series of writers groups throughout
the year at its base in Sloane Square. Additionally the YWP welcomes
unsolicited scripts from all young writers from across the country. 'We are
always looking for scripts for development and possible production (not
film scripts).'

Library Services

Barbican Library
Barbican Centre, London EC2Y 8DS
☎ 020 7638 0569   Fax 020 7638 2249
Email barbicanlib@corpoflondon.gov.uk
Website www.cityoflondon.gov.uk

Open: 9.30 a.m.–5.30 p.m. Monday, Wednesday, Thursday, Friday;
9.30 a.m.–7.30 p.m. Tuesday; 9.30 a.m.–12.30 p.m. Saturday.
Open access.
Situated on Level 2 of the Barbican Centre, this is the Corporation of
London's largest lending library. Study facilities are available plus free
Internet access. In addition to a large general lending department, the
library seeks to reflect the centre's emphasis on the arts and includes strong
collections (including DVDs, videos and CD-ROMs) on painting, sculpture,
theatre, cinema and ballet, as well as a large music library with books,
scores and CDs (sound recording loans available at a small charge). Also
houses the City's main children's library and has special collections on
finance, natural resources, conservation, socialism and the history of London. Service available for housebound readers. A literature events programme is organized by the library which supplements and provides
cross-arts planning opportunities with the Barbican Centre artistic
programme.

BBC Written Archives Centre

Peppard Road, Caversham Park, Reading, Berkshire RG4 8TZ

☎ 0118 948 6281   Fax 0118 946 1145

Email wac.enquiries@bbc.co.uk

Website www.bbc.co.uk/thenandnow

Contact *Jacqueline Kavanagh*

Open: 9.30 a.m.– 5.30 p.m. Monday to Friday.

Access for reference, by appointment only on Wednesday to Friday.

Holds the written records of the BBC, including internal papers 1922–1979 and published material to date. Twentieth-century biography, social history, popular culture and broadcasting. Charges for certain services.

BFI National Library

21 Stephen Street, London W1T 1LN

☎ 020 7255 1444   Fax 020 7436 2338

Email library@bfi.org.uk

Website www.bfi.org.uk

Open: 10.30 a.m.–5.30 p.m. Monday and Friday; 10.30 a.m.–8.00 p.m. Tuesday and Thursday; 1.00 p.m.–8.00 p.m. Wednesday; telephone enquiry service operates 10.00 a.m.–5.00 p.m.

Access for reference only; annual, five-day and limited day membership available.

The world's largest collection of information on film and television includes periodicals, cuttings, scripts, related documentation, personal papers.

Birmingham Library Services

Central Library, Chamberlain Square, Birmingham B3 3HQ

☎ 0121 303 4511

Email central.library@birmingham.gov.uk

Website www.birmingham.gov.uk/libraries

Open: 9.00 a.m.–8.00 p.m. Monday to Friday; 9.00 a.m.–5.00 p.m. Saturday.

Over a million volumes. Research collections include: Shakespeare Library; War Poetry Collection; Parker Collection of Children's Books and Games; Johnson Collection; Milton Collection; Cervantes Collections; Early and

Fine Printing Collection (including the William Ridler Collection of Fine Printing); Joseph Priestley Collection; Loudon Collection; Railway Collection; Wingate Bett Transport Ticket Collection; Labour, Trade Union and Co-operative Collections. Photographic archives: Sir John Benjamin Stone; Francis Bedford; Francis Frith; Warwickshire Photographic Survey; Boulton and Watt Archive. Charles Parker Archive; Birmingham Repertory Theatre Archive and Sir Barry Jackson Library; Local Studies (Birmingham); Patents Collection; Song Sheets Collection; Oberammergau Festival Collection.

British Library National Sound Archive
96 Euston Road, London NW1 2DB
☎ 020 7412 7440   Fax 020 7412 7441
Email nsa@bl.uk
Website cadensa.bl.uk

Open: 10.00 a.m.–8.00 p.m. Monday; 9.30 a.m.–8.00 p.m. Tuesday to Thursday; 9.30 a.m.–5.00 p.m. Friday and Saturday; closed for public holidays.
Listening service by appointment.

Northern Listening Service
British Library Document Supply Centre, Boston Spa, West Yorkshire

Open: 9.15 a.m.–4.30 p.m. Monday to Friday.
Open access.
An archive of over 1,000,000 discs and more than 200,000 hours of tape recordings, including all types of music, oral history, drama, wildlife, selected BBC broadcasts and BBC Sound Archive material. Produces a thrice-yearly newsletter, *Playback*. For information on British Library National Sound Archive collections and services, visit the website.

Witham Library
18 Newland Street, Witham, Essex CM8 2AQ
☎ 01376 519625   Fax 01376 501913

Open: 9.00 a.m.–7.00 p.m. Monday, Tuesday, Thursday, Friday;
9.00 a.m.–5.00 p.m. Saturday (closed Wednesday).
Drama: Dorothy L. Sayers and Maskell collections.

The Mitchell Library
North Street, Glasgow G3 7DN
☎ 0141 287 2999   Fax 0141 287 2915
Website www.mitchelllibrary.org

Open: 9.00 a.m.–8.00 p.m. Monday to Thursday; 9.00 a.m.–5.00 p.m.
Friday and Saturday.
Open access.
One of Europe's largest public reference libraries with stock of over
1,200,000 volumes. It subscribes to forty-eight newspapers and more than
2,000 periodicals. There are collections in microform, records, tapes and
videos, as well as CD-ROMs, electronic databases, illustrations, photographs, postcards, etc. The library contains a number of special collections
including the Robert Burns Collection (5,000 vols.), the Scottish Poetry
Collection (12,000 items) and the Scottish Drama Collection (1,650 items).

City of Plymouth Library and Information Services
Central Library, Drake Circus, Plymouth, Devon PL4 8AL
Website www.pgfl.plymouth.gov.uk/libraries *and*
www.webopac.plymouth.uk

Open access.

Central Library Lending Departments:
Lending ☎ 01752 305912
Children's Department ☎ 01752 305916

Music and Drama Department
☎ 01752 305914
Email music@plymouth.gov.uk

Open: 9.30 a.m.–7.00 p.m. Monday and Friday; 9.30 a.m.–5.30 p.m.
Tuesday, Wednesday, Thursday; 9.30 a.m.–4.00 p.m. Saturday.

The lending departments offer books on all subjects; language courses on cassette and foreign-language books; the Holcenberg Jewish Collection; books on music and musicians, drama and theatre; music parts and sets of music parts; play sets; DVDs; videos; song index; cassettes and CDs.

Reading Central Library

Abbey Square, Reading, Berkshire RG1 3BQ

☎ 0118 901 5955   Fax 0118 901 5954

Email info@readinglibraries.org.uk

Website www.readinglibraries.org.uk

Open: 9.30 a.m.–5.30 p.m. Monday and Friday; 9.30 a.m.–7.00 p.m. Tuesday and Thursday; 9.30 a.m.–5.00 p.m. Wednesday and Saturday. Open access.

Lending library; reference library; local studies library, bringing together every aspect of the local environment and human activity in Berkshire; business library; music and drama library. Special collections: Mary Russell Mitford; local illustrations. Public meeting room available.

Theatre Museum Library and Archive

1e Tavistock Street, London WC2E 7PR

☎ 020 7943 4700   Fax 020 7943 4777

Website theatremuseum.org

Open: 10.30 a.m.–4.30 p.m. Tuesday to Friday.

Access by appointment only.

The Theatre Museum was founded as a separate department of the Victoria and Albert Museum in 1974 and moved to its own building in Covent Garden in 1987. The museum (open Tuesday to Sunday 10.00 a.m.–6.00 p.m.) houses permanent displays, temporary exhibitions and a studio theatre, and organizes a programme of special events, performances, lectures, guided visits and workshops. The library houses the UK's largest performing arts research collections, including books, photographs, designs, engravings, programmes, press cuttings, etc. All the performing arts are covered but strengths are in the areas of theatre, dance, musical theatre and stage design. The Theatre Museum has acquired much of the

British Theatre Association's library and provides reference access to its collections of play texts and critical works.

Westminster Reference Library
35 St Martin's Street, London WC2H 7HP
☎ 020 7641 4636   Fax 020 7641 4606
Email westreflib@dial.pipex.com
Website www.westminster.gov.uk/libraries/libraries/westref
General Reference and Performing Arts: ☎ 020 7641 4636
Art and Design: ☎ 020 7641 4638
Business and Official Publications: ☎ 020 7641 4634

Open: 10.00 a.m.–8.00 p.m. Monday to Friday; 10.00 a.m.–5.00 p.m. Saturday.
Access for reference only.
A general reference library with emphasis on the following: art and design – fine and decorative arts, architecture, graphics and design; performing arts – theatre, cinema, radio, television and dance; official publications – major collection of HMSO publications from 1947, plus parliamentary papers dating back to 1906; business – UK directories, trade directories, company and market data; official EU Depository Library – carries official EU material; periodicals – long files of many titles. One working day's notice is required for some government documents, some monographs and most older periodicals.

Useful Websites at a Glance

The Arts Council of England
www.artscouncil.org.uk

Includes information on funding applications, publications and the National Lottery. (See page 225.)

Author-Network
www.author-network.com

Writers' resource site, operated by Puff Adder Books.

Author-Publisher Network
www.author.co.uk

Services for writers, information network, newsletter and online magazine.

BBC
www.bbc.co.uk

Access to all BBC departments and services.

British Film Institute (bfi)
www.bfi.org.uk

Information on the services offered by the institute. (See page 215.)

British Library
www.bl.uk

Reader service enquiries, access to main catalogues, information on collections, links to the various reading rooms and exhibitions.

Complete Works of William Shakespeare
the-tech.mit.edu/Shakespeare/works.html

Access to the text of the complete works with search facility, quotations and discussion pages.

Dictionary of Slang
dictionaryofslang.co.uk

A guide to slang 'from a British perspective'. Research information, search facility.

The Eclectic Writer
www.eclectics.com/writing/writing.html

US website offering a selection of articles with advice for writers on topics such as 'Proper Manuscript Format', 'Electronic Publishing', 'How to Write a Synopsis' and 'Motivation'. Also a character chart for fiction writers and an online discussion board.

Film Angel
www.filmangel.co.uk

Established in March 2000 by Hammerwood Films to create a shop window for writers and would-be film angels alike. Writers submit a short synopsis which can be displayed for a predetermined period, for a fee, while would-be angels are invited to finance a production of their choice.

Filmmaker Store
www.filmmakerstore.com

Scriptwriting resources, listings and advice.

Guide to Grammar and Style
www.andromeda.rutgers.edu/~jlynch/Writing

A guide to grammar and style which is organized alphabetically, plus articles and links to other grammatical reference sites.

Internet Movie Database
www.imdb.com

Essential resource for film buffs and researchers with search engine for cast lists, screenwriters, directors and producers, film and television news, awards, film preview information, video releases.

Mr William Shakespeare and the Internet
daphne.palomar.edu/Shakespeare

Guide to scholarly Shakespeare resources on the Internet.

New Writing North
www.newwritingnorth.com

Essentially for writers based in the north of England but also a useful source of advice and guidelines. (See page 218.)

PlaysOnTheNet
www.playsonthenet.com

Information and help for new playwrights. Launched in association with Oneword Radio in January 2002, the site offers the chance to get involved, whether as a writer or someone who enjoys reading and listening to new plays. The site features new works that can be downloaded.

PACT (Producers Alliance for Cinema and Television)
www.pact.co.uk

Publications, jobs in the industry, production companies, membership details. (See page 219.)

Scottish Arts Council

www.sac.org.uk

Information on funding and events; 'Image of the Month' and 'Poem of the Month'. (See page 226.)

Screenwriters and Playwrights Home Page

www.teleport.com/~cdeemer/scrwriter.html

A website resource for scriptwriters, maintained by US screenwriter Charles Deemer. Links to a discussion forum and 'Screenwright', an electronic screenwriting course.

Screenwriters Online

screenwriter.com/insider/news.html

Described as the '*only* professional screenwriter's site run by major screenwriters who get their scripts and screenplays made into movies'. Contains screenplay analysis, expert articles and 'The Insider Report'.

Society of Authors

www.societyofauthors.org

Includes FAQs for new writers, diary of events, membership details, links to publishers' and other societies' websites. (See page 221.)

The Arts Council of Wales

www.artswales.org.uk/language.htm

Information on publications, council meetings, the arts in Wales. Links to other arts websites. (See page 227.)

WordCounter

www.wordcounter.com

Highlights the most frequently used words in a given text. Use as a guide to see what words are overused.

Writers' Guild of Great Britain
www.writersguild.org.uk

A wide range of information including rates of pay, articles on topics such as copyright, news, writers' resources and industry regulations. (See page 222.)

Writernet
www.writernet.org.uk

Formerly New Playwrights Trust. Information, advice and guidance for writers on all aspects of the live and recorded performance. (See page 225–6.)

WritersServices
www.WritersServices.com

Established in March 2000 by Chris Holifield, former deputy managing director and publisher at Cassell. Offers fact sheets, book reviews, advice, links and other resources for writers including editorial services, contract vetting and self-publishing (enquiries to info@writersservices.com).

Magazines

Scriptwriter Magazine
2 Elliott Square, London NW3 3SU
☎ 020 7586 4853   Fax 020 7586 4853
Email julian@scriptwritermagazine.com
Website www.scriptwritermagazine.com

Owner *Scriptease Ltd*
Editor *Julian Friedmann*
Circulation 1,500
Launched November 2001. Six issues per year. Magazine for professional scriptwriters covering all aspects of the business and craft of writing for the small and large screen. Interested in serious, in-depth analysis. Maximum 1,500–3,500 words. Email with synopsis sample material and CV. Payment £20 per 1,000 words.

The Stage (incorporating Television Today)
Stage House, 47 Bermondsey Street, London SE1 3XT
☎ 020 7403 1818   Fax 020 7357 9287
Email editor@thestage.co.uk
Website www.thestage.co.uk

Owner *The Stage Newspaper Ltd*
Editor *Brian Attwood*
Circulation 41,500

FOUNDED 1880. Weekly. No unsolicited mss. Prospective contributors should write with ideas in the first instance.

Preference for middle-market, tabloid-style articles, maximum 800 words. 'Puff pieces', PR plugs and extended production notes will not be considered. Profiles, 1,200 words. News stories from outside London always welcome, maximum 300 words. Payment £100 per 1,000 words.

Commissioning Rates and Pay Scales

Subsidized Repertory Theatres (excluding Scotland)

The following minimum rates were negotiated by the Writers' Guild and Theatrical Management Association and are set out under the TMA/Writers Agreement. Theatres are graded by a 'middle range salary level' (MRSL), worked out by dividing the 'total basic salaries' paid by the total number of 'actor weeks' in the year. (Rates correct as of June 2002.)

	MRSL 1	MRSL 2	MRSL 3
Commissioned Play			
Commission payment	£3,487	£2,852	£2,219
Delivery payment	£1,585	£1,268	£1,268
Acceptance payment	£1,585	£1,268	£1,268
Non-Commissioned Play			
Delivery payment	£5,073	£4,119	£3,486
Acceptance payment	£1,585	£1,268	£1,268
Rehearsal Attendance	£46.78	£41.04	£37.83
Options			
UK (excluding West End)		£1,977	
West End/USA		£3,298	
Rest of the World (English-speaking productions)		£2,637	

Television and Film

Television Drama

For a sixty-minute teleplay, the BBC will pay an established writer £7,410 and a beginner £4,703. The corresponding figures for ITV are £9,245 for the established writer and £6,568 for a writer new to television but with a solid reputation in other literary areas. ITV also has a 'beginner' category with a payment of £6,296 for a sixty-minute teleplay. Day rates for attendance at read-throughs and rehearsals is £67 for the BBC and £74.40 for ITV.
N.B. ITV rates under negotiation.

Feature Films

The Writers' Guild and PACT agreement of 1992 (under negotiation) allows for a minimum guaranteed payment to the writer of £31,200 on a feature film with a budget in excess of £2 million; £19,000 on a budget from £750,000 to £2 million; £14,000 on a budget below £750,000. However, many in the industry pay rates which take inflation into account and negotiate a royalty provision for uses instead of fixed percentage payments.